AMERICAN PARTIES
IN DECLINE

AMERICAN PARTIES IN DECLINE

WILLIAM J. CROTTY
Northwestern University

GARY C. JACOBSON
University of California, San Diego

LITTLE, BROWN AND COMPANY
Boston   Toronto

Preface

This book is intended for students in introductory courses on American government and for students in courses on political parties. It is meant as an introduction to the current state and contemporary difficulties of the parties, to supplement the more standardized treatments found in textbooks on American government and on political parties concerning the operations and functioning of political parties in a democratic society.

We are witnessing a decline in the role and significance of political parties in the United States. The reasons for this decline are many: society is changing; a new technology of politics has arisen; an evolving electorate is placing new and unaccustomed demands on the party agencies. The political parties are responding as best they can. The overall result is a period of confusion and an evolving transformation in the party system. In this book we analyze these concerns. In the process, we will attempt to assess the current status and the continuing difficulties facing the political parties.

The book is divided into four parts. The first three carry the burden of the substantive argument. In Part I we review the changes of the last two decades in the mood and composition of the electorate and the implications these have for the political parties. Particularly significant are the rise in issue orientation and the accelerating trend toward independent voting. In Part II we introduce the technology of the new

v

politics. Emphasis is placed on the role of money in winning office, the rising significance of corporate and trade Political Action Committees (PACs), single-issue and ideological groups, and campaign consultants, the gurus of the new politics, and the services they offer. All have contributed significantly to the decline of political parties.

In Part III we analyze the problems of, and the transformations within, the party in the government, and, more specifically, the parties in Congress. Party loyalty is decreasing and this is especially true in Congress. We trace the reasons for this decrease and explore the implications of this trend for presidential-congressional relations and for policy outcomes. The Epilogue is a brief conclusion that reviews some of the issues raised by the weakening of a once vital party system for a democratic form of governance.

William Crotty wrote Parts I, II, and the Epilogue. Gary C. Jacobson wrote Part III on the congressional party.

We wish to extend our particular thanks to Will Ethridge and Greg Franklin, political science editors, Barbara Kane, who oversaw the book's production, all of Little, Brown and Herbert J. Jacob, a friend, a colleague, and an inspiration for this volume.

William J. Crotty
Gary C. Jacobson

Contents

10
**The Congressional Parties: Leaders and
    (Sometimes) Followers**   **202**

11
Congress and the President   **225**

AMERICAN PARTIES
IN DECLINE

I
THE DECLINE OF THE PARTY IN THE ELECTORATE

Introduction

    The American electorate of the late twentieth century is a "turned-off" electorate. It is characterized by: low levels of voter participation; a decline in party loyalty, with a concomitant increase in split-ticket voting and wild and unpredictable swings in outcomes and vote margins from one election to the next; an increasing emphasis on issue voting; and claims, at least, of a more ideological electorate. All have significance for the operations and continued vitality of the party system.

1

Participation in Elections:
A "Turned-Off" Electorate

TURNOUT

The number of nonvoters in the United States is reaching critical proportions.[1] However, the problem of nonvoting is little understood and badly underresearched. It has received little public or political attention. The major voting studies have focused on voting and, more specifically, voter decision making in choosing between candidates and parties in an election year. Little attention has been, or is even now, given to the fact that nonvoting is increasing. Without being unduly alarmist, we may say that it is reaching epidemic proportions. As one

[1] Among the available studies see: Sidney Verba and Norman H. Nie, *Participation in America: Political Democracy and Social Equality* (New York: Harper and Row, 1972); S. Verba, N. Nie, and J. Kim, *Participation and Political Equality: A Seven-Nation Comparison* (Cambridge: Cambridge University Press, 1978); Arthur T. Hadley, *The Empty Polling Booth* (Englewood Cliffs, N.J.: Prentice-Hall, 1978); Penn Kimble, *The Disconnected* (New York: Columbia University Press, 1972); and W. Crotty, *Political Reform and the American Experiment* (New York: Thomas Y. Crowell, 1977).

4

TABLE 1.1
Voter Turnout in Selected Democratic Nations

Country	Turnout	Country	Turnout
Malta	94.4%	New Zealand	82.7%
Australia	92.6	Israel	78.2
Austria	91.9	Ireland	75.7
Sweden	91.4	Canada	74.9
Italy	90.8	Great Britain	72.8
Iceland	90.3	Japan	72.6
West Germany	89.9	India	60.5
Belgium	88.3	United States	54.4
Denmark	88.2	(presidential)	
Holland	87.5	Switzerland	51.7
France	83.5	United States	37.0
Norway	82.8	(midterm)	

Source: Data compiled by the British journal The Economist. Used by permission.

commentator has noted, voting is now a "minority habit."[2] By any standards, the problem is severe.

In contrast to that in other democratic nations, voter turnout in the United States is anemic. In fact, in comparisons with twenty-one other democratic countries, the United States ranks last (Table 1.1). Its position is challenged only by Switzerland, a country whose constant referenda on matters of public concern apparently overtax its citizenry's interest. It is claimed that American voting turnout exceeds that of only one other democracy—Botswana.

Curtis Gans of the Committee for the Study of the American Electorate, a bipartisan, nonprofit research group that concentrates on studying voter turnout, argues,

> The central and perhaps the greatest single problem of the American polity today is . . . the degree to which the vital underpinnings of American democracy are being eroded. The legitimacy of a democratic leadership and the health of the democratic process depend squarely on the informed and active participation of the electorate. Yet the level of political participation is now sinking *and the decline seems irreversible*. [Italics added].[3]

[2] Martin F. Nolan, "The Off-Year Election Blues," *Boston Globe*, October 15, 1978, p. A1.
[3] Curtis B. Gans, "The Empty Ballot Box: Reflections on Nonvoters in America," *Public Opinion*, September/October 1978, p. 54.

These are somber words, but Gans's committee is prepared to back them up. The seriousness of the situation is fully apparent.

— During the last ten years, fully 15 million Americans who were once regular voters have dropped out of the political process.
— Nearly 70 million eligible Americans failed to vote in the 1976 presidential election; more than 100 million eschewed the ballot box in the congressional election of 1974.
— Fewer than 28 percent of Jimmy Carter's fellow citizens voted for him in the presidential election of 1976; Brendan Byrne became governor of New Jersey with a mandate of less than 15 percent of New Jersey's eligible voters; Mayor Koch was the choice of less than 12 percent of New York City's electorate; Senator Henry Jackson won the 1976 New York presidential primary with less than 6 percent of the total vote.[4]

Alarm appears justified. American voting turnout over time is decreasing and it has reached unusual lows (Table 1.2). Moreover, it is not likely to improve significantly in the immediate future. About one-half or a little more of the American people vote in presidential contests, the most highly publicized of elections. Turnout in these elections has been consistently declining from highs of over 60 percent in the 1960s. By the 1970s it was in the mid-fiftieth percentiles. In terms of numbers, rather than percentages, the severity of the decline is more apparent. In a voting age population of 150 million in 1976, over 68 million Americans did not participate in even the most rudimentary form of political expression: casting their ballot for a presidential nominee.

Lance Tarrance has used governmental statistical sources to estimate the number of registered voters in each election since 1928 and the division of the vote among the parties. He has introduced the conception of the "Non-Voter" party, a term that covers the numbers of people not participating in presidential elections.[5] Richard Nixon won a landslide victory in 1972 with the greatest plurality in votes (19 million) ever recorded by a presidential candidate. Yet the "Non-

[4] *Ibid*

[5] V. Lance Tarrance, "Suffrage and Voter Turnout in the United States: The Vanishing Voter," in Jeff Fishel (ed.), *Parties and Elections in an Anti-Party Age* (Bloomington: Indiana University Press, 1978), pp. 77–85.

TABLE 1.2
Turnout in Presidential and Congressional Elections, 1920–78

Year	Office		Year	Office	
	President	U.S. House		President	U.S. House
1920	43.5%	40.8%	1950	— %	41.1%
1922	—	32.1	1952	61.6	57.6
1924	43.9	40.6	1954	—	41.7
1926	—	29.8	1956	59.3	55.9
1928	51.9	47.8	1958	—	43.0
1930	—	33.7	1960	62.8	58.5
1932	52.4	49.7	1962	—	45.4
1934	—	41.4	1964	61.9	57.8
1936	56.9	53.5	1966	—	45.4
1938	—	44.0	1968	60.9	55.1
1940	58.9	55.4	1970	—	43.5
1942	—	32.5	1972	55.5	51.1
1944	56.0	52.7	1974	—	36.3
1946	—	37.1	1976	54.3	49.6
1948	51.1	48.1	1978	—	37.9

Source: U.S. Bureau of the Census, *Statistical Abstract of the United States,* 99th ed. (Washington, D.C., 1978), p. 520.

Voter" party easily won the election with 62 million votes to Nixon's 47 million. In 1976, Jimmy Carter was elected president by 28 percent of the voters. Forty-five percent of the eligible electorate chose not to vote.

The significance of these figures is manifold. The largest number of potential voters is not supporting one candidate or party or the other. Rather, these people are withdrawing from the electorate. The number of nonvoters has always been substantial; but there was solace in the belief that participation rates seemed to be climbing, slowly to be sure but consistently. Unfortunately, this is no longer the case. The rates are falling and the numbers of nonparticipants are increasing substantially. From the 1950s through 1968, the average percentage of eligible voters not turning out was 39 percent and the average number of people not participating was under 43 million. These figures may be high in cross-national perspective, but they look good when compared to those of the 1970s. An expanded electorate exacerbated the problem. Turnout rates in the 1970s are a little over one-half of the eligible adult (18 years and older) population and, most importantly, the number of nonvoters *now averages more than 60 million*. And the figures are still climbing.[6]

The potential impact of these nonvoters (if they participated) in close elections, such as 1976 (or 1968 or 1960), would be decisive, of course. Even the pluralities in the lopsided contests pale in comparison to the numbers who simply do not vote. Any of the election outcomes in the modern era could have been reversed through the participation in sufficient numbers of those who have withdrawn from the electorate. No president in modern American history has been elected by a majority of the electorate. This includes, as indicated, the overwhelming victories of Lyndon Johnson and Richard Nixon.

The thought is sobering. Equally important are the problems caused for an otherwise stable and vigorous democratic order that fails to include sizable portions of its citizenry in its active electorate. It is reasonable to believe that people who consistently do not vote receive minimal representation (at best) of their views. Their ties to the political system are not likely to be strong, and they provide the potential — should the right candidate or combination of circumstances come along — for a major disruption of the American political scene. Nonvoting of this magnitude is not a healthy condition for a democratic society.

LOWER-LEVEL CONTESTS

We might expect presidential elections to have modest turnouts because they are the farthest removed from the individual voter and his concerns. As contests become closer to home, voter interest and familiarity with the candidates and issues should rise, leading to corresponding increases in turnout. This is not the case. Presidential elections consistently excite the most interest and the highest levels of involvement. As one progresses from these contests to the congressional, state, and local races, voters' information about the contests, their enthusiasm for participating, and their rates of involvement drop substantially.[7] For example, as shown in Table 1.1, there is a fall-off in voting for congressional offices during presidential years. In midterm

[6] *Ibid.*
[7] Crotty, *Political Reform*, pp. 49–52.

contests, the voter turnout can drop ten to fifteen percentage points. At present, less than 40 percent of the electorate votes in off-year congressional races. In absolute terms, although the eligible voting-age population increased 5.4 million between 1976 and 1978, voting participation dropped 13 million. Better than 96 million adults did not bother to vote in the 1978 off-year election.

These figures are troublesome, and they get no better as we examine state and local races. The Committee for the Study of the American Electorate, mentioned earlier, noted that the combined turnout (37.9 percent) for all races in the 1978 election year was the lowest since 1942.[8] An analysis of voter involvement in elections in New York, New Jersey, and Connecticut over several decades found that turnout had dropped perceptibly.[9] In presidential elections for 1952–76, turnout was down 11 percent in New York State and 9 percent in both New Jersey and Connecticut. The fall-off was particularly noticeable in the largest cities such as New York, where the decline in voting participation reached 25 percent. In terms of numbers (rather than percentages), and despite the population growth, fewer people voted in New York State in 1976 (6.6 million) than in 1952 (7.2 million). In gubernatorial races in New York between 1958 and 1978, the proportion turning out fell twenty-nine percentage points (and forty points in New York City). The decline in participation rates for gubernatorial elections in New Jersey and Connecticut was fifteen and fourteen percentage points, respectively. The percentage of eligible citizens who registered and voted in these three states in 1978 ranged between 38 and 47 percent of those eligible.[10]

One other distressing fact needs to be reported. Although voter turnout has consistently decreased, the social and demographic factors associated with a higher turnout have actually become more prevalent in the population. Norman Nie has found that although participation rates did not improve between 1952 and 1968,

> during this same period, however, many of the variables which we know to be highly correlated with levels of political participation have been rising, and rising rapidly. Median years of education have risen in this

[8] Report of the Committee for the Study of the American Electorate, December 18, 1978.

[9] Frank Lynn, "Voter Apathy Found Throughout 3 States of Metropolitan Area," *The New York Times*, January 22, 1979, p. 1.

[10] *Ibid*.

sixteen-year period from 9.5 to 12.1, and the proportion of the population who have completed college has just about doubled. Income, which opens the way for a greater variety of leisure activities, has risen dramatically, and the proportion of the population in white-collar occupations has increased by almost 10 percent. Yet levels of participation which are so highly correlated with these factors (income, occupation, and education jointly explain as much as 20 percent of the variance in rates of participation in the United States) have not been substantially altered.[11]

These demographic characteristics continue to become more prevalent, while actual voter participation continues to drop.

OTHER POLITICAL ACTIVITY

If people do not vote, they are not at all likely to engage in any of the other forms of political activity.[12] Table 1.3 illustrates the tendency. The number of individuals engaging in each of the activities is overreported (e.g., the 72 percent claiming to have voted as against the 55 percent who actually did). Nonetheless, the proportionate differences between the types of political behavior engaged in should be approximately correct. The vast majority of respondents claim to have voted. One-third of the voters tried to influence others as to how they should vote and one-fifth to one-fourth wrote public officials or newspaper editors or contributed money to political campaigns.

Nonvoters, in contrast, were not even this moderately involved in political life. In fact they appeared to have little interest in any political input. Better than 90 percent took no part in campaigning in any form, including wearing a candidate's button or placing bumper stickers on their cars. Better than 80 percent did not contribute financially to anyone's campaign, and between 70 and 80 percent have not, at any point in their lives, written public officials or newspapers on matters of

[11] Norman H. Nie, "Future Developments in Mass Communications and Citizen Participation," in Albert Somit (ed.), *Political Science and the Study of the Future* (Hinsdale, Ill.: Dryden, 1975), p. 141, as quoted in Harry Holloway and John George, *Public Opinion: Coalitions, Elites and Masses* (New York: St. Martin's Press, 1979), p. 59.

[12] For analysis of different "modes," of patterns or participation, see Verba and Nie, *Participation in America*.

consequence. Two-thirds of the nonvoters do not become involved at even the lowest and easiest level of participation, attempting to influence someone they come in contact with as to how they should vote. Eighty percent of the nonvoters engaged in no activities whatsoever. The bulk of the other 20 percent participated in only one. One-half of the voters became involved in one or more political acts, beyond voting.

TABLE 1.3
Political Activity of the American Electorate, 1976

I.   Activities

	Engaged in Activity	
	Yes	*No*
Voted	72%	28%
Tried to influence others (how to vote)	37	63
Attended political meetings, dinners, rallies, etc.	6	94
Worked for a political party or candidate	4	96
Wore a campaign button or put a sticker on the car	1	99
Contributed money to campaigns or took a tax check-off (a contributor to the presidential campaign fund)	18	82
Wrote to public officials on political matters at some time in the past	28	72
Wrote letter to editor of newspaper or magazine at some point in the past	19	81

*II.   Summary Index of Political Activities
        (based on above activities)*

	Voters	Nonvoters
No activities	50.6%	79.3%
One activity	35.8	19.0
Two activities	8.6	1.4
Three activities	3.3	0.2
Four activities	1.7	0.1
	100%	100%

(Continued)

TABLE 1.3 *(continued)*

III. *Summary Index of Activities on National Problems*[a]

	Voters	Nonvoters
No activities	67.8%	88.0%
One activity	17.5	8.1
Two activities	9.7	2.5
Three activities	3.1	1.0
Four activities	1.5	0.2
Five activities	0.4	0.2
	100%	100%

IV. *Summary Index of Activities on Local Problems*[b]

	Voters	Nonvoters
No activities	47.9%	73.6%
One activity	22.7	14.9
Two activities	13.8	6.6
Three activities	9.4	3.7
Four activities	4.2	0.8
Five activities	1.6	0.4
Six activities	0.4	0.0
	100%	100%

Source: Data supplied by the Center for Political Studies.

[a]The number of activities on national problems was determined by asking the respondents whether they had:

1. Written a letter to the editor of a magazine or newspaper about some problem.
2. Worked with others or joined an organization trying to do something about some national problem.
3. Spoken to or written their congressman or some other national leader.
4. Signed a petition either for or against action by the national government.
5. Taken part in a sit-in, demonstration, or protest concerned with some national problem.

[b]The number of activities on local problems was determined by asking the respondents the same questions as for national problems, as well as whether they had:

6. Attended meetings of the city council or school board.

When asked what response they had taken to either national or local problems (Table 1.3), nonvoters by and large had taken none. One-third of the voters on the national level (against 12 percent of the nonvoters) and one-half on the local level (as against 26 percent of the nonvoters) engaged in one activity or more to make their wishes known. On the local level, voters appear particularly involved in alternative forms of political expression. Nonvoters are basically inactive on all levels. If people do not vote, the chances are excellent they will not participate in any other form of political processes. In effect, they remain outside the political system, unrepresented and ignored.

THE NONVOTERS

Nonvoters are a fairly predictable lot (Table 1.4). Traditionally, the South, the border states, and rural areas have a lower voter turnout than do other localities. Youth is definitely correlated with low rates of political involvement. Individuals thirty-five and under vote considerably less than those thirty-six to sixty-five, and first- and second-time eligibles are the least involved of any. The Center for Political Studies reported a substantial difference (16 percent) between 18–20-year-olds and 21–24-year-olds in their participation rates in 1972.[13] A similar difference (45 percent of the 18–20-year-olds voted as against 62 percent of the 21–24-year-olds) was evident in 1976. Young voters, and particularly those eligible for the first time, do not participate in large numbers.

Generally speaking also, people of lower occupational achievement, people who are not union members, those who identify themselves as working-class or below, and those of lower incomes vote less than others. Jews, whites, and males have comparatively higher turnout rates than others.

The impact of education on turnout and its role more generally in explaining the increasing issue orientation of the electorate has been a matter of some debate.[14] People with less education vote and participate less in politics. This much is accepted. In Table 1.4, for example,

[13] Arthur H. Miller and Warren E. Miller, "Issues, Candidates, and Partisan Divisions in the 1972 American Presidential Election," *British Journal of Political Science* 5(1975): 429.

[14] For different perspectives, see *ibid.;* Philip E. Converse, "Public Opinion and Voting Behavior," in Fred I. Greenstein and Nelson W. Polsby (eds.), *The Handbook of Political Science*, Vol. 4 (Reading, Mass.: Addison-Wesley, 1975), pp. 75–169; Norman H. Nie, with Kristi Andersen, "Mass Belief Systems Revisited: Political Change and Attitude Structure," *Journal of Politics* 36 (1974): 540–87; and Lester W. Milbrath and M. L. Goel, *Political Participation*, 2nd ed. (Chicago: Rand McNally, 1977), pp. 98–102.

TABLE 1.4
Voting and Nonvoting in the 1976 Presidential Election

I. Demographic Characteristics

Region	Voters	Nonvoters
New England	78.8%	21.2%
Middle Atlantic	70.8	29.2
East North Central	81.2	18.8
West North Central	78.7	21.3
Solid South	64.1	35.9
Border States	68.6	31.4
Mountain States	81.7	18.3
Pacific States	72.6	27.4

Size of Place	Voters	Nonvoters
Twelve largest cities	74.8%	25.2%
Other large cities	73.3	26.7
Suburbs of twelve largest cities	74.7	25.3
Other suburbs	72.5	27.5
Adjacent areas	74.3	25.7
Outlying areas	67.5	32.5

Age	Voters	Nonvoters
18–24	55.7%	44.3%
25–35	68.2	31.8
36–50	81.6	18.4
51–65	80.3	19.7
66–	71.7	28.3

Education	Voters	Nonvoters
Eighth grade or less	60.7%	39.3%
Some high school	59.8	40.2
High school	69.4	30.6
High school plus noncollege schooling	75.8	24.2
Some college	83.8	16.2
College graduate	86.4	13.6
Advanced degree	92.2	7.8

Occupation	Voters	Nonvoters
Professional	88.9%	11.1%
Managerial	82.3	17.7
Clerical or sales	78.4	21.6

Occupation	Voters	Nonvoters
Craftsman-foreman	74.1%	25.9%
Operatives	65.7	34.3
Services	60.9	39.1
Laborers	59.6	40.4
Farming	71.7	28.3

Union Membership	Voters	Nonvoters
Member	78.6%	21.4%
Nonmember	71.2	28.8

Class Identification	Voters	Nonvoters
Lower class	40.0%	60.0[a]%
Average working class	65.7	34.3
Working class	60.0	40.0
Upper working class	74.6	25.4
Average middle	79.9	20.1
Middle class	63.0	37.0
Upper middle	83.4	16.6

Income Level	Voters	Nonvoters
Under $2000	41.0%	59.0%
$2000–4999	61.0	39.0
$5000–9999	68.1	31.9
$10,000–14,999	72.8	27.2
$15,000–19,999	76.4	23.6
$20,000 and above	87.6	12.4

Religion	Voters	Nonvoters
Protestant	73.8%	26.2%
Catholic	74.9	25.1
Jewish	83.7	16.3

Sex	Voters	Nonvoters
Male	78.3%	21.7%
Female	69.1	30.9

Race	Voters	Nonvoters
White	73.9%	26.1%
Black	65.5	34.5

[a] Only five people identified themselves as lower-class.

(Continued)

TABLE 1.4 (*continued*)

II.   *Party and Political Measures*

Party Identification	Voters	Nonvoters
Strong Democrat	82.0%	18.0%
Weak Democrat	68.9	31.1
Independent Democrat	72.7	27.3
Independent	57.3	42.7
Independent Republican	76.3	23.7
Weak Republican	75.4	24.6
Strong Republican	92.3	7.7

III.   *Information on Politics*

Follow public affairs	Voters	Nonvoters
Most of the time	86.5%	13.5%
Some of the time	78.9	21.1
Only now and then	56.2	43.8
Hardly at all	38.9	61.1

Watch evening national news broadcasts on television	Voters	Nonvoters
Frequently	77.9%	22.1%
Sometimes	67.7	32.3
Rarely	66.9	33.1
Never	65.1	34.9

Read a Daily Newspaper	Voters	Nonvoters
Yes	78.7%	21.3%
No	58.0	42.0

Source: Data supplied by the Center for Political Studies.

education is strongly associated with voting. People with a high school education or less are markedly less likely to vote than those with some college or advanced degree work. Arthur Miller, Warren Miller, and their associates at the Center for Political Studies have reported that turnout fell disproportionately between 1964 and 1972 for the lower-educated while holding relatively stable among the higher-educated. Voting was down ten percentage points for the grade-school-educated, eight points for the high-school-educated, and only two points for the college-educated.[15] They suggest that the drop in participation rates is due mostly to those with the least formal education, in effect accentuating the trend toward the underrepresentation of those of low socioeconomic status.

Miller, Miller, Raine, and Brown's explanation for the increasing importance of education as a predictor of turnout has significance for the discussion of the increasing importance of issues in elections:

> As the focus of analysis moves across educational levels from grade school to college, the bulk of the explanatory power shifts from candidate image to issues and ideology. Voters with college educations are better informed politically, generally more cognizant of policy differences between the candidates and, therefore, more likely to make a decision on the basis of policy preferences than are less well educated individuals. It is apparently far easier for college-educated individuals to translate issue attitudes into a vote decision than for the relatively less well educated who use the candidate as an intervening focus for their ideology.[16]

An issue-oriented electorate has less room for the poorly educated. One of the functions of a strong party system includes mobilizing the vote, expanding the electorate to represent as many people as possible. The American party system did this imperfectly, but apparently a good deal better than other less vigorous party systems now in the offing.

Another function of the party for the individual was to structure the vote; to allow him a point of reference in making his choice that minimized the need for an extensive investment of time and effort to acquire information, organize it, and relate it to the political world. Perhaps an electorate in which the party system no longer fulfills the function of structuring information and providing powerful cues to influence the individual's vote is one that makes the costs and personal investment needed to participate too high for those with fewer resources (in this case, formal educational achievements) to meet. Electoral decision making may become increasingly uncomfortable for them, and they may drop out to join the expanding ranks of the nonvoters.

[15] Arthur H. Miller, Warren E. Miller, Alden S. Raine, and Thad A. Brown, "A Majority Party in Disarray: Policy Polarization in the 1972 Election," *American Political Science Review* 70 (1976), as reprinted in Richard G. Niemi and Herbert F. Weisberg (eds.), *Controversies in American Voting Behavior* (San Francisco: Freeman, 1976), pp. 176–95.

[16] *Ibid.*, p. 193.

In terms of attitudinal measures, independents and weak Democrats are among those least likely to vote. Strong party identifiers, led by the especially impressive vote of strong Republicans, have the highest participation rates. People who are weakly socialized to politics — that is, whose parents had little political interest — vote decidedly less than those who report one or both parents with a good deal of interest. Correspondingly, among those individuals with least interest themselves in political events, less than one-half vote. Among the most interested, 85 percent vote. Individuals with low levels of trust, those who can find little to be proud of in American government, who have little concern about the election outcome, and who either sporadically or rarely follow public affairs, have a depressed voter turnout.

The informational questions indicate that those who watch Walter Cronkite, or John Chancellor and David Brinkley, on the evening news frequently are likely to vote. An even stronger predictor of the vote may be the newspaper. People who habitually read a daily newspaper appear to be considerably different from those who do not. In terms of the vote, 78 percent of the newspaper readers as against only 58 percent of the nonreaders vote.

Overall then, those on the lower end of the social ladder — the less-educated and those of lower economic status, occupational achievement, and income potential — and the young are disproportionately represented among the nonvoters. These are the same people with less input into the political system — through such things as contributions to campaigns, personal access to party officials and public officeholders, outlets for their views through the media and representation through established professional and economic interest groups — than others. It is a fact of political life that those least likely to vote are also those least likely to participate in politics in any other form.

REASONS FOR NONVOTING: STRUCTURAL

It is presently unfashionable to blame registration requirements for the low voter turnout. The rules have been improved significantly since the passage of the Voting Rights Act in 1965, and its reenactment each five years (as required in the original law).[17] Congress has made

[17] Crotty, *Political Reform*, pp. 72–100.

an effort to lighten the requirements for qualifying to vote in federal elections, and it has also attempted to modernize some of the proce- dures (as, for example, in filing absentee ballots). However, it has been most reluctant to go much further. It has proven hostile to the Carter administration's proposals to reduce registration barriers to the bare essentials and to require only election-day registration in federal con- tests. If Congress had adopted such a plan, many (perhaps most) states and localities would have been forced to go along for reasons of practi- cality and the added cost of administering two separate systems (state and national).

Congress refused to adopt the plan and, after the initial rebuff, the Carter administration reassigned it a low priority. Both Congress and the state legislatures — and, in fact, most practicing politicians — fear the impact of drastic registration changes that would redefine the elec- torate by substantially increasing its numbers. Politicians are content to maintain an electorate they understand and with which they have had success. Self-interest favors retention of the familiar and the safe.

There is another reason also for the antipathy to registration reform. Congress and most of the states still distrust schemes promoting too easy participation. Meeting the hurdles posed by registration practices is seen as a matter of faith. The privilege (as against right) of being eligible to participate in elections is perceived as something a citizen should gain on his own initiative. The concept is a throwback to a theme that has dominated the thinking concerning registration and one that has produced a strain between the nation's democratic impulse and the desire for a restricted franchise.[18]

The present jumble of registration practices was introduced be- tween 1890 and 1920. These practices were adopted in response to the political muscle exercised by an odd coalition of reformers and practical politicians. The Progressives wanted strict standards for qualifying vot- ers in order to institutionalize within the electorate the middle-class virtues they represented. Through these measures they hoped to cor- rect many of the machine abuses of the day by, in part, denying the vote to the urban ethnic groups that constituted the machine's base. Machine politicians accepted registration requirements as a means for ensuring a restricted and controllable electorate, sensitive to their wishes. Machines feared large voter turnouts that could result in

[18] *Ibid.*, pp. 3–45.

unpredictable election outcomes. Finally, there were the southern whites who wanted to regain control of their region's politics. Stiff registration standards allowed them constitutionally to disenfranchise blacks (and lower-class whites also, if need be) and to again assume the political reigns within their states. All three elements of the coalition gained what they wanted with the resultant jumble of procedures and requirements coming on down to our own time.[19]

Registration practices were not invented in the Progressive era. They were universally applied to elections during that time, however. The idea underlying the institution of such rules went back to colonial times and the belief in the qualitative vote: an individual should prove himself worthy of participation in community affairs. Voting, in effect, was a reward for good citizenship. The practice goes back to pre-Revolutionary times, when the right to have a voice in community decisions was restricted in some colonies to the company shareholders who put up the money for the venture and in other colonies to the members of the recognized Church ("the elect"). Admission to these ranks was not bestowed frivolously.

At various points in American history, qualifying provisions were adopted that related to property holding, wealth, moral behavior, education (or the ability to read and interpret parts of a state or federal constitution to the satisfaction of an election official), and so on. Such laws disenfranchised at various times the poor, ethnics, blacks, Orientals, members of various religious groups (Jews, for example), institutionalized populations, the highly mobile, unmarried couples, Indians, and people who committed certain types of criminal acts. Many of those laws and the screening procedures used to enforce them are still on the books. The registration barriers have given way reluctantly. It took the civil rights revolution in the South in the early 1960s to bring about fundamental change and to spearhead the attack against the worst vestiges of the old order.

Over the last decade, the courts have become increasingly unsvm-

---

[19] *Ibid.*, pp. 11–42; Philip E. Converse, "Change in the American Electorate," in Angus Campbell and Philip E. Converse (eds.), *The Human Meaning of Social Change* (New York: Russell Sage, 1972), pp. 263–337; Walter Dean Burnham, "Theory and Voting Research: Some Reflections on Converse's 'Change in the American Electorate,'" *American Political Science Review* 68 (1974): 1002–23; and Jerrold G. Rusk, "The American Electoral Universe: Speculation and Evidence," *American Political Science Review* 68 (1974): 1028–49.

pathetic to registration barriers. The present rule of thumb in the federal courts is that registration laws that do not serve "a compelling state interest" are voided under the "equal protection" clause of the Fourteenth Amendment. The Supreme Court took this position in *Dunn* v. *Blumstein* (1972), a case that struck down unreasonably long residency requirements (of six months' to two years' duration) in state and local elections. The ruling brought state practices in line with federal procedures as mandated in the Voting Rights Act of 1970.[20]

Nevertheless, the old traditions die hard. Congress has rejected attempts either to minimize the barriers or to facilitate registration through governmental initiatives in reaching and enrolling voters (as is done in most other democratic nations). As a consequence, registration formulas persist that deny each citizen equal access to the polls.

A study by Steven Rosenstone and Raymond Wolfinger of turnout in the 1972 presidential election estimated that registration laws reduced voting by about 6 to 10 percent. The regulations had their greatest impact in the South and more generally on the poorly educated. Less restrictive procedures could increase the participation of southern blacks by approximately sixteen percentage points and southern whites by almost as much. Elsewhere, the authors estimate that an increase in turnout across the board of roughly nine percentage points would constitute a reasonable expectation.[21] Arthur Hadley, who executed the most comprehensive analysis of nonvoting in the 1976 election, feels that more facilitative registration procedures might increase turnout among some groups by up to eighteen percentage points.[22]

The biggest structural barrier to the vote continues to be registration requirements. Registration has priority over voting and is a more difficult challenge to meet. Registration provisions are poorly understood and enrollment periods often occur at times when people's political interest is dormant. By the time many prospective voters become aware of the candidates, their platform, and the issues of the day, and develop some interest in the election, it is often too late for them to meet registration requirements. As a consequence, they are unable to vote. This is more true of past elections when registration practices

[20] Crotty, *Political Reform,* p. 35

[21] Steven J. Rosenstone and Raymond E. Wolfinger, "The Effects of Registration Laws on Voter Turnout," *American Political Science Review* 72 (March 1978): 22–45.

[22] Hadley, *Empty Polling Booth,* p. 119.

were more onerous, but it is still a problem. Data on the 1976 presidential election compiled by the Census Bureau indicate that 82 percent of the people not voting failed to register (Table 1.5). Seemingly, the first and most obvious step in increasing turnout would be to simplify the registration barriers or possibly to eliminate them altogether. Curiously, such barriers are the ones most amenable to immediate relief, if the politicians so willed it.

Registration alone, of course, is not the total cause of the problem. Its effects cannot be dismissed, but the malaise that has infected all aspects of American political life has certainly influenced the willingness of people to both register and vote.

REASONS FOR NONVOTING: ATTITUDINAL

A principal cause of nonvoting clearly is the psychological malaise that dominates contemporary politics. Simply put, American voters appear "turned off" to virtually everything associated with politics. This theme pervades the current studies of the subject. Political parties, candidates, and elections are seen as irrelevant to the personal concerns of citizens and to the problems that plague the nation. People distrust governmental institutions and feel that they exercise no influence over what their government does and whom it serves. Voting, for such people, becomes a meaningless act. Robert Teeter, a pollster prominent in Republican party circles, reported to a meeting of the nation's governors in the early phases of the 1978 election that the most prevalent attitude found among prospective voters in his polls was the feeling that the individual could no longer influence the course of government action.[23] The result was that many people simply dropped out of the electorate. His Democratic counterpart told the same group, "The voter sees no link between his taxes and government spending." Although young people have failed to participate in large numbers, the most bitter group were those "between the ages of 50 and 64 who had

[23] F. Richard Ciccone, "Voters in Sour Mood, Pollsters Tell Governors," *Chicago Tribune*, August 29, 1978, Section 1, p. 5.

TABLE 1.5
Reasons for Nonvoting in the 1976 Presidential Election *(In percent)*

I.	*Registration and Turnout*			
	A. Registered	66.7	Not reported	33.3
	B. Voting	59.2	Not voting	40.8
II.	*Reasons for Not Voting*			
	A. Not registered			82.0
	B. Registered, but not voting because:			

1. Unable to vote:

No way to get to polls	4.0
Illness or emergency	20.0
Could not take time off work	7.0
Machines not working, lines too long	2.0
Out of town, away from home	14.0
Other unable to vote	6.0
Subtotal	**53.0**

2. Did not want to vote or not interested

Did not prefer any candidate	11.0
Politicians not interested in my problems	1.0
Believed vote would not make a difference	1.0
Don't want to get involved	1.0
Not interested in election this year	7.0
Other not interested	1.0
Subtotal	**22.0**

3. Other

All other reasons	17.0
Don't know and reason not reported	8.0
Subtotal	**25.0**
Total (Registered, not voting)	**100.0%**

Source: Bureau of the Census.

planned for their retirements and now find their futures plucked from their hands."[24] The latter group should represent the core of a stable, reasonably satisfied electorate.

[24] *Ibid.*

Follow-up analysis of the 1978 election proved the pollsters correct. Examples of the disillusionment of the voters abounded. A former peace activist in the 1960s said, "Politicians are not doing their job. I don't give two cents for the whole lot of them. I've just lost interest in politics. Apathetic, I guess that's the word. I won't sit around arguing for the next ten years the way I did for the last ten."[25] A clerk in a department store in New Jersey: "You don't get anything for your taxes; it's just a bunch of garbage. I'm off today. I have no excuse, but I just don't feel like voting."[26] A nurse in Maryland: "It doesn't matter who gets elected. They can't do what they want. They're controlled by the people around them. So it doesn't matter whether I vote."[27] A patron of a beauty salon in New Jersey: "I really don't think there's much you can do about anything. It's getting to be frustrating. I'm just a little person who doesn't have much pull. But that's the way of the world, I guess."[28]

The message seems clear enough. The confusion, disinterest, and frustration of the individual is apparent. The government and its leaders appear remote, unconcerned with the problems of the person in the street. The thought of controlling politicians, making them responsive to the citizen, and directing the course of government through the vote seems incomprehensible.

Curtis Gans of the Committee for the Study of the American Electorate believes that nonvoting is associated with fundamental weaknesses within the political system. These include

> the decay of political and social institutions, most notably the political party; the growing impotence felt by the citizen in the face of large public and private institutions and increasingly complex problems; [and] the role that mass media, especially television, has in creating confusion in the minds of some.[29]

In short, they include almost everything related to modern American politics. Walter Dean Burnham, a political scientist who specializes in

[25] Steven V. Roberts, "Electorate's Majority Prefers Sidelines," *The New York Times*, November 8, 1978, p. 18.

[26] *Ibid*.

[27] Steven V. Roberts, "100 Million Didn't Vote — Some Express Disillusions," *The New York Times*, November 12, 1978, p. 26.

[28] *Ibid*.

[29] Quoted in Adam Clymer, "Nov. 7 Voter Turnout Was 37.9%, Lowest Since '42," *The New York Times*, December 19, 1979, p. A13.

election analyses, predicts that if turnout "gets much lower, we will hit rock bottom."[30] Another academician and a political activist, historian Richard Wade, can see no reason why the slide will not continue. What can be done about it? "The first thing to do is to let people know how bad it is."[31] It does not seem like much, but perhaps it is a start.

[30] Robert Reinhold, "Portrait of American Electorate: It Is Large, Young, and Reluctant," *The New York Times*, November 8, 1978, p. 1.

[31] Quoted in Lynn, "Voter Apathy Found."

2
Party Loyalty

PARTY IDENTIFICATION

Party identification is a psychological measure of voter identification with a political party. It is grounded in the individual's personal development and his exposure to such things as the influence of his parents, schooling and its impact, the views of business associates and the demands of making a living, and the network of friends and acquaintances that comprise the social setting in which a person lives and matures. Among all of the influences acting on partisan identification, the family is the strongest. The political ties picked up from the parents and then influenced by later learning and life experiences form the basis for a number of political attitudes. Among the strongest of these is party identification. Because the socialization to political parties begins so early and because the attachments once formed are both strongly resistant to change and highly predictive of political behavior, partisan affiliation can be compared to religious choice or ethnic ties. Party identification is an important measure of the stability and vitality of the party system.

The indicator of party identification is used in voting analyses to gauge the direction (Democrat, Republican, or independent) and intensity (strong, weak) of support for the political parties. It is a powerful measure not subject to random fluctuation and, since its introduction in the early 1950s, it has proven to be the most significant of the three indices (issue orientation and candidate appeal being the other two) devised to explain voting behavior.[1]

The evidence is that party loyalty, as measured by party identification, is changing. The trend is obvious and has been continuous since the measure was introduced. Personal identification with a party is becoming less common and less important. Fewer people are identifying with either of the political parties, and even among those who do, the intensity of their identification is falling off markedly. The newest members of the electorate have the weakest ties to the party system. And for most people who have identified with either of the parties in the past, the strength of their identification has atrophied over the years. As a consequence, party identification has become less meaningful for predicting the vote. Loyalty to a party and its candidates has declined seriously. The electorate has begun to lose the factor of greatest significance in producing an order and predictability to election behavior. As party identification has declined in importance, the number and significance of independent voters has increased substantially. In return, the unpredictability and volatility of the vote returns attest to the weakening of party ties and the decline of party loyalty.

Survey data collected by the Center for Political Studies of the Institute for Social Research of the University of Michigan document the erosion of support for the parties. As Table 2.1 shows, the attachment to the parties has decreased in both proportion of those identifying and the intensity of the affiliation over time. Three out of four adults identified with the major political parties in the 1950s:

Partisan Identification by Decade

	1950s	1960s	1970s
Partisans	74.2%	72.2%	63.5%
Strong	35.5	33.0	26.0
Weak	38.7	39.2	37.5
Independents	21.8	25.8	34.8

Source: Data supplied by the Center for Political Studies.

[1] Angus Campbell, Philip Converse, Warren Miller, and Donald Stokes, *The American Voter* (New York: Wiley, 1960).

TABLE 2.1
Strength of Party Identification Over Time, 1952–76

Year

	1952	1954	1956	1958	1960	1962	1964	1966	1968	1970	1972	1974	1976
Strong Democrat	22%	22%	21%	23%	21%	23%	26%	18%	20%	20%	15%	17%	15%
Weak Democrat	25	25	23	24	25	23	25	27	25	23	25	21	25
Independent Democrat	10	9	7	7	8	8	9	9	10	10	11	13	12
Independent	5	7	9	8	8	8	8	12	11	13	13	15	14
Independent Republican	7	6	8	4	7	6	6	7	9	8	11	9	10
Weak Republican	14	14	14	16	13	16	13	15	14	15	13	14	14
Strong Republican	13	13	15	13	14	12	11	10	10	10	10	8	9
Apoliticals: Don't Know	4	4	3	5	4	4	2	2	1	1	2	3	1
	100%	100%	100%	100%	100%	100%	100%	100%	100%	100%	100%	100%	100%

Source: Data supplied by the Center for Political Studies.

The attachments eroded slightly during the 1960s, but the significant decline became evident in the 1970s. The fall-off was pronounced among strong party identifiers, down from 35 percent to 26 percent over two decades.

The trend has affected the parties differently. The Republican party's coalition is small to begin with and can be expected to have strong and persistent ties since they have remained stable in the face of social pressures that have worked since the New Deal to the advantage of the Democrats. Apparently, this is the case. The overall decline in Republican identifiers is modest at best. Where the party has lost support is among the "strong" identifiers, whose proportions have decreased from 13 to 15 percent during the earlier years to 8 or 9 percent in more recent elections. The number of "independent Republicans" (people who claim to be independent but favor the Republican party) has increased slightly to where it now about equals the strong identifiers. The modal group among Republicans is the "weak" identifiers.

The Democratic party's coalition is considerably larger (claiming 16 to 20 percent more of the party identifiers over time) and far more malleable than the Republican's. Although the same pattern holds true for the Democrats as for the Republicans, their losses are more severe. The proportion of party identifiers that made the biggest drop (about 7 percent) is found among "strong" party identifiers. The number of "independent Democrats" has increased, and the party's modal group is "weak" identifiers. The trend then is for fewer people to identify and for those who do identify (or are already psychologically committed to support the party) to have their ties loosen as time passes.

Independents have increased markedly to the point where they now rank in number equal to or slightly behind the Democrats and well ahead of the Republicans. The day is not far off when independent will clearly be the identification preferred by Americans. In fact, there is nothing to indicate a substantial reversal or leveling off of the trend shown. Thus, independents will most likely continue to increase in significance and number with each passing election year. From an electorate in which 75 percent of its members loyally associated themselves with the major parties to one (in future elections) in which the majority may well claim to be independents is a major transition that, in itself, has changed, and will continue to change, the practice of American politics.

The decreasing frequency and intensity of identification with the parties is alarming (for party sympathizers) on a number of counts. The figures presented in Table 2.1 and on page 27 probably underestimate the extent of the defections. Party attachment is, as noted, an attitudinal force of considerable strength and durability. It is nurtured in the family and transmitted through the parents (primarily) to the emerging adult. The dynamics of the process are not unlike those through which other traditional and social values that earmark the individual's personal world are passed on in a society. The socialization process is strong enough that values once passed on are not easy to modify. Attitudinal identification with a party would be the one indicator of party loyalty most resistant to change. Yet an individual has to make some concession to a changing political environment and, potentially at least, to the perceived failure of the parties to offer him meaningful choices in elections and a continuing sense of direction for his political activity. The individual's life experiences and the political climate of the times in which he matures politically would influence the direction and nature of his political affiliations.

The process would be gradual. The likelihood is that pressures created by the perceived political environment in conflict with the family socialization processes would lead first to a change in behavior (in this case, the vote) and only later, as the behavior and the attitude conflict, to a gradual decrease in importance of the attitude. This, in turn, would lead to a modification of the attitude (a decrease in intensity of the identification or a drift from a "strong" or "weak" identification toward independence). The process of reconciling attitudes and behavior may take years, and, because of the intensity of the socializing forces, probably several generations.[2] Attachments would weaken over time and new members entering the electorate would exhibit far weaker partisan ties, products of changing socialization cues and a restructured political environment. Thus, although the decline in party identification shown here is troublesome enough, it may in actuality mask both the actual extent of the erosion and its seriousness.

There is evidence to support these contentions. The data presented in Table 2.2 suggest an increasing disparity between identification and the vote. There is an increasing willingness on the part of many party members to break with their party and its candidates and to vote for

[2] Paul Abramson, *Generational Change in American Politics* (Lexington: D. C. Heath, 1975); and Kristi Andersen, *The Creation of a Democratic Majority, 1928–1936* (Chicago: University of Chicago Press, 1979).

TABLE 2.2
Defection Rates Within Categories of Party Identification, 1952–76 *(In percent)*

I. By Year:

Democrat	1952	1956	1960	1964	1968	1972	1976	Average, 1952–76
Strong	17[a]	15	9	5	11	26	9	13
Weak	39	37	28	18	38	52	25	34

Independent	1952	1956	1960	1964	1968	1972	1976	Average, 1952–76
Democrat	40	33	15	11	49	44	24	31
Independent	—	—	—	—	—	—	—	—
Republican	7	6	13	25	19	14	14	14

Republican	1952	1956	1960	1964	1968	1972	1976	Average, 1952–76
Strong	1	1	2	10	3	4	3	3
Weak	6	7	13	43	12	9	22	16

II. By Decade

Democrats		1950s	1960s	1970s
Strong		4.3	8.0	17.5
Weak		18.2	22.4	38.5

Republicans		1950s	1960s	1970s
Strong		3.7	1.2	3.5
Weak		16.2	19.6	15.5

Source: Data from the Center for Political Studies as reported in Arthur H. Miller and Warren E. Miller, "Partisanship and Performance: 'Rational' Choice in the 1976 Presidential Election" (Washington, D.C.: Annual Meeting of the American Political Science Association, September 1-4, 1977), p. 12. Reprinted by permission.

[a] Entry is the proportion of the voters whose vote for president was other than for the candidates of the party with which they identified.

the opposition. An examination of the trend in these regards makes the development unmistakable. The strength of party identification has traditionally proven to be an excellent prediction of the individual's vote. The number of defections by even weak party identifiers (Table 2.2) was small during the 1950s and up through most of the 1960s. A vote for the opposition by a strong party identifier was virtually un-thinkable. Approximately 80 percent of the weak identifiers and well over 90 percent of the strong identifiers consistently voted for their party's presidential candidate during these years.

The pattern is changing (Table 2.2). The 1976 presidential election appeared to represent a return to a stronger party-based vote than either of its two predecessors. Better than one-third to one-half of the weak Democratic identifiers voted for the Republican nominee in 1968 and 1972, and they were joined in the latter election year by one out of four strong Democratic identifiers. In the same election years, almost half of the "independent Democrats" supported the Republican pres-idential candidate.

The larger Democratic coalition is more likely to defect than is the smaller group of Republican identifiers. The strong Republican identi-fiers remain a solid, if embattled, group of party believers with a consistently impressive 96 percent of its dwindling members religious-ly supporting its party's standard-bearer. Weak Republican defections are variable, peaking in the Goldwater race of 1964 with 43 percent. Roughly one-fifth (22 percent) broke ranks in 1976 to vote for Jimmy Carter. "Independent Republicans" defect at about the same rate as weak Republicans.

The progressive decay in party allegiance is most apparent from a comparison of the rates of defection for party sympathizers by decade (Table 2.2). Allowing for variations introduced by the response to indi-vidual candidacies, the Republican figures are fairly consistent over time. The Democratic rates are not. The proportion of strong party identifiers who defected doubled from the 1950s to the 1960s and doubled again from the 1960s to the 1970s, whereas the proportion of weak Democratic identifiers voting Republican increased by over twenty percentage points to where an average of one out of three supported the opposition party in the 1970s.

John Petrocik has extended this analytic avenue by comparing the strength of partisan identification with the individual's vote over time in presidential, House, Senate, and gubernatorial races.[3] Defections range on the average between 5 percent and 35 percent for the various

[3] John R. Petrocik, "The Changeable American Voter: Some Revisions of the Revi-sion." Paper presented at the Annual Meeting of the American Political Science Associa-tion, New York, August 31–September 3, 1978.

types of contests, and the trend is toward less consistency between the psychological attachments of an individual and his party vote. The one exception appears to be the 1976 presidential vote, which seemed to show at least a short-run drop in defections. In Petrocik's analysis, the pattern evidenced in the 1976 presidential election is close to that found in the 1950s. The election, it appears, is but an aberration. This is not true for the House, Senate, or gubernatorial contests in 1976 when the defections equaled or exceeded those for the 1960s. Petrocik goes on to plot the correlation between party identification and the vote. The decline is consistent and dramatic for all races (president, House, Senate, governorships) over time (1952–76). The author concludes:

> Party identification is no longer the robust predictor of the vote that it was in the 1950s. The evidence for this is so overwhelming and widely recognized that the point is easily belabored. . . . Through 1960, party preference accounted for about fifty percent of the variance of the vote for these offices, by the late 1960s it was down to about thirty-six percent of the variance, and in the 1976 election party identification accounts for barely a third of the variance in the vote for the different offices.[4]

UNPREDICTABILITY IN THE VOTE

If this thumbnail sketch of the decline in party identification is relevant for elections, it is reasonable to expect party to be less meaningful as a referent in structuring the vote. This is exactly what happens. Voters, as noted earlier, are not inclined to turn out, but when they do vote, they are considerably less likely to vote the party label for all offices on the ballot. The changes are striking. Unequivocal party support appeared to be the norm in the 1950s and early 1960s. For example, it seems extraordinary within the context of today's politics, but among Democrats and Republicans better than 70 percent supported their party's presidential candidates in the 1950s. In the 1960 and 1964 presidential elections, the figure for partisan identifiers still hovered at an impressive two out of three. By the 1970s it had dropped

[4] *Ibid.*, p. 18.

to roughly one-half. In other words, the odds are not much over fifty-fifty today that a party identifier will vote for his party's presidential nominee. Republicans are little different from Democrats in this regard.

SPLIT-TICKET VOTING

Party members are also considerably more likely to split their tickets (i.e., to vote for candidates of different parties) at successive levels of contests. The frequency of split-ticket voting, another measure of the instability of partisan attitudes and contemporary politics, has increased significantly since the beginning of systematic academic surveying in the 1950s.

About a third of the Republicans and half of the independents and Democrats (in the Eisenhower victory of 1952, the percentage rose for Democrats) split their tickets between the parties. Goldwater's candidacy created difficulties for some Republicans, but it was not until the election of 1968 that split-ticket voting clearly began to claim a majority of participants. In the 1970s, between two-thirds and three-quarters of the independents and the Democrats and one-half of the Republicans divided their ballots between the parties at one point or another. Split-ticket voting has replaced the straight party vote as the norm for the American electorate — one further sign of the volatility present within the electorate and the decay of party influence.

Charles Hadley and Susan Howell have pressed the examination of split-ticket voting further than most.[5] Political scientists have argued that split-ticket voting is not only a sign of political instability, but that it may also be the forerunner of major upheavals within the electorate and possibly of a political realignment. Increases in the amount of split-ticket votes, for example, appeared in the 1890s and the 1920s,

[5] Charles Hadley and Susan Howell, "Split Ticket Voting in the Northeast, 1952–1976: Partisan Realignment, Dealignment, or Status Quo." Paper delivered at the Annual Meeting of the Midwest Political Science Association, Chicago, April 20–22, 1978.

periods that preceded a major, and even crucial, shift in electoral alignments.[6]

With this in mind, Hadley and Howell have probed below the surface of national politics to investigate whether there are differing patterns of voting loyalty associated with regions of the United States. They found that most Americans tend to vote for the same party in presidential and congressional races. From 1952 through 1968, on the average only 15 percent of the people divided their vote between the parties for these offices. To emphasize how rare splitting the ticket was, they point out that the region with up to five times as great an incidence as the others in presidential and congressional races was the South. The area was just beginning to evidence results of the powerful transformation toward a more competitive two-party politics closer to the national model.[7] In 1952, over 90 percent of nonsoutherners consistently voted for the same party at the presidential and congressional level.

By the 1970s split-ticket voting in these contests had increased to one-quarter or better for the nation as a whole (29 percent in 1972; 25 percent in 1976). The pattern was pronounced in all regions, although the South and the Northeast had the highest rates of defection.

In state and local races, the trend was similar. Less straight party voting could be expected in these contests, and less occurred. Nonetheless, the figures testifying to party loyalty for the early period (1952–60) are impressive. Only about one in four (27 percent) split their votes at these levels in these races. The trend is quite different after that. In the elections from 1960 to 1972 (the question was not asked in 1976), first 40 percent, then 48 percent and, by 1972, 58 percent, had divided their support between the parties in lower level contests.[8] The evidence of party instability is not confined to the national races only. It has permeated all levels of politics.

---

[6] Walter Dean Burnham, *Critical Elections and the Mainsprings of American Politics* (New York: Norton, 1970); Burnham, "The Changing Shape of the American Political Universe," *American Political Science Review* 59 (March 1965): 7–28; and Burnham, "The Appearance and Disappearance of the American Voter." Paper prepared for the Conference on the Future of the American Political System, Center for the Study of Democratic Politics, University of Pennsylvania, April 12–13, 1979.

[7] William C. Havard (ed.), *The Changing Politics of the South* (Baton Rouge: Louisiana State University Press, 1972); Jack Bass and Walter DeVries, *The Transformation of Southern Politics* (New York: Meridian, 1977).

[8] Hadley and Howell, "Split Ticket Voting," pp. 7–12.

INDEPENDENTS

The most noted aspect of the changing allegiance to political parties has been the rise in numbers and influence of the independent voter. The trend has been remarkable and has helped change the American political landscape from one dominated by party loyalties to one increasingly subjected to the whim of unattached and uncommitted (in partisan terms) electors.

The growing ranks of independents introduce an increasing unpredictability into election outcomes. The party label anchored the vote for identifiers. It was (as shown in Table 2.2) a reliable guide to the individual's political intentions. In what Philip Converse has called the "steady-state" period of party hegemony (1952–64),[9] it was both difficult and unusual for a member to break with his party to support an opposition candidate. Independents operate under no such constraints. By definition, their vote (and, for that matter, whether they choose to vote at all) is not anchored by party ties. It responds to short-term influences associated with the candidates and the issues in the campaign or the political climate peculiar to the given election year. It is an unstable vote (and turnout) that is basically unpredictable over time, and introduces into elections an increased volatility that today's fluid politics do not need.

The increasing number of independents cannot be disputed. As Table 2.1 demonstrates, independents have increased from about one-fifth of the electorate in the 1950s to better than one-third in the 1970s. The independents stand in numbers just behind the Democrats and well ahead of the Republicans. The trend is clear and the future favors the independents. It is likely that each successive election will witness a swelling of their ranks.

The independent vote is up for grabs. It has no allegiances. Its volatility and malleability does little to ease the concern of those who value stability and order in American politics. As Table 2.3 illustrates, the turnout of "pure" independents is normally well below that of partisans. This has been particularly true of the elections from 1964 onward. The effects of the expansion of the electorate through the introduction of the eighteen-year-old vote can be seen in 1972 and

[9] Philip Converse, *The Dynamics of Party Support* (Beverly Hills: Sage, 1976).

TABLE 2.3
Voter Turnout in Presidential Elections and Partisan or Independent Affiliation, 1952–76

	1952	1956	1960	1964	1968	1972	1976
Partisans	79%[a]	77%	85%	83%	81%	79%	77%
Independents[b]	74	77	77	62	65	53	57

Source: Data supplied by the Center for Political Studies.

[a] Figures have been rounded.

[b] "Independent Democrats" and "independent Republicans" (or "leaners") have been omitted.

1976. Not only did the number of independents grow, but their participation fell to modest levels (57 percent), comparable in many respects to the poor turnouts following the advent of female suffrage in the 1920s.[10]

The independent vote is fluid. It tends to drift from one candidate and party to the other, depending on what happens to excite the fancy of the voter. Apparently, the independents were strongly attracted to Dwight Eisenhower in 1952 and 1956, awarding the Republicans better than 80 percent of their vote (Table 2.4). The independents reacted negatively to Barry Goldwater in 1964 and George McGovern in 1972. In both cases, their opponents received 70 percent or more of the independent vote. The surges and the equally pronounced drop-offs in the proportion of votes cast for the parties and their candidates from one election to the next indicate the changeability and unreliability of this increasingly significant bloc of electors.

To add to the confusion, not only is the number of independents increasing, but their composition is changing. The new independents coming into the electorate are not the same as the old independents. Originally, it was felt that independents were the classic embodiment of the democratic spirit. It was believed that in the best civics textbook fashion they voted the man, not the party, and that they did so on the basis of issues and the common good. The assumptions were that they were not blinded by party, that they weighed the issues and candidates in a campaign, and that they then made their choice based on their own

[10] William Crotty, *Political Reform and the American Experiment* (New York: Crowell, 1977), pp. 20–22.

TABLE 2.4
Swings in the Independent Vote, 1952–76, as Measured by Support for the
Democratic Presidential Nominee

1952	1956	1960	1964	1968	1972	1976
20%	16%	46%	77%	24%	30%	22%

Source: From Herbert B. Asher, *Presidential Elections and American Politics: Voters, Candidates, and Campaigns Since 1952.* © The Dorsey Press, 1976. Reprinted by permission. 1976 figure from Center for Political Studies 1976 presidential election survey.

values and the information received from the media and other sources during the campaign.

The early voting studies demolished the myth. The independent voter was found to be the individual with the weakest ties to the political system (hence his failure to identify with one of the major parties), the least interest in and knowledge of politics, and the greatest likelihood not even to vote. The picture was not a pleasant one.

Political conditions have changed and many people have begun to question the bleak assessment of the independent found in the traditional voting studies. The reexamination of the independent is not intended to disown the commonly accepted characterization. Rather, it is intended to suggest that the picture drawn of the independent may not be accurate for substantial numbers of independents. The group is too large and too complex for that.

Beginning with an analysis of the 1964 election, Walter Dean Burnham has suggested the emergence of a "new" independent, quite different in social characteristics and political concerns from the "old" (or traditionally described) independent. The "new" independents, says Burnham, "may have declined to identify with either major party not because they are relatively politically unconscious, but because the structure of electoral politics at the present time turns upon parties, issues, and symbolism which do not have much meaning in terms of their political values or cognitions."[11]

Burnham finds that independents, although as a group ranking low in income, occupational achievement, and education (as would be ex-

[11] Burnham, *Critical Elections*, p. 127

pected from the classical model), have a bloc of highly educated adherents. It is also true that independents rank low on participation but (and this could not be predicted from the earlier voting studies) they exhibit both a high and a low distribution on indices of political efficacy, a measure of perceived ability to affect the political environment. The measure is important for understanding political behavior and correlates highly with involvement, political competence, and knowledge. The bloc that scores high in efficacy ranks second only to "strong" Republican identifiers, a surprising outcome. He also found that the policy views of independents are not as inchoate as had been assumed. Rather, they normally fell somewhere between the two parties' position, a location that gives some credence to Burnham's views.

Finally, Burnham looked at those defecting from Democratic ranks to independent status. He found them to be among those who rank the highest on social and demographic measures of socioeconomic status. Additionally, the young seemed particularly attracted to the independent category.[12]

An examination of data from the 1976 presidential election appears to support the depiction of a new, evolving, and younger independent coalition. For example, in examining the proportion of independents by age group (Table 2.5), one finds a strong association between age and partisanship. The older the person, the more likely he is to have identified (and to continue to identify) with a political party. Conversely, the younger the person, the greater the likelihood that he will be independent.

Recent elections show a much greater incidence of first-time electors claiming independent status.[13] The change is sharp and is not explained by the eighteen-year-old vote, whose impact was first felt in 1972. On the contrary, the jump in independents became pronounced between 1964 and 1968 and has held steady since then. This suggests that changes in the political environment fundamentally affected the way people viewed politics and their willingness (or lack thereof) to associate with either of the major parties. Once the move toward independence gathered momentum, it continued to be strong. With

[12] *Ibid.*, pp. 123–26.

[13] See Norman Nie, Sidney Verba, and John R. Petrocik, *The Changing American Voter* (Cambridge, Mass.: Harvard University Press, 1976), Table 4.3, p. 60, and text discussion, pp. 59–73.

approximately 8 percent of the electorate new each presidential election year and with the refusal to identify with parties strongest among the young, continued growth in the proportion and importance of the independent vote is highly likely.

YOUTH AND THE PARTIES

It has been argued that as people mature and assume the economic and familial responsibilities of life, their political views become more conventional and they begin to assume their political responsibilities. The argument could be extended to contend that the young adults will then associate with one of the political parties and the trend toward independence will be blunted; in effect, that trend is an artifact of an extended and an increasingly younger electorate. Clearly, the strength of party identification is significantly different among age groups as Table 2.5 shows.[14] Comparing the oldest and youngest age cohorts in the presidential electorate in Table 2.5, one uncovers some remarkable differences in affiliation. Half of those under thirty claimed some type of independent status, and the other half affiliated with a political party. Among the oldest voters (those first eligible to vote in 1916 or before), 78 percent identified with a political party, and of these 40 percent were classified as "strong" identifiers. Only 9 percent of the most recent voters could be called "strong" identifiers. A relatively small 22 percent of the oldest category claimed independent status.

Any change toward increased partisanship by the new voters of the last decade is unlikely. The point cannot be proven, obviously, but it is likely that strong partisanship for older voters is a product of the time and political conditions in which they entered the electorate. Different generations of voters are socialized in different states of political party significance. As they mature their political ties become stronger. New voters have weaker ties. The political situation at present encourages independence; the political parties do not attract the new voters. Un-

[14] For comparative data and related findings, see Arthur H. Miller and Warren E. Miller, "Partisanship and Performance: 'Rational' Choice in the 1976 Presidential Election." Paper presented at the 1977 Annual Meeting of the American Political Science Association, Washington, D.C., September 1–4, 1977, p. 25.

TABLE 2.5
Age and Party Status, 1976

Party Identification	18–20	21–25	26–30	31–35
Democrats	34%	31%	32%	32%
Strong Democrat	(7)	(8)	(10)	(9)
Weak Democrat	(27)	(23)	(22)	(23)
Independents	52%	47%	50%	43%
Independent Democrat	(16)	(17)	(19)	(11)
Pure Independent	(21)	(18)	(19)	(21)
Independent Republican	(15)	(12)	(12)	(11)
Republicans	14%	22%	18%	25%
Strong Republican	(2)	(7)	(6)	(8)
Weak Republican	(12)	(15)	(12)	(17)
	100%	100%	100%	100%
N	86	202	238	170

Party Identification	36–40	41–50	5–60	61 and older
Democrats	31%	40%	47%	47%
Strong Democrat	(9)	(18)	(18)	(22)
Weak Democrat	(22)	(22)	(29)	(25)
Independents	40%	36%	29%	22%
Independent Democrat	(11)	(11)	(10)	(7)
Pure Independent	(16)	(14)	(8)	(9)
Independent Republican	(13)	(11)	(11)	(6)
Republicans	29%	24%	24%	31%
Strong Republican	(11)	(10)	(12)	(13)
Weak Republican	(18)	(14)	(12)	(18)
	100%	100%	100%	100%
N	150	268	300	453

Source: Data supplied by the Center for Political Studies.

less there is some unforeseen upheaval, these conditions are not likely to change. Partisanship is dying. The strongest party identifiers are consistently being phased out of the electorate. Time is on the side of the independents.

ELECTORAL SWINGS

Let us look at one further piece of evidence on the decreasing impact of political parties in elections. Party loyalty tended to anchor an electorate. Drastic changes in the vote from one election to the next were unlikely. If party support is less important to the voter, then sharp (even wild) swings in the proportion of the vote cast for each of the parties would appear a likely consequence. This, again, is happening (Figure 2.1). Historically, elections go through different phases. A

FIGURE 2.1
Swings in Presidential Election Outcomes, 1876–1976

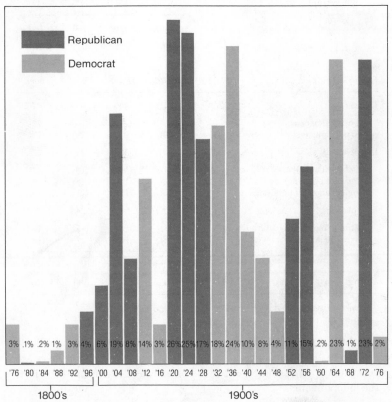

Source: From Everett C. Ladd, Jr., " 'Reform' Is Wrecking the U.S. Party System," *Fortune* (November 1977), p. 179. Redrawn from art provided by permission from *Fortune* art department.

period of highly competitive and close elections will be followed by one in which one party has a distinct advantage. The distinguishing characteristic, however, has been the consistency of a given pattern for an electoral era.

This is not true for the contemporary period. Beginning in 1960, there has been a dizzying succession of close elections followed by landslides, then by toss-up races, and so on. To confuse matters further, the shifts can benefit one party or the other, almost on whim. In 1960 the Democrats won an extraordinarily close contest. Four years later they won in a landslide. Could the party have been on its way to recouping its losses and establishing itself as the dominant party in a one-party era? Not so. In 1968 Richard Nixon and the Republicans came back to win the presidency in a very close contest. Four years later Nixon won in a landslide comparable to Johnson's in 1964. Perhaps the Republicans were on their way to reemerging as the dominant coalition, as many of their adherents claimed. However, the party's immediate fate was much the same as that of the Democrats in the mid-1960s. Four years later the Republicans lost a close contest to Jimmy Carter and the Democrats.

The wild variations in the vote are further indications of the rootlessness of contemporary American politics. Party loyalty has declined precipitously. Nothing has replaced it that could give elections the structure and certainty evident only a few decades ago. For better or worse, the contemporary scene is one of fluidity and uncertainty with no change in the dominating patterns in sight. The politics of the present, whatever its shortcomings, will be the politics of the immediate future. If anything, the changes traced here and their ramifications should become more pronounced.

3
The Rising Significance of Issues in Elections

ISSUE VOTING

As party has become less important in structuring the individual's vote, policy questions have been assuming a new significance. Researchers have found that voters have a new coherence in evaluating issues, and that they attach more significance to issues in making their decisions.[1]

Most of the contemporary debate over issues and their importance in elections revolves around methodology such as the conceptualization of such studies, the proper wordings of questions and interpretation of replies, the appropriate criteria for accepting and judging an issue-related vote, and the assumptions the researcher brings to the

[1] The literature on this point is extensive. See, as examples: Norman H. Nie, Sidney Verba, and John R. Petrocik, *The Changing American Voter* (Cambridge, Mass.: Harvard University Press, 1976); Gerald Pomper, *Voters' Choice* (New York: Dodd, Mead, 1975); and Benjamin I. Page, *Choices and Echoes in Presidential Elections* (Chicago: University of Chicago Press, 1978).

44

analysis. The debates are technical and have a good deal to do with the way in which the research findings are evaluated and the weight that should be given the results.[2] The general trend is clear, and virtually everyone involved in investigations of voting behavior would agree: voter reliance on the issues in campaigns and the stands taken by the candidates has significantly increased since the mid-1960s. As party identification has declined, voters have relied more on issues to fulfill the functions once served by the parties. That trend began in the election of 1964 when voters were offered clear choices on a policy basis between candidates (Barry Goldwater and Lyndon Johnson) and political parties. The break with the past elections studied in depth by academicians since the advent of modern survey technology (1952–60) was sharp. In this sense 1964 may have represented something akin to a "critical" election: one that provokes (or institutionalizes) a break with the past that endures beyond the immediate election.[3] In effect, a critical election redirects the course of American electoral behavior.

The trend toward an increased reliance on issues has endured. The elections of 1968, 1972, and 1976 saw a greater consistency and predictability among individual beliefs and a greater impact of these on the election. The exact causes (and their relative impacts) that explain these changes are debated and the comparative importance of issues as against party identification in contributing to the election outcome is argued by "revisionists" (those who emphasize the change toward an

[2] As examples, see: James A. Stimson, "Belief Systems: Constraint, Complexity, and the 1972 Election," *American Journal of Political Science* 19 (1975): 393–417; David RePass, "Issue Salience and Party Choice," *American Political Science Review* 65 (1971): 389–400; Gerald Pomper, "From Confusion to Clarity: Issues and American Voters, 1956–1968," *American Political Science Review* 62 (1972): 415–28; Benjamin I. Page and Richard A. Brody, "Policy Voting and the Electoral Process," *American Political Science Review* 66 (1972): 979–95; Richard W. Boyd, "Popular Control of Public Policy: A Normal Vote Analysis of the 1968 Election," *American Political Science Review* 66 (1972): 429–49; John H. Kessel, "The Issues in Issue Importance," *American Political Science Review* 66 (1972): 459–65; and David M. Kovenock, James W. Prothro, et al., *Explaining the Vote*, 2 vols. (Chapel Hill, N.C.: Institute for Research in Social Science, 1973).

[3] Pomper, "From Confusion to Clarity"; Mark A. Schulman and Gerald Pomper, "Variability in Electoral Behavior: Longitudinal Perspectives From Causal Modeling," *American Journal of Political Science* 19 (1975): 1–18; John C. Pierce, "Party Identification and the Changing Role of Ideology in American Politics," *Midwest Journal of Political Science* 14 (1970): 25–42; John Field and Ronald Anderson, "Ideology and the Public's Conceptualization of the 1964 Election," *Public Opinion Quarterly* 33 (1969): 380–98; and Walter Dean Burnham, "American Voting Behavior and the 1964 Election," *Midwest Journal of Political Science* 12 (1968): 1–40.

issue-oriented electorate) and "traditionalists" (those whose past concern has been with the dominant role of party identification in influencing vote outcomes).[4] The controversy may be one of degrees rather than trends. The greater reliance on issues in affecting the vote decision and thus the election outcome is clear enough and, as a trend, not a basic point of dispute.

Essentially, recent investigations have found that the public's awareness of issues and their relevance to the vote has increased markedly since the 1950s; that the public has a better conception of the differences between the two parties on the issues; and that issues are assuming a greater importance in explaining the voter's decision. Although party identification is still a potent contributor to the voter's decision, the increasing impact of issues has coincided with a decline in significance of party identification in explaining election outcomes. And, surprisingly, the changes observed have come about in a relatively short period of time (since the election of 1964, as noted) and contrast sharply with the interpretations of voting behavior of an earlier period (1952–1960).

Gerald Pomper has been a leader in the line of inquiry. He has shown in his work the sharp divergence between two sets of presidential elections, 1956–1960 and 1964–1968, in the perception of party differences on policy matters of traditional concern to the Democratic and Republican party coalitions (i.e., aid to education, medical care, job guarantees, fair employment, school integration, and foreign aid). These are issues that have provided a basis for continuing cleavage between the national parties. Beginning with the 1964 election, far greater numbers of voters began to perceive the contrasting party stands on these issues and the individual voter's party identification and policy support positions began to be more consistent than in the past.[5] In a related investigation, Pomper and Mark Schulman were able to show for the presidential elections of 1956, 1964, and 1972, that though the correlation of party identification with the vote declined 30 percent, the association between issues and voting increased almost fourfold.[6] Figures of this nature can be misleading, especially because

---

[4]The debate is reviewed in Philip E. Converse, "Public Opinion and Voting Behavior," in Fred I. Greenstein and Nelson W. Polsby (eds.), *Handbook of Political Science*, Vol. 4 (Reading, Mass.: Addison-Wesley, 1975), pp. 75–169; and Herbert Asher, *Presidential Elections and American Politics* (Homewood, Ill.: Dorsey, 1976).

[5]Pomper, "From Confusion to Clarity."

[6]Schulman and Pomper, "Variability in Electoral Behavior."

of the complexity of the analysis being done and the uncertain extent to which parties and candidates themselves are perceived in an issue context. In the Pomper and Schulman analysis, party identification and candidate appeal maintained formidable associations with voting, even exceeding that for issues. The direction of the changes, nonetheless, is the important clue to the way in which the electorate is moving.

Norman Nie, Sidney Verba, and John Petrocik have authored the most comprehensive reexamination of voting behavior since the classic *The American Voter*, published in 1960.[7] In their book (suitably entitled *The Changing American Voter*), they have put the matter simply and well:

> Party voting has declined for two reasons: the number of Independents (who cannot cast a party vote) has risen, and the number of party identifiers who defect when they vote has gone up as well. At the same time, issue voting has increased for two similar reasons: more citizens have consistent issue positions on the basis of which they can vote; and more citizens are guided by these issue positions in casting their vote.[8]

Norman Nie and Kristi Andersen have examined voting behavior for 1956–72 in an attempt to determine the associations among issues, voting, and attitudinal constraint (a measure of ideological conceptual ability).[9] Their analysis is broader than the efforts to associate individual sets of issues with voting. By introducing attitudinal constraints in reexamining the assumptions concerning the electorate's conceptual abilities found in the pioneering work of Philip Converse,[10] the authors are attempting to chart the movement in consistency and predictability among, for example, domestic, foreign, and civil rights clusters of issues and their association with both party identifications and the vote.

Nie and Andersen found, as have others, that the correlation between party identification and the vote fell consistently between 1956 and 1972. For the elections of 1956–60, the association between the vote and party identification averaged a very high 0.89 and for the elections of 1964–72, 0.69. Meanwhile, the association between polit-

[7] Nie, Verba, and Petrocik, *The Changing American Voter*; and Angus Campbell, Philip Converse, Warren Miller, and Donald Stokes, *The American Voter* (New York: Wiley, 1960).

[8] *Ibid.*, p. 291.

[9] Norman H. Nie with Kristi Andersen, "Mass Belief Systems Revisited: Political Change and Attitude Structure," *Journal of Politics* 36 (1974):540–87.

[10] Philip Converse, "The Nature of Relief Systems in Mass Publics," in David Apter (ed.), *Ideology and Discontent* (New York: Free Press, 1964), pp. 206–61.

ical attitudes and the vote rose from lows of 0.16 and 0.21 in 1956 and 1960, respectively, to an average of 0.52 for the elections of 1964–72.[11]

The changes observed do not appear to be transitory. They mark a pronounced shift in correlates of voter decision making that, since 1964, have seen the increase in importance of issue stands in voter choice. Correspondingly, although this need not be the case (an individual's party affiliation and his position on issues could reinforce each other and both could correlate strongly with the vote), party identification has declined significantly as an influence on voting.

The changes in voter response have resulted from a different political climate. The relative complacency of the 1950s was shattered by a series of major social and economic upheavals during the 1960s that have continued to this day. The following have left their mark:

the civil rights revolution
the Vietnam War
demonstrations and civil violence
concern over crime in the streets
the burning of cities
the bitter disappointment over the Great Society programs
government misconduct
the excesses of the FBI, other governmental invasions of the rights of
    individuals (e.g., wiretapping)
CIA involvement in the overthrow of the Chilean regime
the assassinations of John and Robert Kennedy
two attacks on an incumbent president (Ford)
the assassination of the preeminent civil rights leader (Martin Luther
    King)
the shame of Watergate and the resignation in disgrace of a president
recession, unemployment, and inflation
the decay of the cities
the rise in taxes
the women's rights revolution
the pollution of the environment
the energy crisis

and so on. Americans became issue-conscious and issues became more closely associated with their vote choices.

[11] Nie and Andersen, "Mass Belief Systems Revisited."

As the political environment changed, so did the nature of the candidates. Presidential contenders began to take stands on issues of broad concern and to offer voters a choice. When they did, and as voters began to perceive differences of consequence on policy concerns between parties and candidates, their views on questions of policy began to exercise an increasing influence on their votes.[12]

Although party identification supplied the primary explanation for the outcomes of presidential elections during the 1950s and early 1960s, the tide had begun to turn in 1964. By 1972, the Center for Political Studies of the University of Michigan, the group whose work was employed as the cornerstone of the debate and the most consistent defender of the traditionalist position, was willing to concede that major changes had taken place. The center used multivariate analytic techniques that included "proximity measures" (an assessment of where an individual stood on an issue compared to where the candidate or political party was perceived to stand) to measure voters' conceptual abilities and policy concerns and to correlate these with the vote decision. The authors of the center's report on the 1972 election wrote, "The proximity measures, when taken together as reflecting ideology [conceptual abilities] and policy voting, were substantially more important as direct explanations of the vote than was party identification."[13] The researchers went on to test their conclusion through a path analytic approach and concluded that "we found the total effect of party identification to be .51, whereas the issue effect was .55. *As an explanation of the vote in 1972, issues were at least equally as important as party identification*" (emphasis in the original).[14]

The 1976 presidential election seemed to feature a return to a stronger party-based vote. Any assumptions of a decrease in issue voting may be misleading, however. The Center for Political Studies's report on the 1976 election, prepared by Arthur Miller and Warren

[12] Pomper, "From Confusion to Clarity"; Page, *Choices and Echoes;* Nie and Andersen, "Mass Belief Systems Revisited."

[13] Arthur H. Miller, Warren E. Miller, Alden S. Raine, and Thad A. Brown, "A Majority Party in Disarray: Policy Polarization in 1972 Election," *American Political Science Review* 70 (September 1976): 753–78, as reprinted in Richard G. Niemi and Herbert F. Weisberg (eds.), *Controversies in American Voting Behavior* (San Francisco: Freeman, 1976), p. 190.

[14] *Ibid*., pp. 191–92.

[15] Arthur H. Miller and Warren E. Miller, "Partisanship and Performance: 'Rational' Choice in the 1976 Presidential Election" (Washington, D.C.: Annual Meeting of the American Political Science Association, September 1–4, 1977).

Miller, makes a number of points.[15] First, between 1972 and 1976 the level of attitudinal consistency and ideological thinking among the American voters remained essentially unchanged. Party association, nonetheless, appeared stronger in its correlation with the vote. The authors explain the apparent paradox as follows:

The presidential candidates in 1976 (as opposed to 1972) chose to deemphasize issues. Jimmy Carter, in particular, may have obscured his position on many policy concerns. An assessment of candidate strategy in this regard is somewhat conjectural.[16] Voters did not perceive the clear differences between candidates that they had four years earlier. In such uncertainty, voters tend to return to their party moorings for direction. Since there are more Democrats than Republicans, such strategy clearly helped Carter's candidacy.

The issues that were stressed in the campaign tended to relate to economic concerns, the basic dividing point between the Democratic and Republican coalitions. This emphasis would again reinforce a party-oriented vote. It served another function for the Carter campaign. It provided the one solid rallying point for the large and heterogeneous Democratic coalition and, at the same time, avoided inflammatory concerns such as those introduced into the McGovern campaign, which severely divided Democrats.

Issue perceptions and party affiliations may be more closely associated than many believe. The authors conclude that their research has provided

> solid evidence for the theoretical expectation that when voters are uncertain about the issues positions espoused by the candidates, they employ a partisan issue ideology in their electoral decision-making. The important point here is not simply that this partisan ideology is used to reduce uncertainty and resolve the electoral choice, but that it is apparently based upon policy considerations, and not an empty and habitual response to party labels.[17]

Issue voting lives. If the association between issue positions and party choice is anything like what Miller and Miller have suggested, then it would behoove the parties to take clear and attractive stands on

---

[16] James Wooten, *Dasher* (New York: Summit Books, 1978); Jules Witcover, *Marathon* (New York: Viking, 1977); and Martin Schram, *Running for President 1976* (New York: Stein and Day, 1977).

[17] Miller and Miller, "Partisanship and Performance," p. 62.

the major policy concerns of the day. In the past, political parties have not served well as vehicles of policy representation and articulation. They will have to change. In an age of increased issue concern, the very existence of the parties may well depend on it.

While the trend towards the increasing importance of issues in presidential elections is clear, a few caveats are in order. Initially, candidate orientation was posited as one of the three most important influences on the presidential vote (along with party identification and issue orientation). Candidate image is a short-run factor influencing individual elections. Its effect from one presidential race to the next could be expected to vary greatly. It is a difficult concept to measure and may in fact be associated in national elections with the voter's issue perceptions. As an example, a voter who strongly favored a law and order position in 1972 logically would have supported Richard Nixon, whom he would also be likely to perceive personally in favorable terms; a voter strongly opposed to the Vietnam War in 1972 would have backed George McGovern, and this support could color, to a degree, his perception of the candidate and his qualities. Because of the ambiguities in the concept and the increasing emphasis on issues in presidential elections, candidate orientation as a factor in explaining presidential election outcomes has been stressed less and at present the concept is undergoing experimental attempts to redefine it as a measurement tool. The end result could be a clearer indication of its impact on national-level voter decision-making.

It should be noted also that in congressional (and perhaps other levels of elections) both the voter's perceptions of the candidates and a habitual party vote may assume greater importance. This tendency is discussed later in this book in relation to congressional elections where policy positions are often of far less importance in explaining election outcomes. On the presidential level, however, there has been a decided move in voter decision-making toward an increased reliance on issues in determining for whom to vote.

4

Liberalism/Conservatism

An increasing turn toward conservatism, many observers believed, marked the elections of the late 1960s and the 1970s. Early on, it was focused on the revolt against lawlessness; the decline in adherence to traditional moral and social values; crime in the streets; the campus disruptions; cities in flame; the hippie life style and the "me generation" syndrome; the disrespect for authority and the vilification, in particular, of the police; and the mass demonstrations and continuing acts of civil disobedience sparked by the Vietnam War. The nation's social fabric seemed to be unraveling. The revolt coincided with, and helped feed, an increasing cynicism concerning the value and objectives of the massive government spending programs and the social welfare priorities of the Johnson-Kennedy years. The beneficiary of this revolt in its first stages was Richard Nixon, the Republican nominee for president in 1968. Nixon won narrowly, but he did beat the dominant Democratic party and he ended its eight-year control of the presidency.

As president, Nixon interpreted his "mandate" broadly and attempted to build a conservative coalition of sun-belt states, Republicans, and about anyone dissatisfied with the Democratic programs and the seeming moral decay and political anarchy rampant in the society. The chief focus of the new conservative resurgence was to be the "silent majority" — those quiet Americans, basically conservative in social and fiscal policy, that Nixon's people believed represented the mainstream of political thinking.

Nixon and his policies went too far, resulting in a repressive government posture that eventually forced the president's resignation under threat of impeachment. Gerald Ford, the vice-president, assumed the top office. Ford, a conservative, was a twenty-six-year veteran of the House of Representatives who had faithfully mirrored the values of his midwestern constituency.

Ford, in turn, went down to a narrow defeat in 1976 at the hands of Jimmy Carter, the Democratic candidate. Carter appeared to be a moderate. In office, his policies of fiscal restraint, reduced social programs, tight money, decontrol of the oil industry, and moderately increased defense spending placed him closer to the Ford-Nixon policy emphasis than to that of the more traditional Democratic programs of Johnson and Kennedy.

By the late 1970s the rise of interest rates, a decade of increasing inflation, and the corresponding decline in the standard of living had voters in a sour mood. Although the off-year election of 1978 was hailed as a victory for conservatism, the Republicans did not significantly increase their seats in either the House or Senate. The election year did, however, give birth to the Proposition 13 mentality. There was an effort to limit taxation through legislative initiative, or state or national constitutional amendment if necessary. The Kemp-Roth bill was introduced in the Congress to cut taxes across the board by one-third. It quickly became a popular political debating point. Who could be for taxes? California Governor Jerry Brown, one of Carter's rivals for the 1980 Democratic presidential nomination, endorsed the idea (favored mostly by rightists and some Republicans) of a new constitutional convention to rewrite into the Constitution limits on taxation and possibly federal spending. The hero of the new public mood was Howard Jarvis, a previously unknown conservative activist, who in his later years (he was over seventy) had risen to prominence as co-sponsor and principal lobbyist for Proposition 13. With the ratification by California voters of the proposition, Jarvis became the highly publicized political guru of the new revolt. The media proclaimed the rise of conservatism among voters and the new mood that had taken control of political life. Were Americans becoming more conservative? Had a conservative philosophy of government come to dominate the views of Americans?

The characteristics of the period appeared to be:

the move to cut taxes
the belief that social welfare and spending programs did not work
the reactions to big government
a "get-tough" attitude toward crime and criminals
renewed support for the death penalty and its reconstitution in many
    states
the prolonged opposition to busing and new civil rights legislation
support for defense spending
the antiabortion crusade
the faltering drive for ERA (Equal Rights Amendment)
a hardening line toward the Soviets and any SALT (Strategic Arms
    Limitation Treaties) pacts.

The signs could be misleading however. As with most things, the reality was more complex and, as fits the American character, more pragmatic than the media, the immediate reaction to issues, or the pundits' instant analysis would lead one to expect.

First, as to the conservatism of the American population in general, poll results raised doubts about the commitment to a new conservatism. Louis Harris and Associates had been asking Americans to characterize themselves as "Liberal," "Middle-of-the-Road," and "Conservative" for years. An examination of the Harris data for 1968–78 (Table 4.1) shows an actual decrease in the proportion of respondents considering themselves conservative. The drop came between 1968 and 1972, and since the early 1970s the number of conservatives had stabilized around 35 percent. The proportion of self-identified liberals had remained relatively constant at 22 percent. The major increase had been in those classed as middle-of-the-roaders, up from 36 percent to 45 percent. There is not much support for a conservative resurgence in these figures.

The picture becomes more complex when individual issue areas are examined. Americans did appear frustrated by and angered with big institutions of every kind over which they exercised little control (Table 4.2). The increase in those who believed that government had become too powerful was dramatic, from 44 percent of a national adult sample in 1964 to 69 percent by 1976. A majority in the 1970s believed the unions were too strong and a majority also felt that corporate profits should be controlled (up from 25 percent in 1962).

TABLE 4.1
Ideology of the American Electorate, as Measured by Harris Surveys, 1968–78

	Ideology		
Year	*Conservative*	*Middle-of-the-road*	*Liberal*
1968	43%	36%	22%
1972	35	38	26
1974	33	47	20
1975	40	40	21
1976	36	41	23
1977	36	45	20
1978	35	45	21

Source: Surveys by Louis Harris and Associates as reported in *Public Opinion* (September/October 1978), p. 23. Reprinted by permission of Elsevier North Holland, Inc.

The public, nevertheless, tended to strongly support government-sponsored social welfare programs. Between 74 and 81 percent indicated that they felt the government should help everyone who wanted a job find work and that it should assume responsibility for assisting people to acquire low-cost health care. Although sentiment favoring the death penalty did increase during the 1970s, so did support for liberalized positions on such social concerns as legalization of marijuana, the propriety of premarital relations, careers for married women, and a woman for president. Those favoring the ERA resolution remained in a majority. The number of proabortionists continued fairly stable (but at less than a majority), and those willing to make divorce easier, another indication of the attitude toward permissiveness and moral questions in the society, fluctuated, but stayed well ahead of comparative levels of response for the 1960s.

Attitudes toward racial questions (outside of busing) appeared to have liberalized remarkably. Better than 70 percent of the population disapproved of state laws against interracial marriage (up from 49 percent in 1965); 84 percent would support a black for president (up from 51 percent in 1963); and 93 percent believed that blacks had a right to live any place they chose (up from 71 percent in 1960). These statistics represent pronounced changes in attitudes toward blacks. They are paralleled by the rise in support for civil liberties. In 1954, at the height of the McCarthy era, a social scientist, Samuel Stouffer, surveyed Americans as to the strength of their support for libertarian qualities in

TABLE 4.2
Public Views on Major Social Questions *(Percentage agreeing)*

I. *Reactions to Big Institutions*

1. The government is getting too powerful.

1964	1968	1972	1976
44.0	55.0	57.0	69.0

Source: Data supplied by the Center for Political Studies.

2. Should the government put a limit on the profits companies can make in industries where there is no competition?

1962	1971	1973	1975	1977
25.0	33.0	40.0	55.0	55.0

Source: Opinion Research Corporation.

3. Labor unions have grown too powerful.

1971	1975	1977
55.0	50.0	51.0

Source: Opinion Research Corporation.

II. *Social Welfare Positions*

1. The government should help in getting doctors and hospital care at low cost.

1960	1964	1968	1978
65.0	58.0	61.0	81.0

Source: Data supplied by the Center for Political Studies; CPS/*New York Times* Survey, January 8–12, 1972.

2. Government should guarantee people jobs.

1956	1960	1978
62.0	64.0	74.0

Source: Same as above.

3. Favor the death penalty.

1960	1965	1966	1969	1971	1972	1976	1978
51.0	45.0	42.0	51.0	49.0	57.0	65.0	62.0

Source: Gallup Polls (American Institute of Public Opinion).

4. Legalize marijuana.

1969	1973	1975	1978
13.0	19.0	21.0	31.0

Source: Gallup Poll and National Opinion Research Center.

5. Approve sex education courses.

1965	1969	1970	1977
69.0	71.0	65.0	77.0

Source: Gallup Polls.

6. Approve of sex relations before marriage.

1969	1972	1978
23.0	51.0	59.0

Source: Gallup Polls, National Opinion Research Center.

7. Married women should be allowed to work.

1970	1972	1975	1978
60.0	64.0	70.0	72.0

Source: Same as above.

8. Would support a woman for president.

1967	1969	1971	1972	1978
59.0	58.0	69.0	74.0	81.0

Source: Same as above.

9. Support ERA (Equal Rights Amendment).

1975	1976	1977	1978
51.0	66.0	56.0	55.0

Source: Harris, Louis. *The Harris Survey*. New York: The Chicago Tribune–New York Syndicate, July 17, 1978.

III. *Racial Issues*

1. Would support black for president.

1963	1965	1967	1969	1971	1972	1977	1978
51.0	63.0	57.0	74.0	75.0	73.0	82.0	84.0

Source: Gallup Polls, National Opinion Research Center.

2. Reject laws against interracial marriage.

1965	1970	1972	1977
49.0	62.0	61.0	72.0

Source: Same as above.

3. Blacks have a right to live anywhere (and a right to fair treatment in jobs and housing).

1960	1968	1978
71.0	63.0	93.0

Source: Data supplied by the Center for Political Studies.

(Continued)

TABLE 4.2 *(continued)*

(Percentage agreeing)

IV. *Support for Civil Liberties*

Year	Allow anti-religion speaker	Keep anti-religion book in library	Allow socialist speaker	Permit social-ist teacher to hold job	Keep social-ist book in library
1954	37.0	35.0	59.0	33.0	53.0
1977	62.0	59.0	62.0	57.0	69.0

Source: Samuel A. Stouffer, *Communism, Conformity, and Civil Liberties* (Garden City, New York: Doubleday, 1955); and National Opinion Research Center.

V. *Liberal and Conservative Differences on Selected Issues*

Self-identification	Approve of sex education courses	Approve of government guarantees of fair jobs and housing for blacks	Restrict sale of handguns	Allow sale of pornography to adults
Liberal	85.0	79.0	71.0	68.0
Middle-of-the-Road	81.0	73.0	59.0	59.0
Conservative	69.0	67.0	55.0	51.0

Self-identification	Approve quotas for minorities	Government help poor with abortions	Allow sale of marijuana	Government help with medical costs
Liberal	45.0	60.0	56.0	91.0
Middle-of-the-Road	41.0	47.0	44.0	85.0
Conservative	35.0	38.0	34.0	82.0

Self-identification	Government guarantee jobs for all	Government set safety standards for factories	Support government regulation of business	Increase spending for domestic programs	Agree Great Society programs make things better
Liberal	81.0	77.0	49.0	44.0	40.0
Middle-of-the-Road	79.0	72.0	36.0	32.0	36.0
Conservative	71.0	69.0	27.0	23.0	30.0

Source: Data compiled in *Public Opinion* (September/October 1978), pp. 33–39.

Source: Information from The Gallup Poll; Louis Harris and Associates, Inc.; and Elsevier North Holland, Inc., reprinted by permission.

a variety of projected situations (permitting antireligion or socialist speakers to address gatherings in the community; keeping antireligion or socialist books in the local library; allowing a socialist to be a teacher). The mean level of support favoring the civil liberty positions was 43 percent in 1954. Two decades later, a survey asking the same questions found that the support level had risen to a mean of 65 percent.

To confound matters, a majority of conservatives supported many liberal positions. These included government guarantees of jobs and housing for blacks, restrictions on the sale of handguns, approval of sex education courses, and allowing pornographic materials to be sold to adults. Conversely, on such issues as quotas for minorities, support of government regulation of business, increases in domestic spending, and a belief that the Great Society programs made life better, a majority of liberals took positions normally associated with conservatives. On other issues (government-supported abortions; restrictions on the sale of marijuana) conservatives were conservative and liberals were predictably liberal.

If anything, in most of the issues surveys Americans appear to be moderately liberal. Yet there is some truth to talk of a conservative revival. Surely, the rhetoric of the 1970s involved typically conservative issues (inflation, economic recession, decreases in the standard-of-living, government spending) and the solutions proposed by Democrats and Republicans alike tended to be conservative (cut taxes, restrict government expenditures, balance the budget, tighten the money supply, trim social welfare programs). Liberals and traditionally liberal programs were very much on the defensive.

Perhaps the answer lies more in the changing nature of politics during the 1970s than in any pronounced shift in voter attitudes. It is true that conservative issues dominated political debate. It is also clear that conservative groups and causes became better organized and aggressively militant. Such groups benefited from the political exhaustion of the times and the seeming disarray of liberal groups. They also made quick use of the new campaign laws that encouraged business and ideological group financing and used extensive media campaigns to retake the political initiative during a confused and party-weakened period. Although the number of conservatives may not have increased during the 1970s, the proportion of conservatives becoming attached to the more ideologically militant wing of the group did appear to increase. Warren Miller and Teresa Levitin report, for example, that the proportion of "strong conservatives" in their study of political activists (those in the electorate who tried to persuade others to support their candidate or views) rose by 50 percent between the 1972 and 1976 presidential elections to where this group accounted for almost half of all conservatives (47 percent) and approximately a fifth of all political activists.[1]

Whereas liberal assumptions and programs appeared under sustained attack, the conservative movement was buoyed by the emergence of the American Enterprise Institute (AEI), a conservative Republican-oriented think-tank in Washington, D.C. Within a few years, and with sustained financial support from the Nixon administration, AEI became aggressively outspoken on political issues confronting the nation. Its staff had increased to over 100 of the best-known academics and political figures on full-time status and a large number of others under contract for specific projects. Its $8 million budget exceeded that of its older, somewhat staid and moderately liberal rival, the Brookings Institution.[2]

One writer has described the conservative (or, as he calls it, neoconservative) intellectual and policy-oriented movement as

> a child of the Sixties — the Other Child, the one that didn't turn on, tune in, and drop out; that didn't join the commune in California, march on Washington, or boo Hubert Humphrey in Chicago. Neoconservatism sets itself against the Sixties, against social turbulence, political conflict, and cultural experiment. From its beginnings, neoconservatism has been fiercely attached to political and cultural moderation, committed to stability, pessimistic about the possibilities for long-range — or even short-range — change in America, and imbued with a foreboding sense of our civilization's decline. Because neoconservatism didn't fit the conventional image of the times, its gathering strength was ignored. Yet in the end, neoconservatism may be the most enduring political legacy of the "radical Sixties," of the very Eden so many liberals claim as their own.[3]

In a period of intense voter disillusionment and continuing public apathy, conservatives at least were on the move. It may be that a low

[1] Warren E. Miller and Teresa E. Levitin, *Leadership and Change: Presidential Elections from 1952 to 1976* (Cambridge, Mass.: Winthrop, 1976).

[2] Peter Steinfels, "The Reasonable Right," *Esquire*, February 13, 1979, p. 29.

[3] *Ibid.*, p. 29.

level of political involvement coupled with a political situation (the ineffectiveness of parties, the rise of new sources of business and ideological funding) provides a receptive climate for conservative politics. Or, it may be that the issues of the day favored conservatives; that the liberal coalition was in turmoil, a continuing legacy of the devisive 1960s; and that in the vacuum that evolved, a well-financed and intellectually aggressive conservative voice drew new attention.

II
THE DECLINE OF
PARTY IN CAMPAIGNS

Introduction

The role of the political party in campaigns has given way to the technology of television-centered campaigns built on polls and run by media and public relations experts. The evolving politics is a candidate-centered, technocratic exercise in impersonal manipulation. It is also a politics of extraordinary expense.

The new technology costs a great deal of money and, as a result of the recent campaign financing laws, a new source of funds has emerged: the Political Action Committees (PACs). These business, labor, and ideological groups constitute a new and continually more significant source of funding for political races. Most often they invest in candidates to secure specified economic or other policy ends. Since 1974 they have completely overshadowed the party organizations in supplying campaign funds. The PACs and the modern campaign technology have encouraged the emergence of new single-interest groups (on abortion, the gun lobby, Proposition 13) and ideological interest groups that have an increasing impact on the parties, the conduct of campaigns, and the nature and policy commitments of elected public officials. These developments are all very recent (since 1974), but their impact is already clear. Although a growing source of political influence, these groups — their motives and methods — are little understood at present.

The partyless campaign is a slick and expensive exercise that can often result in forceful, well-built, and highly professional candidate organizations. As soon as the election is over, win or lose, the candidate organizations are disbanded and the professional consultants move on to their next job. A similar expense of money and effort in creating permanent party organizations would result in lasting benefits. Unfortunately, that cannot happen. By definition, the professionalized candidate organizations are bought by one man's money and committed to only one man's success. They are basically antiparty and contribute one more factor to the eroding base of the party in campaigns.

In this section we will look at: television and the politics of the media; polling and other professional consulting services; the escalating cost of politics and the role of the business and labor PACs and ideological issue groups in funding political contests; and, briefly, the efforts to equalize resources and return political races to the public domain. The latter is the concern behind the present efforts to legislate federal (and to a lesser extent, state) funding of congressional and other elective races. The section concludes with an analysis of the parties' response to the realities of a changing political environment.

5
Television and the Politics of the Media

Television is the new political god. It has supplanted the political party as the main conduit between candidate and voter. It is the principal influence acting on the voter in a campaign and his chief source of information. It is the medium of information he is most dependent on and the one he trusts most implicitly. However, it is both an expensive and unpredictable master.

Television allows those candidates who can command the necessary financial resources to mount impressive challenges tò incumbents at all levels. Such candidates are not dependent on the political party to sponsor their careers. A political organization and the mastery of a ladder-like succession of political offices are no longer prerequisites for nomination and election to higher political offices. A prospective candidate with sufficient personal wealth or PAC resources can run for office whenever he decides. He need have no previous political experience, no ties to the party whose nomination he seeks, and no particular roots in the community or bonds to the people he seeks to represent. All he needs is the ability to use television, to follow the advice of his consultants, and to pay for the services rendered. The last is the most important.

THE PERVASIVENESS OF TELEVISION

Television is the great American pastime. Americans have become television junkies to an alarming extent. The Federal Communications Commission reveals that 97 percent (73.3 million) of American homes (of a total 75.3 million) contain at least one television set. The average home has its set(s) turned on about six hours a day. With such a communications vehicle available, it is not surprising that politicians have been quick to take advantage of it.

The rise in television's influence can easily be documented. The presidential election of 1952 saw the first, tentative use of television on a broad scale in national campaigns. Republican Dwight Eisenhower's campaigners experimented in this election year (and later in 1956) with employing television to humanize the general and to personalize his virtues. Through television use the Republicans attempted to communicate a sense of Eisenhower's integrity, honesty, and forthrightness. The efforts largely succeeded. Adlai Stevenson chose to focus on televising polished oratorical addresses on issues of national concern and delivered before large audiences in auditoriums or prescheduled rallies. The approach was conventional and it was stilted. It is fair to say that the Stevenson people, unlike Eisenhower's, never fully utilized the new medium and, in fact, failed to grasp its potential.

Building on the Eisenhower success, other candidates evolved strategies that came to depend more and more on television as the centerpiece of their campaign efforts. At the same time, television began to emerge as the dominant source of campaign information for the voter. Between 1952 and 1956 alone, the number of voters identifying television as the most important source of their political information jumped from 36 to 56 percent. By the 1960s two-thirds of the electorate relied mostly on television. Newspapers came in a poor second, commanding approximately one-fourth of the voters' allegiance; and radio declined from about one-third to where it, along with magazines, became relatively insignificant as a source of campaign news.

Yet it can be argued that those who depend on newspapers for their news receive a quite different level of information: more thorough and sophisticated, with the issues and the contending positions and their implications sharply defined. Those relying on newspapers tend to have a stronger informational base and are more resistant to transitory opinion changes than are those who depend on television for guidance.[1] They tend also to be of higher socioeconomic status, which may account for their choice. Concurrently the use of television has paralleled a decrease in reliance on multiple sources for political news. It would appear that as television has become more prominent in political campaigns it has also fostered a dependence on it that works to the increasing exclusion of other sources of information. It is a safe, easy, and sanitized way to acquire political information.

The hegemony of television in transmitting political news is singularly unfortunate. There are a number of things about television that help place its role in communicating political information in perspective. First, television and television news are big business. The corporations that control the major networks are multibillion-dollar conglomerates whose interests in addition to owning networks and individual television and radio stations nationwide extend to publishing houses, entertainment parks, real estate, movie corporations, sports franchises, and about anything else that will return a profit and is not illegal.

Individually owned television stations return a handsome profit also. A representative of a consumer federation told Congress in mid-1979, "The average station earns about 100 percent on investment every year, and network-owned stations earn three times that. . . . [Advertising] rates for time go up every year; 1980 is substantially sold out at all-time high prices."[2]

Entertainment programming, of course, is a highly profitable venture. But the profits extend also to news. Such programming is both prestigious and quite lucrative. It is a moneymaking enterprise that networks and independent stations have no intention of jeopardizing. Unfortunately, the entertainment psychology extends to much of news programming. Entertain, Amuse, Do not shock (or worse, bore) appear to be the rules of the day. Controversial issues are watered down in presentation, and the less conventional side usually receives limited attention. The "happy talk" news shows on local stations epitomize the

[1] See Thomas E. Patterson and Robert D. McClure, *The Unseeing Eye* (New York: G. P. Putnam's Sons, 1976); and Patterson and McClure, "Television and Voters' Issue Awareness," in William Crotty (ed.), *The Party Symbol* (San Francisco: W. H. Freeman, 1980).

[2] Joan Hanauer, "New Look at Old Law," *Boston Globe,* June 12, 1979, p. 29.

tendency, but the network news programs — the most prestigious of television programs — show the same tendencies.

The examples are many. Despite the euphoria and self-congratulations spawned by the (eventually) successful investigations and revelations of the *Washington Post* reporting team of Carl Bernstein and Bob Woodward on Watergate, their type of reporting (and impact) is far more the exception than the rule.[3] The results were duly (and rightly) lionized. It is not by accident that Woodward and Bernstein's reports appeared in a newspaper. Television (and for that matter most newspapers) confined itself to reporting the official White House rebuttals to the Bernstein-Woodward accusations and only tangentially addressed themselves to the serious charges of criminal and governmental misconduct that they revealed. Television, in time, was a major influence in educating the country to the extraordinary constitutional abuses of the Nixon administration: a sign of its tremendous potential for developing an informed and responsive electorate. It did this, however, only after the revelations concerning Watergate refused to disappear. And television did this by covering live the Ervin Committee hearings documenting the allegations and the Rodino Committee deliberations on impeachment. In effect, it could not avoid covering in depth what then was the biggest news story of the decade and one of the most disturbing in the nation's political history.

Television likes to justify its dominant public role and think of itself as providing a public service of extraordinary consequence. Luckily, both the Ervin and Rodino hearings were good theatre as well as good news, and both were good public relations. It is more fruitful to ask what role CBS, NBC, and ABC news played in revealing the basic abuses of governmental and constitutional safeguards by Richard Nixon and his associates before the major governmental agencies acted. What did television contribute to the education of the public on these issues before national concern forced major congressional investigations?

In these areas the contribution of television is far less impressive. Individual television reporters (Dan Rather and Daniel Schorr of CBS come to mind) did take the lead in forcing revelations and placing the

[3] Carl Bernstein and Bob Woodward, *All the President's Men* (New York: Simon and Schuster, 1974); and Woodward and Bernstein, *The Final Days* (New York: Simon and Schuster, 1976). On Watergate more generally, see: J. Anthony Lukas, *Nightmare: The Underside of the Nixon Years* (New York: Viking, 1976).

Nixon administration on the defensive for its actions. They were atypical. More prevalent would be the approach of the news anchors and the television news editors on the major networks. Walter Cronkite is an example. The best-known and most trusted newsman in the country, Cronkite is a celebrity in his own right; his personal life and avocations are covered by the media for their own news value. Cronkite is a centrist with a sense of obligation to the role and mission of television as he sees it. His approach and sensitivities on what constitutes acceptable news programming are not significantly different from those of corporate heads such as William Paley, who directs the CBS network. Network executives are more concerned with bottom-line profits, the noncontroversial presentation of issues, and good relations with political leaders. They are aware that such leaders can do much through the Federal Communications Commission and congressional legislation to punish unfriendly television outlets.

Watergate is as good an example of the role of television in news reporting and its extraordinary sensitivity to political pressures as any. CBS news decided to do a more in-depth analysis of the Watergate scandals immediately prior to Election Day 1972 in an effort to tie together the various reports of political abuse and to place them in a context meaningful to the voter. The report was to be delivered in several relatively lengthy installments on the "CBS Evening News" (the average story runs thirty to ninety seconds). The principal reporters were to be Daniel Schorr and Dan Rather.

The report did not uncover more information, and it did not add much to the pool of knowledge available. This was not its purpose. It was an attempt to apply perspective to the problems addressed and, as originally filmed, it was explicit. "They [spokespersons for the Nixon administration] keep issuing general denials; they are depending on that, and silence, to make the allegations go away," reported Rather.[4]

The first segment was broadcast. The remaining reports had been scheduled to follow immediately but were postponed. Eventually they did appear in highly abbreviated form with much of the substance and commentary deleted.

Why this occurred is a matter of controversy. The White House did contact Paley at CBS and various news officials with power over news programming. This much seems clear. What exactly the role of the

[4] Daniel Schorr, *Clearing the Air* (New York: Houghton Mifflin, 1977).

White House was and how much weight the CBS officials placed on its threats is in debate. Nonetheless, the Nixon administration got most of what it wanted, and the presentation was seriously cut. The episode illustrates the sensitive role of television news reporting and its vulnerability on matters of importance to official pressures.

The Nixon administration used threats against individual reporters (for example, through FBI investigations into the background of media critics such as Daniel Schorr) and networks. It threatened CBS with a variety of reprisals, from loss of access to government decision-makers to support for policies that would strike directly at the financial base of the networks (encouragement of challenges to the licensing renewals of network-owned stations; divestiture of company-owned stations; proposals for the federal licensing of networks; government promotion of alternative communication channels such as cable TV).[5] The administration's successful efforts to weaken public broadcast television and to move its emphasis from public affairs (potentially a source of embarrassment to the administration) to nonpolitical cultural and local programming illustrates the extent to which it was willing to go.[6] Television is particularly vulnerable to these types of official retribution.

Nixon, in his campaigns and while in office, received generally good press, despite his beliefs to the contrary and his sensitivity to any criticism, however mild. His attacks on the commercial networks paid dividends. The emasculation of the Rather and Schorr report is but one example. The other two networks did far less than CBS. As a consequence, the news source most listened to and most trusted by the American people did little in the 1972 campaign to foster an understanding of an issue that would eventually topple a president.

Nixon also managed to command national air time for news conferences, speeches, and announcements, as do all presidents. The opposition (whether it be Republican or Democrat) is rarely given a meaningful chance to employ television to rebut a president or his stand. Such

[5] Other accounts of relevance to this discussion include: *ibid.*; David Halberstam, *The Powers That Be* (New York: Knopf, 1979); William S. Paley, *As It Happened: A Memoir* (New York: Doubleday, 1979); Dan Rather and Mickey Herkowitz, *The Camera Never Blinks* (New York: Morrow, 1977); Gary Paul Gates, *Air Time* (New York: Berkley, 1979); William Crotty, *Political Reform and the American Experiment* (New York: Crowell, 1977), pp. 139–67; *The Senate Watergate Report*, 2 vols. (New York: Dell, 1974); and *The Impeachment Report* (New York: New American Library, 1974).

[6] "A Bid to Establish a Nixon Network," *The New York Times*, February 2, 1979, p. 4E.

was certainly the case with Nixon. His opponents were afforded little or no opportunity to speak before national television audiences to counter the president's messages.

The Nixon White House managed to stifle a good deal of dissent — specifically as voiced on national television. The administration even orchestrated a campaign against the network reviews and assessments ("instant analysis," as the White House pejoratively referred to it) that followed major Nixon addresses, successful enough to force them to drop those efforts to inform the public and to place the events that had transpired in some context.

The Nixon assault on television raises questions about the role of the nation's most powerful communications medium in transmitting ideas and subjecting these to informed criticism and debate. Television did not fulfill this function well during the Nixon years.

Nixon's job in controlling the media, or at least in forcing a more receptive hearing for his position, may not have been as difficult as it seemed. The media have an image of themselves as independent, fearless, and professionally neutral conveyors of information: vital links in the chain of democratic governance. In reality, as already noted, journalism is corporate business at the highest level. It is also a business heavily dependent on the good will and access provided by official decision makers. How much publishers and electronic and print reports rely on official entrée is just beginning to be understood. Herbert J. Gans, a sociologist, has recently completed an assessment of what becomes "news" and how the choice process operates.[7] He found, among other things, that in two of the nation's most prestigious newspapers, *The New York Times* and the *Washington Post*, 78 percent of the 2850 domestic and foreign stories he examined came directly from public officials.

Gans divided the stories examined into "knowns" and "unknowns" in terms of the source and/or subject categories. The political, business, social, and cultural celebrities account for 70 to 85 percent of the final news content. "Unknowns" manage to break into print usually for criminal offenses. Gans comments that those who are powerless on important issues must often resort to civil disturbances to obtain access to news outlets.[8]

---

[7] Herbert J. Gans, *Deciding What's News* (New York: Random House, 1979).
[8] See the review by Richard Rovere in "Political Books" in *The Washington Monthly*, March 1979, pp. 60–61.

This may not be too surprising. It may be more impressive, and worrisome, that the president alone accounts for 20 percent of all domestic news and that the president's cabinet accounts for another 20 percent. A monopolization of news channels to this extent raises serious questions, again, about the role and contribution of television, and the news media more generally, to an informed contemporary electorate.

Beyond the problems of access and establishment monopolization of communications channels, there is another: the superficiality of television news reporting. This problem is also serious. In part, it is a function of the medium and in part it relates to the cultural role television has carved for itself in society. Either way, it directly affects the quality of political decision making and the intensity and relevance of information shared by voters.

Americans turn to television for relief from their daily lives and its tensions. They seek diversion and amusement, and television has proven very successful in providing a low-level escapism. More than entertaining its viewers in any provocative manner, television fills up their time: it anesthetizes them, blocks out other sensations, and provides for the passage of time. Television entertainment — the "$1.98 Beauty Show," "Starsky and Hutch," the "Gong Show," and so on — strives for (and obtains) the lowest common denominator. A listing of the top shows for the 1978–79 television season makes the point (Table 5.1). The most popular television fare included "Laverne and Shirley," "Three's Company," "Mork and Mindy," and "Happy Days." Only one news program, CBS' popular "60 Minutes," cracked the top thirty. It would be surprising if the psychology of show business values, and quick profit turnover from television's entertainment ventures, did not affect its approach to the news.

Technically, television is a visual medium. It needs pictures — and the more active and personalized the better — to tell its story. It does not deal well with issues, the varying positions on a dispute, the arguments and evidence available to the protagonists, and the implications of the proposed alternatives. This is a cerebral and fairly abstract type of information better conveyed on the printed page. Television demands movement, color, and associations made with the eye. This has led to a certain type of news orientation. Issues are crammed into a brief (minute or so) segment. An edited tape of a proponent making a

TABLE 5.1
Most Popular Television Programs 1978–79 Season (September–May)

Rank	Program	Network
1	"Laverne and Shirley"	ABC
2	"Three's Company"	ABC
(tie) 3	"Mork and Mindy" and "Happy Days"	ABC
5	"60 Minutes"	CBS
(tie) 6	"M*A*S*H" and "Angie"	CBS & ABC
8	"The Ropers"	ABC
(tie) 9	"All in the Family" and "Taxi"	CBS & ABC
(tie) 11	"Eight Is Enough" and "Charlie's Angels"	Both ABC
13	"The Little House on the Prairie"	NBC
14	"Alice"	CBS
15	"Barney Miller"	ABC
16	"The Love Boat"	ABC
17	"One Day at a Time"	CBS
18	"Soap"	ABC
19	"The Dukes of Hazzard"	CBS
20	"Fantasy Island"	ABC
21	"Vega$"	ABC
22	"Barnaby Jones"	CBS
(tie) 23	"CHiPs" and "13 Queens Blvd."	NBC and ABC
25	"Stockard Channing — Just Friends"	CBS
(tie) 26	"Monday Night Football" and "Diff'rent Strokes"	ABC and NBC
28	"What's Happening"	ABC
29	"Lou Grant"	CBS
30	"Battlestar Galactica"	ABC

Source: Nielsen prime time audience rating, released in June 1979. Reprinted by permission of the A. C. Nielsen Company.

quick statement and someone speaking on the other side is shown, and the show moves on. It would be extraordinarily difficult for a viewer to pick up any meaningful information that would help him to make an informed judgment from such an exposure. Yet this is what he must cope with.

An example will make the point. An individual turns on the television and finds that there is an oil crisis. Long lines of car owners seeking gasoline in eastern states are shown; violence at several stations is reported; a story is presented on many service stations restricting fuel purchases to three or five dollars; and a reporter says the situation is likely to get worse. A story is then introduced about independent truckers striking against higher diesel prices. Reports show truck stops and major highways blockaded by truckers; the state police in several states are shown trying to break the blockade; a trucker is reported killed in one state; and, in another, the governor calls out the national guard. The president is shown demonstrating a solar heating system on the roof of the White House to supply part of its energy load and lauding it as a future possibility. The secretary of energy comes on to say that the crisis will get worse as oil import prices increase, but there should be plenty of gasoline for the summer. The televised news moves on to other subjects.

What is a viewer to think? What has he learned? He knows there is a gasoline shortage. He realizes that people are angry and that violence has occurred. He can associate the shortage with OPEC, but that may be as far as his knowledge goes. He will learn little from this television program on matters concerning the role, profits, and alternatives of the oil companies; the potentially competing energy proposals and their feasibility; the long-run implications of the crisis; the differences in proposals being put forth in Washington by oil, government, and consumer groups; and so on. Yet, to reemphasize, television is the dominant source of news. It communicates headlines and feelings about problems but little beyond this. This is the level of information on which most people, not exposed to other sources of news, must rely.

Television has further reduced the role of the political party as a communicator of news and as a shaper of the public will. It has replaced the political party and the printed media as the dominant source of issue information. Yet television gives news a certain, often superficial, emphasis, and it is open to subtle, but powerful influences on its operations. Whether the reliance on television is an improvement over the old ways is debatable.

TELEVISION AND POLITICAL CAMPAIGNING

Television's coverage of political campaigns is much the same: superficial with emphasis on the visual. Television focuses on the obvious. It is not concerned with the extended exploration of policy issues, relative differences in positions, or even in-depth investigations of an individual's background and previous policy stands. In the pre-nomination phase, the media focus on the primaries and, specifically, the first of these, New Hampshire.[9]

Overall, the media — and television would be the leader in this regard — emphasize the sporting aspect of races. They are concerned with transmitting the lowest level of information — who is ahead, who is catching up, what tactics are being used, what the latest developments are.

Thomas E. Patterson, who has studied this area in depth, reports that more than half of the media outlets he analyzed, and over 60 percent of the reports given on television's evening news, stressed the "horse-race" aspect of the campaigns at the expense of issue analyses, in-depth reports on candidates or developments, background briefings, or much of anything else of substance (Table 5.2).[10]

Candidates for office, of course, are well aware that television is a visual and entertainment-oriented medium. It wants action-oriented shots and simple messages, and they supply them. The best way to achieve television exposure is not to give a speech on a major policy concern or to issue position papers. The most direct course is to do something that is colorful and has human interest potential. Candidates are much concerned with television's needs and become highly skilled in attracting as much TV exposure as possible.

GETTING THE MEDIA'S ATTENTION

Free Television

It is possible for a candidate of some public standing or with substantial backing to receive free television exposure to make a statement of consequence on a national issue of major concern. However,

[9] Michael J. Robinson, "Media Coverage in the Primary Campaign of 1976: Implications for Voters, Candidates and Parties," in Crotty, *The Party Symbol;* and Rhodes Cook, "Media Coverage of the 1976 Nominating Process," in Crotty, *The Party Symbol*.

[10] Thomas E. Patterson, "The Media Muffed the Message," *Washington Post*, December 5, 1976, p. B1, as quoted in Harry Holloway and John George, *Public Opinion: Coalitions, Elites, and Masses* (New York: St. Martin's, 1979), p. 250. See also Patterson and McClure, *The Unseeing Eye;* Ron Powers, *The Newscasters* (New York: St. Martin's, 1977); and Ben H. Bagdikian, *The Information Machines* (New York: Harper Torchbooks, 1971).

TABLE 5.2
Press Coverage of the 1976 Presidential Campaign[a]

	Network Evening News		Los Angeles Times		Erie (Pa.) Times		Time and Newsweek	
The Horse Race:								
Winning and losing		16%		17%		25%		19%
Strategy, logistics, and support	62%	22%	51%	19%	57%	18%	55%	28%
Appearances and crowds		24%		15%		14%		8%
The Substance								
Candidates' issue positions		10%		13%		6%		9%
Candidates' characteristics and backgrounds	24%	6%	30%	7%	24%	7%	31%	13%
Issue-related (e.g., party platforms)		8%		10%		11%		9%
The Rest:								
Campaign events calendar	14%	2%	19%	4%	19%	6%	14%	3%
Miscellaneous (e.g., election procedures)		12%		15%		13%		11%
	100%		100%		100%		100%	

Source: From Thomas E. Patterson, "The Media Muffed the Message," *The Washington Post*, December 5, 1976, p. B1. © 1976 The Washington Post. Reprinted by permission.

[a] Figures based on random selection of at least 20 percent of the coverage by each news source. Figures include opinion and analysis as well as regular news reports.

this happens rarely. Incumbents, and especially presidents, dominate the news. Others need to develop ways to dramatize what they say or what they stand for. Inventing such means has become something of an art. Attracting media attention is a vital part of any candidate's run for office.

Here are a few guidelines for the aspiring politician:[11]

1. Assignment editors, not reporters, determine what stories or candidates will be covered and what gets on television. Cultivate the assignment editor.

[11] Based on a study by Rick Neustadt and Richard Paisner, "How to Get on TV," as reported by Bob Greene, "How Politicians Get That Free TV Time," *Chicago Tribune*, April 10, 1979, Sec. 2, p. 1; and Neustadt and Paisner, "How to Run on TV," *New York Times Magazine*, December 15, 1974, pp. 20ff.

2. Schedule the event you want covered so that it is convenient for television to cover it. The best time is between 10:00 A.M. and 2:30 P.M. on weekdays. This allows for TV crews to record and edit the session for the 5:00 and 6:00 evening news. Most news seen on the late news (10:00 or 11:00 P.M.) is a rehash of the earlier programs. Weekends are normally poor times for news coverage. Most stations operate with skeleton crews.

   The scheduling of events to maximize television coverage is sometimes carried to extremes. Reporters covering the civil war in Lebanon between Christians and Moslems reported that both sides in Beirut would wait for the television crews to arrive and the cameras to be in place before shelling the enemy. They would also position their guns to get the type of pictures and background effect they wanted recorded. In this case, and many others, the images sent via television to the world were more important than any immediate military advantage from the bombardment.

   Daniel Schorr told how the late Hubert Humphrey called him and asked him if he could set up a spare television camera in his committee room. It turned out that Humphrey was holding a hearing and no other senators had turned up. He reasoned that if a television camera were present the absent senators would troop in and the business of the Senate could go on.

   In another case, a congressional aide called Schorr to warn him of an upcoming committee meeting on a health and welfare issue that would have witnesses from women's groups, blacks, Hispanic-Americans, and Native Americans in full Indian dress. When Schorr's crew could not make the meeting, the aide offered to reschedule it for television's convenience.[12]

3. Come up with good visuals. The job here is to make the visuals attractive to television and its audience and, secondly, to make sure they get across the message the candidate wants. The wrong visual can draw attention away from the candidate and what he is saying, or even contradict his message.

4. If a television crew is scheduled to cover the event, wait until it arrives. Usually these crews run late. Rather than pressing them to speed up or going ahead with the event as scheduled, wait. The print media and the audience may be inconvenienced, but

[12] Reported in David B. Wilson, "Medium Not the Message; It's the Power," *Boston Globe*, December 3, 1978, p. A7.

television is the target. Most people depend on it for news; the other groups are secondary concerns.

5. Keep your statement short (usually about ninety seconds). In this way you can dictate what television will run on the evening news. Do not introduce confusing facts and figures. Pause every twenty seconds to allow for easy editing and cutting. Pass out a press release that repeats what you said. More often than not whatever is read to accompany the story will come directly from what you release.

6. If you are asked tough or embarrassing questions by reporters while the cameras are on, be vague, unstructured, and longwinded in your replies. This will make the television film or tape unusable.

7. End the event or press conference quickly. Say what you have to say and terminate the proceedings. This guards against mistakes.

8. If you did make a mistake and let something slip that was not intended, do not worry. Often it is buried in the long answers to the unscheduled questions, and television reporters, in particular, are unlikely to realize its significance or news value. Television reporters usually do not know anything about the stories they cover. Their job is to record and report on a variety of occurrences for the evening news. These range from traffic tieups and local crime news to political races. Unlike newspaper reporters, they are not well prepared and they are not familiar with the implications of any one story.

Television favors men and women who look attractive on camera. Journalistic ability is not the major concern in their hiring. This affects their preparation for every news story and the amount of critical editing they are likely to do.[13]

Finally, approximately ninety seconds of air time is allotted to a story. The television reporter is concerned with introducing the event and briefly touching on its significance. The margin for candidate error in such a situation is limited.

Gimmicks

To attract free television time and to distinguish themselves from the welter of other contenders and their demands, candidates are willing to try almost anything. The flashier and more novel the event, the

[13] Powers, *The Newscasters*.

likelier the media attention. With more candidates than ever running (for example, from 1960 to 1976 candidacies for congressional seats increased by 40.9 percent in toto and for open seats by 76.1 percent), the competition for the valuable television exposure has become stiffer. Incumbents normally have little difficulty in attracting attention for official statements and for the coverage of official duties. For the challenger, however, TV time is a problem.

In the 1970s, the major gimmick appeared to be walking from one end of a state to the other. The candidate would dress in work clothes and then trek from town to town and media market to media market. The idea was to show a populist concern with the people and their wishes and to contrast the folksy challenger with the seemingly remote officeholder. The strategy worked. Lawton Chiles, an unknown, won a Florida Senate seat at the beginning of the decade in this manner. Others were quick to copy his success. In a major upset, Dick Clark defeated a Republican Senate incumbent in Iowa in 1972 with the same approach. Dan Walker, a maverick Democrat, won his party's gubernatorial nomination and the Illinois governor's office in another upset by exploiting the tactic.

As the novelty of walking candidates faded, others searched for new gimmicks to replace it. Cliff Finch, a Democratic candidate for governor of Mississippi, needed to build an identification with the working class in his state, a constituency he hoped would propel him into the governorship in 1975. He succeeded by scheduling "blue-collar workdays" in which he would work at different blue-collar jobs on selected days. These efforts received wide television coverage.

Bob Graham, a candidate for the Democratic nomination for governor in Florida, refined the approach in 1978. Graham was an underdog in a crowded six-candidate field. To attract attention and build a constituency he vowed to work in 100 jobs before the primary. In the course of his efforts he worked on the sponge docks in Tarpon Springs, as a Tallahassee policeman, a nursing home orderly, a shrimp fisherman, a stable boy, and an airline attendant. As part of one stunt he appeared as a corpse in a college theatre production, an effort that attracted national TV attention. In another he substituted as a bellboy and ended up carrying the luggage of the wife of one of his principal opponents.

The efforts may appear frivolous. Graham did not think so. He combined the free television with a well-designed television advertising campaign that was built around the film clips of the work sessions.

He also used the outings to attack the state administration and make his own policy positions known (greater support for the police, renewed efforts to promote the state's fishing industry, and so on).[14]

The approach worked. Graham finished second in the primary field and qualified for the run-off. He beat the favorite and went on to win the governorship in the general election. He had overcome a lack of name recognition, the absence of a broadly based constituency, and an association with large wealth (he had a personal fortune of $4 million made in real estate and the dairy business).

Other candidates try other tacks. James "Big Jim" Thompson, the incumbent governor of Illinois and a media favorite, took his newborn daughter to the state fair. The event captured widespread coverage in his reelection bid. Unfortunately, the child caught pneumonia. She recovered in time to spend the evening in front of the television lights at her father's campaign headquarters, bottle in mouth, with the band playing "Rock-a-Bye Baby," the night he won the election.[15]

Lee Dreyfus, an unconventional contender for the Wisconsin governorship in 1978, proved a formidable candidate. Dreyfus was a college administrator with no political experience or basis of support. With little funding ($36,000 — "not even gas money" according to his campaign manager[16]) and despite the pleas of his friends and political associates, Dreyfus ran. A year before the election 97 percent of the state's population did not even recognize his name.

Dreyfus proved to be a personable candidate with a good sense of comic timing. What he needed was media exposure. He gained this by campaigning across the state in a red vest from the back of an old school bus redesigned to look like a steam engine. The modified bus had a platform for speech-making and room for bands and entertainers. The bus attracted the media attention Dreyfus needed to get his message across to the voters. He went on to win his party's nomination and become the state's first Republican governor since 1966.

Strom Thurmond, whose political versatility is legendary, added another chapter to his personal saga in 1978. Thurmond, seventy-five

---

[14] Charles W. Hucker, "Political Stunts: Working Replaces Walking," *Congressional Quarterly*, October 21, 1978, pp. 3060–61.

[15] Sean Foolan, "Samantha Jayne Aids in Dad's Victory Scene," *Chicago Tribune*, November 8, 1978, p. 15.

[16] Joseph Sjostram, "Gov.-Elect in Wisconsin is a Man of Blunt Words," *Chicago Tribune*, November 12, 1978, Sec. 3, p. 24.

years old, was seeking reelection to his Senate seat from South Carolina. He was facing a young and articulate Democrat with a proven
vote-getting ability in the state (he had been denied a chance for
victory in the governor's race a few years earlier on a residency techni-
cality). Thurmond's age became an issue in the campaign.

The senator outfitted a "Strom-trek" van and took his family barn-
storming across the state. He outfitted his wife, a thirty-one-year-old
former beauty queen, and his four young children in campaign T-
shirts. The children's shirts read "Vote for my Daddy." During the
campaign he held a birthday party for one of his children and to the
delight of the TV cameramen repeatedly slid down the firepole to show
how fit he was.

His efforts were sufficient to turn back the age issue and to convince
the voters of South Carolina of his physical durability. Thurmond, a
Republican, went on to win another term with 56 percent of the two-
party vote.

More conventional is the effort to attract media attention through
endorsements from sportspeople and other celebrities. Joe Garagiola, a
network baseball announcer and former ballplayer, campaigned with
President Gerald Ford in 1976 and served as master of ceremonies for
many of his paid television programs. St. Louis Cardinals football
coach, Bud Wilkenson, had performed the same function for Richard
Nixon in his presidential campaigns. Among other celebrities in 1978,
football's Fran Tarkenton backed Albert H. Quie for governor of Min-
nesota, and the Boston Red Sox's Carl Yastremski supported Edward
King for governor of Massachusetts. The Yankees' Reggie Jackson fa-
vored incumbent governor, Hugh Carey, in New York, and the Los
Angeles Dodgers' Steve Garvey and Don Sutton endorsed Republican
Evelle Younger in California. Muhammad Ali campaigned for Charles
Percy for senator in Illinois ("If you want to do good, then listen to Ali.
Vote for Percy, pull Lever B-1.") and Charles Evers for senator in
Mississippi. Baseball's Ted Williams and Billy Martin endorsed Bob
Short, the loser in a race for a Minnesota Senate seat. A number of Bill
Bradley's old New York Knicks teammates backed his successful bid for
the Senate in New Jersey. Other athletes, including Pete Rose, Johnny
Bench, Arnold Palmer, Sonny Jurgenson, Billy Kilmer, Chris Evert,
Dorothy Hamill, Peggy Fleming, and Richard Petty, campaigned for
various candidates during the election year.

There is a certain predictability to this. Sports figures command media attention. Simply receiving their endorsement is news. Many athletes appear regularly in campaign after campaign and several (Jack Kemp for one) have cashed in their fame to the extent of running for office (congressman). Most athletes tend to favor the conservative alternative in any race. There are exceptions, but the general rule holds true. Perhaps this should not be surprising. As one commentator wrote in 1978, except for Jackson and those who supported Bradley, and with the "partial exception" of Ali,

> Every sports superstar I know of who brought his influence to bear upon a congressional or gubernatorial race favored the more conservative choice, whether Democrat or Republican. Famous athletes tend to have a lot of money and to feel they deserve it, they tend to be involved with good-sized business concerns, and they tend to have spent the afternoons of their formative years with Tom Lasorda or Woody Hayes.[17]

A Massachusetts GOP state chairman attempting to draw early support in 1978 for his candidate for president, the little-known conservative, Congressman Phil Crane, had his wife do a belly dance for 400 Republican leaders in Michigan. The stunt did attract attention.[18] Richard Cheney, a Republican candidate for Congress in Wyoming, came up with an unusual, and unwanted, means of attracting public attention. He had a heart attack. He was only 37, but it looked like his yet-to-be-born political career was finished. Surprisingly, polls taken after the attack showed that as a result of the publicity his name had become a household word in the state. It helped rather than hurt him in the campaign, and he went on to win the office.

Gimmicks sometimes can backfire. One gubernatorial candidate hired a baseball stadium and held a barbecue for 16,000 people. They ate his food, but they voted for his opponent. Another candidate for the Senate in New York was hospitalized with an infection that severely limited his campaign time. He had become ill diving into the Hudson River for the television cameras to dramatize his concern with water pollution.

"Big Jim" Thompson, in the wake of the public outcry over Proposition 13, came up with Proposition "0." It was to be put before the

---

[17] Roy Blount, Jr., "Late Returns," *The New York Times*, November 13, 1978, p. C6.
[18] "GOP Chairman's Wife Does the Belly Dance," *Boston Globe*, July 23, 1978, p. 21.

state's voters in the November election in 1978. In it they were to indicate whether they voted yes or no to have their taxes cut. Unfortunately, the proposition was only advisory and had no power over any governmental body. Thompson received a good deal of publicity over the amendment before its full nature became known. As interest slackened, pressure was put on party workers to come up with the necessary signatures to qualify the proposition for a ballot position. In their haste, party workers forged a large number of signatures. As this became known, it presented one of the few obstacles to Thompson's reelection.

Television exposure is crucial. The more free TV time for a campaign the better, and candidates will go to great lengths to attract it. When all else fails, a person running for office could do what Evelle Younger, the Republican candidate for governor of California in 1978, did and declare himself "normal, usual, unstrange."[19] This did attract media notice. Younger was running against Governor Jerry Brown, a maverick politician, a former seminarian, and a practitioner of Zen. Among other idiosyncrasies, Brown dated rock star Linda Ronstadt and forsook the governor's mansion to sleep on a mattress in an inexpensive apartment. Brown was good copy. Against that caliber of competition for media attention, Younger was reduced to declaring himself "normal."

Buying Media Exposure

A second way to get on television is to buy time for commercial advertising. This can be expensive.

The first and fundamental rule is that adequate media exposure costs a great deal of money. In the Chicago area television costs alone increased 600 percent between 1972 and 1978. These figures are probably not out of line with those nationwide. A thirty-second commercial in prime time (7:00 to 10:00 P.M. in the midwestern market) on Chicago television costs $5250. This is for air time alone, of course, and does not include production costs, media consultants, script writers, cameramen, equipment, and so on. A "minimum buy" of $30,000 for a two-week period is considered necessary to have any effect.

Robert Agranoff estimates that a one-time showing of a spot commercial on network television costs upward of $20,000 and one

[19]*Chicago Sun-Times,* November 8, 1978, p. 6.

half-hour of network air time upward of $75,000 to $80,000.[20] Production expenses run about 20 percent of the air-time costs of the TV program, although they can run as high as the time costs. The advertising agencies that arrange for the placement of TV commercials charge roughly 15 percent of the air costs, in addition to such expenses as travel and creative costs.

To complicate matters, many television stations do not want political advertising. They do not need the money — the air time is much desired by less controversial clients — and they find commercial advertisers more dependable and predictable (although all television advertising must be prepaid). NBC in Chicago permits only one spot per week in prime time, and the other stations have similar, if less stringent, restrictions on prime-time political advertising. The stations also can limit the total number of political commercials they will accept, and many do. In Chicago, the CBS outlet permits only nine per week, NBC five, and ABC eight.

For comparison purposes, the cost of a one-page advertisement in a magazine such as *Time, Newsweek, U.S. News and World Report,* or *Sports Illustrated* would range from $18,000 to $37,000. A one-page, black and white advertisement in the Chicago edition of one of these magazines would cost about $3500. The Chicago ad would reach an estimated 106,000 readers. Television has the capability of reaching almost everyone in the 3.5 million-person metropolitan area.

On a different level, it would cost about $6000 a week in a densely populated congressional district for major advertisements in all weekly newspapers. Each paper would reach about 60,000 people per issue. A newsletter statewide runs about $125,000. At the very lowest level, car-top advertisements cost only twelve dollars per automobile and, of course, would be seen by the fewest number of people.

There is a certain economic logic for the larger races in focusing on television. However, a major problem with television, beyond cost, is that it indiscriminately reaches many viewers not in the intended market area. For example, many major media markets encompass several states. New York City television reaches people in Connecticut and New Jersey. Chicago television has viewers in Indiana, lower Wisconsin, and western Michigan. Boston TV reaches parts of all of the New

[20] Robert Agranoff, "The New Style of Campaigning: The Decline of Party and the Rise of Candidate Centered Technology," in Robert Agranoff (ed.), *The New Style in Election Campaigns* (Boston: Holbrook, 1972), pp. 31–33. See also Agranoff, *The Management of Election Campaigns* (Boston: Holbrook, 1976).

England states. A candidate for statewide office, in effect, "wastes" a good deal of the exposure he is paying for if the voters cannot participate in that state's election. Similarly, in congressional campaigns, television advertising can reach voters in dense market areas that cover many congressional districts. Nonetheless, despite this relative inefficiency and its cost, the recent trend is toward a greater reliance on television in congressional campaigns. Its lure and its potency cannot be ignored.

In 1978 Gordon Humphrey, a little-known airline pilot and the conservative Republican candidate for the Senate in New Hampshire, bought large chunks of Boston TV to beam his message back to his state. This was a first for New Hampshire politics. It was costly, and most of the voters reached by Humphrey's advertising did not live in his state. His opponent, incumbent Democrat Thomas McIntyre, disdained the new departures, but Humphrey's tactics worked. In an upset Humphrey beat McIntyre by 5000 votes. Lessons like this are not lost on politicians. Whatever its cost, television is worth it. A serious candidate cannot afford to ignore it.

It is not unusual today for campaigns of any consequence (United States Senate, governor and other statewide offices, president) to rely almost totally on the media. The emphasis has shifted from developing a party organization and conducting a door-to-door campaign to employing television to reach as wide a possible audience in the shortest possible time with the least organizational effort.

The new campaigns bypass the party and contribute to its further erosion. They do allow for an abundance of new candidates in any given election; there is no need to work through party channels or to satisfy party leaders in order to be slated for public office. The new technology also allows for a flexibility in campaign strategy not possible before. The strengths and weaknesses of a totally media-oriented campaign can be illustrated by reference to one contest.

THE PERCY-SEITH CAMPAIGN: A TELEVISION EXTRAVAGANZA

In 1978, Charles Percy was a popular Senator from Illinois believed to be unbeatable. He had entered the United States Senate in 1966 by defeating incumbent Paul Douglas, a much-respected liberal and a former professor of Percy's. He had won reelection in 1972 by overwhelming the Democratic candidate, a veteran congressman, Roman Pucinski, with 62 percent of the vote. No political figure of any stature in the Democratic party wished to damage his career by challenging Percy in 1978. As a consequence, he was conceded reelection by the media and by his opponents in both parties. His own thinking paralleled that of others and he began by running a perfunctory campaign.

The prevailing conditions allowed Alex Seith, a young and wealthy lawyer, to win the Democratic nomination with little difficulty. Seith, a newcomer to elective politics, ran a media campaign to develop his name recognition. He also began a walking tour of the state's 102 counties a year before the election. The idea was to listen to the people and acquaint them with his two major proposals: a "take-home pay protector," which would tie taxes to inflation, and a "revenue-keeping" plank that would require more federal tax funds to stay within the state. Seith was attempting to capitalize on the voters' tax revolt mood and the increasing inflation. His proposals were obscure. His only previous political office had been as head of the Cook County Zoning Board of Appeals. It was a nonelective and little-publicized position. His earlier policy stands appear to have come from his experience and his concern with "tax indexing." They were little understood and did not play a role in the campaign.

Once he won the nomination, Seith had the funds to hire nationally known consultants and to launch a massive, and effective, media blitz. The television emphasis was crucial to Seith's campaign. Almost all of Seith's budget was projected for television. As Seith's campaign manager explained, "It's extremely important because Percy never had a challenger who could give to the voter information about Percy's record. [Television] gets Seith recognition and it provides information."[21]

Seith caught Percy unawares and eventually forced him on the defensive. As a new, and as it turned out, articulate candidate, Seith began to receive media attention. He used the opportunity to attack Percy for being out of touch with the state and its constituency. This argument would have a telling effect. The fact that Percy was seldom in

[21] F. Richard Ciccone and William Griffin, "TV Blitzes Give Contests Added Flavor," *Chicago Tribune*, October 22, 1978, Sec. 1, p. 48.

the state to campaign, preferring instead to remain in Washington to attend to his legislative duties, did not help the senator's position. As the campaign went on, it was learned that Percy did not own a home in Illinois (he used his mother's residence for voting purposes). He did own a home in Washington, and he was actively engaged in a public lobbying effort in the District of Columbia to reduce his property taxes.

Seith had tapped a large reservoir of discontent with the senator and his performance. To capitalize on it, Seith decided to move to the right. His belief was that Democrats and liberals would likely vote for him because they had little place else to turn. He felt that by taking a conservative and essentially Republican position on taxes and the budget, as well as on social issues, he could isolate Percy and undercut his support. The strategy was not necessarily successful — there was little difference between Seith and Percy on most issues — but it did serve to demonstrate the topsy-turvy nature of politics in the late 1970s. In a more structured political situation the Democrat could be expected to present the more liberal alternatives and the Republican the more conservative. In Illinois the battle — to the extent issues were involved — was fought out on the moderate right. The left was unrepresented. Eventually, dissatisfied more with Seith's tactics than his murky positions, many Democratic liberals came out for Percy, a moderate. An examination of the voting results suggests this is how many Democrats voted, and their vote may have been decisive in the campaign.

Seith's most potent issue was that voters were disillusioned with politics in general and Percy in particular. Seith was a new face with no political ties. In 1978 this was an advantage. If he could have kept the pressure on Percy, been vague on policy questions, and not alienated significant blocs of Democratic voters (a strategy used successfully by Jimmy Carter in 1976), he might have pulled off the year's biggest upset. Unfortunately for him, he began to push too hard and a reaction set in.

To capture the black vote, Seith recorded two radio messages to play on predominantly black radio stations. The first message linked Percy to Earl L. Butz, a Republican and former secretary of agriculture. Butz had been removed from office by President Gerald Ford after making an intemperate remark about blacks. Percy, in a speech during the 1978 campaign, well after Butz's removal from office, indicated he thought highly of Butz. Seith's commercial therefore linked Percy to Butz and through him, by inference, to racism. It said:

> Do you think Senator Charles Percy is a friend of black people? Well, remember Earl Butz? He was secretary of agriculture who made a racist and obscene joke about blacks. We can't repeat his words on the air, of course, but they were so offensive that he had to resign. . . . Senator Percy said of Earl Butz . . . "I wish he was secretary of agriculture still today." . . . Senator Percy wants the black vote. With friends like this, you don't need enemies.[22]

Seith then followed up with a second radio commercial. The spot began:

> Do you remember the commercial we ran a few weeks ago, the one that told how Senator Charles Percy wanted Earl Butz back again? Butz—the former secretary of agriculture who made such an outrageous racist joke that he had to resign? Well, since then, people have asked what the secretary of agriculture has to do with people in the inner city, anyway.

The spot went on to say that such programs as food stamps and school lunches are administered by the Department of Agriculture. It then concluded,

> But Earl Butz didn't care about these programs. He used them as dumping grounds for excess agricultural products. And when the present secretary of agriculture came to Chicago, he had to straighten out the food-stamp and free-lunch programs, which suffered under Earl Butz's neglect. And Senator Charles Percy says he would like to see Earl Butz back in office. All right. That's why this is documented, paid for and authorized by the Seith for Senate Committee. What does this say about Senator Percy?[23]

The ads caused an uproar. Many black leaders, including Muhammad Ali and the Rev. Jesse Jackson, began to work on behalf of Percy.

At about the same time the radio spots were causing controversy (the middle to end of October), a respected newspaper poll, the *Chicago Sun-Times*'s Straw Poll, was published showing Percy losing to Seith

---

[22] G. Robert Hillman, "Seith Swaps Lie Charges With Percy," *Chicago Sun-Times,* October 25, 1978, p. 3.

[23] G. Robert Hillman, "2d Seith Ad Pitch to Blacks Links Percy, Butz," *Chicago Sun-Times,* October 27, 1978, p. 16.

by seventeen percentage points. The commercials and the poll results suddenly focused attention on an election most people had conceded to Percy. It became a hot item, commanding headlines. Journalists followed both candidates and reported on them in depth. Talk show hosts attempted to have both appear. The events galvanized financial and voter support for Percy, both of which had been languid until this point, and allowed him to redirect his efforts in the last two weeks of the campaign. He was able to raise immediately $450,000 (mostly loans from his own funds) and to command between $1 and $1.5 million in the closing days of the campaign. It all went into a new media blitz.

Seven days before the election, Percy was able to put a totally new media campaign on the air. It had three themes. First, it showed a "humble" Percy saying he had "gotten the message." He admitted having been out of touch and not reflecting the wishes of the voters. He apologized and asked to be returned to the Senate to use his experience and knowledge to fight for what the voters wanted. This was the central thrust of the new media effort, and it appeared to work. Percy surged ahead and eventually beat Seith. The day after the election, Percy followed through on this theme by flying around the state to thank the people for their support and to tell them that he had received a "clear message."

A second thrust of the media campaign was Percy's prominence and experience. It was carried out in a series of commercials essentially similar to the earlier media efforts, except that they emphasized endorsements by television and radio stations and newspapers statewide. The new ads selected references in the endorsements that mentioned Percy as "one of the taxpayers' better watchdogs in the U.S. Senate" and "his outspoken criticism of inefficiency in government"; his fights for "reduction in the bureaucracy"; his "courageous" fight on behalf of the state and against "big-money pressure groups"; and his identification with the citizens of Illinois.

Third, and more controversially, Percy attacked Seith. Mike Royko is Chicago's favorite columnist. He had written several columns on Paul Marcy, who had been convicted of failure to pay taxes on a $55,000 bribe he took from a builder who wanted a zoning case fixed. This type of thing is not unusual in Chicago, and perhaps in most American cities. Marcy, however, was the brother of a known syndicate hoodlum. He was also secretary of the Cook County Zoning Board of Appeals, which Seith chaired, and according to Royko, Seith's "top aide" on the board. Seith had appeared as a character witness for Marcy.

In his own defense, Seith claimed no knowledge of the bribe. Seith said his position was appointive and nonsalaried and he had no power to fire Marcy, although he hoped Marcy would resign.

The Royko columns appeared on October 29 and November 1. The Percy campaign reprinted the columns during the final week of the election in full-page advertisements in the leading Chicago newspapers under the heading "Pulitzer Prize Winner Mike Royko Tells More About The Mobs, The Chicago Machine and Alex Seith."[24] The story and the controversy that followed were the major campaign news heading into election day.

Seith was enraged. He accused Percy of the same type of innuendo and lack of ethics that Percy had charged him with in the controversy over the ads to black voters. Percy replied that he saw nothing wrong with the ads, although he did subsequently delete the lead-in referring to the mobs and Seith.

Immediately preceding the election Seith and Percy appeared on radio and television interview programs on which they accused each other of cheap shots, gross distortions, and unethical conduct. One particularly bitter confrontation on a television program was recorded from the time the candidates entered the studio building until they departed, still hurling accusations at each other. To add to the drama, after leaving the studio (but while still being covered by TV cameras), Percy fainted. The session was treated as the major news of the day by the television stations, and the entire interview program was scheduled twice during the final weekend of the campaign.[25]

Percy recovered and won the election with 54 percent of the vote. The entire campaign, on both sides, was a creature of the media. It had all the elements — personalities, drama, horserace aspects — that make for exciting television. It had very little to do with issue positions, performance while in office, the representation of party coalitions, personal contact with the voter, or the major issues of the day. In

[24] See, as examples, the full-page advertisements in the *Chicago Sun-Times* of November 3, 1978, p. 41 and November 5, 1978, p. 12.

[25] For one account of the episode, see Gary Deeb, "The Turning of the Tide for Percy, Via Video Stage Manager Jacobson," *Chicago Tribune*, November 13, 1978, Sec. 3, p. 9.

these regards it is not dissimilar to the media-oriented campaigns being conducted in all parts of the United States.

After the election, Seith was asked why he, an unknown and a newcomer to politics, should have done so well against an established vote-getter like Percy. He made the point that he was the first candidate Percy had faced with the financial resources needed to hire first-rate consultants and launch the comprehensive media campaign needed to be effective. The cost was high for both sides. The Seith campaign cost approximately $1 million and the Percy effort $2.4 million.

Seith's point is well taken. The first prerequisite of effective political campaigns in the media age would seem to be funding; the second, the luck to hire competent professional consultants; and the third, the ability to follow their advice.

PROFESSIONAL CONSULTANTS

The number of consultants available to a candidate is enormous. Robert Agranoff, who has studied the new politics in depth, has listed the twenty-seven categories of consultants a candidate might wish to hire.[26] These range from advertising agents and advance men to graphic designers and computer programmers. The variety of types and the services they can perform are impressive. A campaign consulting firm, or an individual consultant with the necessary authority and funds, can create for a candidate an organization comparable to the most efficient and streamlined of modern political parties. President Nixon's Committee to Re-Elect the President in 1972 developed an organization on paper and in practice that far excelled anything available to the Republican or Democratic parties. The uses it was put to are, of course, a different matter. It does serve as the most elaborate of its type and a model (less the ethical connotations) that other candidates attempt to duplicate.

Senatorial candidates regularly develop, in effect, their own political parties. They are candidate-centered organizations established in the

[26] Agranoff, "The New Style of Campaigning," p. 17.

short run to serve the immediate end of an individual's election. Although impressive, they are expensive and wasteful. Immediately after the election the organization is dismantled and the consultants move on to their next job. The same time and effort invested in political party organizations would have long-run beneficial consequences. This, however, is not the trend. If anything, the candidate-centered, technocratic, short-lived, and election-oriented organizations are on the rise. It is not unusual to see them now in congressional races.

One year before the national nominating conventions, the Republican National Committee held its semiannual meeting. Normally, this would be a fertile ground for prospective presidential contenders to solicit votes among the movers and shakers of the party. However, the gathering was boycotted by a number of the principal contenders for the party's presidential nomination, including Ronald Reagan, Howard Baker, Jr., and John Connally. Why? The answer reflects the tenor of the times. One observer wrote, "Although those who stayed away gave various reasons for doing so, some party leaders said the contenders were so busy setting up organizations outside the party that they saw little point in making personal appeals to the regular party leaders."[27]

The Pollster and the Polls

The most publicly visible of the consultants are the pollsters. This is a tribute both to the importance polls have assumed in campaigns and the ability of the pollsters to promote their own interests. Pollsters, unlike other campaign consultants, can become nationally known. Louis Harris, George Gallup, Daniel Yankelovich, Peter Hart, Robert Teeter, and, most recently, Patrick Caddell have acquired national reputations. They become celebrities in their own right, and all attract lucrative contracts for their polling services from corporations, trade groups, newspapers and television stations, and even foreign governments. This is in addition to whatever party and candidate polling they might do.[28]

[27] John Herbers, "G.O.P. Ends Its National Meeting With An Optimistic View of 1980," *The New York Times*, June 27, 1979, p. A14.

[28] A critical assessment of polling is contained in Michael Wheeler, *Lies, Damn Lies, and Statistics* (New York: Dell, 1976). See also Harold Mendelsohn and Irving Crespi, *Polls, Television, and the New Politics* (Scranton, Pa.: Chandler, 1970).

Polls are expensive. The least costly for a congressional district or state begin at $10,000 to $15,000, and the costs run up from there. Packages of polls delivered at specified times during a campaign can come to a quarter of a million dollars. Richard Nixon, who depended heavily on polling information in both 1968 and 1972, awarded individual polling agencies campaign contracts of over $400,000 and $200,000 respectively.

Whatever the price, polls are considered essential to a serious candidacy. They serve a number of functions. A candidate can use a poll to establish such things as his name identification and his prospects of victory in a race. How many people know him? What types of knowledge (personal? political?) do they have of him? Is it positive? Will it work to his advantage in a campaign? How well known are his opponents? What are their strengths and weaknesses? Where are they vulnerable? If the results are discouraging — a candidate is not widely known and the incumbent looks unbeatable — he may decide not to make a race. In the long run, the time and money saved may well make the poll a bargain.

If a candidate is intent on running, a poll can identify his support in the electorate and the groups among whom he is weak. It can tell him the issues that are of concern to the voters and the types of solutions they favor. A sophisticated poll analysis can project the support among groups a candidate is likely to pick up or lose with different types of policy stands.

A poll can point out the weaknesses in a candidate's image (or his opponent's) and suggest ways to improve it. It can tell a candidate if a stand of his is going over as anticipated or if it may need modification. It can reveal the voters' reaction to crucial events in a campaign (unanticipated charges of misconduct or corruption, for example) and indicate how best to handle these. A poll can demonstrate if a candidate is failing to educate a constituency to his positions or if a vague policy stand might actually work to his advantage. In these regards, a poll can dictate campaign strategy.

As an example, Hubert Humphrey entered the 1972 contest for the Democratic presidential nomination belatedly. He decided to challenge the front runner, George McGovern, in the last major primary of the nomination season, California. At this point, the battle looked hopeless. McGovern was far ahead in the delegate count and it appeared that he had his party's nomination all but ensured.

Humphrey, however, if he wanted any chance at the nomination, had to challenge in California. At this point several polls played a major influence in the race.

First, a respected statewide poll showed that McGovern would win a highly decisive victory. After the publication of the poll, anything less than an overwhelming McGovern vote would be taken by the media as a moral defeat. The poll also had the tendency to relax the McGovern activists. The outcome seemed foreordained.

Humphrey had his own pollster, the late Oliver Quayle, who conducted some private samplings on his behalf. What Quayle and Humphrey found was that much of McGovern's support was soft and many of his prospective voters did not know their candidate's stand on the issues. This decided Humphrey's strategy. He went after McGovern relentlessly on a series of issues and managed to provoke heated controversy in several head-to-head debates, televised in California and nationwide. In the course of his attacks, he showed that McGovern had not thought through the implications of several of his policies, a revelation that weakened his candidacy. McGovern won an unexpectedly close vote, but the initiative taken by Humphrey helped undermine McGovern's credibility. McGovern captured the nomination, but the problems begun in California continued and his candidacy never became a serious threat to incumbent Richard Nixon.

Michael Dukakis, governor of Massachusetts, encountered a situation in 1978 somewhat analogous to McGovern's in California. His early polls, as well as those published in the newspapers, showed him far ahead of any potential opponents. However, he lost the primary nomination to an opponent, Edward King, who had no experience in elective office and seemingly little support among Democrats. Dukakis believed the polls: "The early polls had me ahead so far in the primary that it was impossible to get the voters to take the race seriously."[29] The early poll returns also encouraged other major Democratic candidates who aspired to the governorship to bypass the race, believing Dukakis invincible.

Polls can also be used to measure a candidate's progress as the campaign wears on and, near the end, to predict which one is the likely winner. A private poll (on occasion, doctored poll results) can be released by a candidate if it shows him doing unusually well (or at least

[29] "Notes on People," *The New York Times*, January 19, 1979, p. 49.

better than the published poll results). The intention is to build a wave of support, a "bandwagon effect," behind a given candidacy. Encouraging private poll results can also be used to stimulate activists and to bring in campaign funds. A campaign manual, typical of the breed, advises: "Reproduce a favorable poll, give a quantity of copies of it to your fundraising chairman and let him use it as a tool to generate money. Everyone likes to back the winner; if your poll shows you to be the frontrunner, those campaign dollars will come easier."[30] They surely will. Contributors like to invest in successful enterprises.

Polls and pollsters are vital to campaigns. They affect every aspect of it and in the process have restructured not only the campaign process, but (along with television) the entire communication process between voter and candidate.

The Future of Consultants

Political consultants are controversial. Many believe that their services lend themselves to abuse. Nonetheless, they can be highly effective. They can help, as consultant Michael Kaye of Los Angeles did, to turn a professional basketball player like Bill Bradley into a United States senator. Bradley employed television commercials to emphasize repeatedly the special bond needed between officeholder and voter. The appeal was effective.

Consultants can also be employed, as in Nelson Rockefeller's campaigns, to turn a negative image into a strong endorsement for reelection. Rockefeller was an unpopular governor at the beginning of each of his reelection campaigns. In large part, he believed this resulted from people not understanding his accomplishments as governor. He had the money to do something about it, and the advertising campaigns that resulted are considered among the best and most effective in recent political annals.

The fears of those who mistrust political consultants and their influence in elective politics can be illustrated by the 1978 gubernatorial campaign of a candidate in Hawaii. His major campaign presentation was a thirty-minute film shown repeatedly on the state's television. In

---

[30] Hank Parkinson, *Winning Your Campaign: A Nuts and Bolts Guide to Political Victory* (Englewood Cliffs, N.J.: Prentice-Hall, 1970), p. 158.

it, the candidate, George Ariyosha, was shown with his parents, falling in love, visiting various places on the island and, in the film's major emphasis, courageously overcoming a serious speech impediment. Not mentioned was the policies Ariyosha supported or what he intended to do as governor. Yet Ariyosha at the time of the campaign had already served as governor for six years.

The tactic worked. The governor went from a 15 percent approval rating at the beginning of the campaign to victory in the general election. The consultant who engineered the project, Michael Rowen of San Francisco, happily reported that Ariyosha was the "perfect candidate because he never asked us what we were doing, never asked to see the file and read whatever lines we gave him to read."[31] The fears of many critics of the new campaign technology are implicit in that statement.

The future of consultants looks very promising. If anything, their influence appears to be spreading. As president, Jimmy Carter contracted with Robert Squire, previously associated with the presidential bids of Senator Edmund Muskie, to coordinate picture coverage of one of his administration's biggest accomplishments, the Camp David summit meeting between Israel and Egypt. As his administration continued to flounder, Carter turned to Gerald Rafshoon, an Atlanta advertising man who had handled the president's media advertising during his 1976 election bid. Rafshoon's most striking contribution during the campaign had been an artistically and politically successful series of commercials and paid television programs personally introducing Carter the man. These showed Carter at his warehouse in Plains and walking through peanut fields and introduced his military career, educational background, family and so on. The idea was both to introduce Carter to the American public and to develop a warm, positive, and personal feeling for him. The media work was considered ingenious.

Rafshoon was placed on the White House payroll and given the job of improving Carter's presidential image and coordinating the White House public relations in anticipation of the 1980 campaign. One of his earliest contributions was a theme to place administrative policies in some context. After rejecting such slogans as "Beloved Community,"

[31] Richard Reeves, "White House Gunslingers," *Chicago Sun-Times*, April 9, 1979, p. 32.

"Moral Force," "Bold Mission," and "New Progressivism," Rafshoon settled on "Building New Foundations." The new theme was introduced in Carter's 1979 State of the Union message.[32]

Let us add a final note on the pervasiveness of consultants and the new technology in campaigns. John Connally, in seeking the Republican nomination for president in 1980, introduced a new wrinkle into such campaigns. Traditionally, the candidates have emphasized personal-contact campaigning and organizational development during the early stages of such efforts. This approach was believed to be particularly important in cultivating the voters of the nation's first primary state, New Hampshire. Connally took a new tack. He began blanketing the state in the summer of 1979 (the earliest ever) with television ads decrying the "declining respect for America." He then asked anyone moved by his appeal to sign up with his campaign by calling a toll-free number in Oklahoma.[33]

[32] Harry Kelly, "Rafshoon Waves a Wand of Power," *Chicago Tribune*, April 15, 1979, Sec. 2, p. 14.

[33] Adam Clymer, "New Hampshire Hardly Notices as Presidential Hopefuls Set Stage for 1980 Primary," *The New York Times*, June 24, 1978, p. 180.

6

The Spiraling Cost of Politics

The new political technology is very expensive. In fact, it is based on money. Without money, the new politics is not possible. The rise in campaign expenditures indicates the increasing reliance on new political technology.

Campaign costs rose dramatically from 1952 to 1972 in presidential races and continue to rise in other contests.[1] The Citizens' Research Foundation reported that campaign expenses came to $140 million in 1952. This figure had climbed to $425 million by 1972. Presidential races cost between $2 million and $5 million up through 1948. The Democratic and Republican presidential contenders combined in 1948, for example, spent a total of $5 million. This figure rose to $12 million in 1952, the first year that television played a major role in campaigns. With this race the escalation of costs had begun in earnest. In 1972 it topped out. The two presidential contenders in 1972 spent a total of roughly $100 million (Nixon $61.4 million; McGovern $42 million).

[1] For overviews, see: William Crotty, *Political Reform and the American Experiment* (New York: Crowell, 1977), pp. 103–90; Herbert E. Alexander, *Financing Politics: Money, Elections and Political Reform* (Washington: Congressional Quarterly Press, 1976); and Herbert E. Alexander (ed.), *Political Finance* (Beverly Hills, Calif.: Sage, 1979).

TABLE 6.1
Campaign Costs, All Levels of Elections, 1952–76 (in millions of dollars)

1952	1956	1960	1964	1968	1972	1976
$140	$155	$175	$200	$300	$425	$500

Source: Federal Election Commission.

By 1976 the costs of the presidential races stabilized at $50 million ($23 million for Carter; $25 million for Ford). This was due to the new campaign finance laws. But while the cost of the races of the principal contenders fell, the totals for the election year again increased. Herbert E. Alexander, the director of the Citizens' Research Foundation and the most prominent student of campaign finance, has estimated that the money spent in the 1976 election came to over $500 million (Table 6.1). This figure represented a $75 million increase over that of four years earlier, despite the newly inaugurated federal funding of (and limits on) presidential races. The 1976 costs are a 357 percent increase over those for the first of the modern presidential campaigns in 1952 and an increase of 250 percent in less than a decade (1968–76).

As Table 6.2 shows, the sums spent by Carter and Ford are misleading. Overall, the federal government made approximately $72 million available to the presidential candidates. This sum includes the money spent by the two nominees, Carter and Ford, in the general election, as well as the payments to the national committees of the Republican and Democratic parties to subsidize their nominating conventions and subsidies to the fifteen candidates who ran in the primaries and qualified for assistance (thirteen as Democrats, two as Republicans). Among the latter group, only Ronald Reagan received the full $5 million in matching funds for which he could qualify.[2] Ford came close ($4.6 million) and the other thirteen contenders received between 5 and 75 percent of their maximum possible amount. Overall, one-third of the funds for the presidential primary campaigns came from public funds; the remaining two-thirds was in private donations (averaging about $27 per contribution).

[2] "Statement of the Federal Election Commission," *Federal Election Reform Proposals of 1977*, Committee on Rules and Administration, U.S. Senate (Washington, D.C.: U.S. Government Printing Office, 1977), pp. 420–46.

TABLE 6.2
Federal Funding of the 1976 Presidential Primary and General Election Campaigns

Candidate	Number of submissions	Number of contributions submitted	Average amount submitted	Total amount submitted	Percentage of total request matched	Total amount certified	Amount originally rejected	Percentage of request matched prior to resubmission of rejected amount	Amount resubmitted	Final amount rejected
Bayh	17	6,988	$66.02	$475,335.94	98.70	$469,199.54	$36,134.95	92.39	$30,309.55	$6,136.40
Bentsen	3	6,767	84.98	575,062.94	88.86	511,022.61	64,030.33	88.86	—	64,030.33
Brown	9	20,089	34.35	694,174.87	83.64	580,629.65	134,177.23	80.00	22,278.01	113,545.22
Carter	21	94,419	41.09	3,880,118.84	89.31	3,465,584.89	522,827.93	86.52	152,892.83	414,533.95
Church	18	18,812	33.50	630,151.01	98.82	622,747.04	12,566.97	98.00	5,485.50	7,403.97
Ford	21	114,661	43.06	4,937,232.99	94.32	4,657,007.82	611,218.93	87.62	330,993.76	290,225.17
Harris	13	56,021	11.74	657,813.91	96.24	633,099.05	147,519.90	77.58	122,805.04	24,714.86
Jackson	7	58,372	35.45	2,069,042.97	95.72	1,980,554.95	613,002.81	70.38	524,514.79	88,488.02
McCormack	8	14,161	18.08	256,093.60	95.32	244,125.40	25,974.37	89.85	14,151.17	11,966.20
Reagan	19	238,266	23.11	5,507,153.24	92.40	5,088,910.66	436,801.80	92.06	18,559.22	418,242.58
Sanford	3	1,960	126.07	247,100.32	99.71	246,388.32	712.00	99.71	—	712.00
Shapp	11	4,416	69.61	307,403.71	97.28	290,066.21	12,947.50	95.79	4,610.00	8,337.50
Shriver	8	2,745	104.12	285,822.19	99.73	285,069.74	14,417.45	94.95	13,740.00	752.45
Udall	22	97,764	21.84	2,135,263.72	88.92	1,898,686.96	295,910.76	86.14	59,922.00	236,376.76
Wallace	6	240,052	14.75	3,539,579.86	92.98	3,291,308.81	870,737.36	75.39	622,466.31	248,271.05
Subtotal	186	975,493	26.86	26,197,340.11	92.65	24,273,401.65	3,798,980.29	85.49	1,922,728.18	1,923,938.46
Democratic National Committee convention payments				2,180,869.79		2,180,869.79				
Republican National Committee convention payments				1,963,800.00		1,963,800.00				
Subtotal				30,342,009.90		28,418,071.44	3,798,980.29	(3)	1,922,728.18	1,923,938.46
General election payments:										
Carter				21,820,000.00		21,820,000.00				
Ford				21,820,000.00		21,820,000.00				
Total				73,982,009.90		72,058,071.44	3,798,980.29	(3)	1,922,728.18	1,923,938.46

Source: Federal Election Commission.

Despite what appear to be major costs, the federal subsidies of elections seem popular. The money comes from tax dollars made available directly by the taxpayer who can check off on his tax returns whether one dollar of his tax payment (two for joint returns) can go into a special fund to subsidize presidential contests. The program got off to a rocky start (the Nixon administration actively discouraged it during its early years) but has proven durable since.

The federal funding of presidential elections is an attempt to contain campaign costs within reasonable limits, while still providing enough leeway for a challenger to make a competitive bid for the nation's highest office. It is also an effort to introduce serious public scrutiny into presidential campaigns and to minimize the influence of single-issue groups, PACs, and wealthy individuals or contenders.[3]

The revelations as to where the money comes from in elections — and the implicit quid pro quo — are factors of consequence in making the public funding of campaigns so attractive. There are no public subsidies for congressional or state-level races. There are, also, no controls over total expenditures. One consequence is that costs have soared. The 1978 congressional elections were estimated to cost over $200 million. That figure is the highest in history, twice the cost of the 1974 off-year elections and well above the 1976 estimated outlay for the same races of $125 million.

The total expenditures for United States Senate races came to $26,443,964 in 1972 and $27,904,495 in 1974. The $38.1 million spent on Senate campaigns in 1976 included eight candidates who spent $1 million or more on their races. Three candidates spending more than $1 million, incumbent senators John Tunney (Dem.) in California and Bill Brock (Rep.) in Tennessee and former congressman William Green (Dem.), seeking the Senate from Pennsylvania, lost. In Green's case his opponent H. John Heinz III, heir to his family's catsup fortune, won the race with a $3 million expenditure (the highest for the year). Incumbent Senator James Buckley, the Conservative-Republican candidate in New York, invested $2.1 million in his reelection bid but still lost to newcomer Daniel Patrick Moynihan.

In the 1978 off-year elections the average Senate race cost $570,000, although expenses of $1 million or more were common. The average for the United States House races approached $100,000, and forty-one

[3]Crotty, *Political Reform*, pp. 168–90; and Bruce F. Freed, "Political Money and Campaign Finance Reform, 1971–1976," in Jeff Fishel (ed.), *Parties and Elections in An Anti-Party Age* (Bloomington: Indiana University Press, 1978), pp. 241–55.

campaigns came to over $300,000. Eleven candidates for the United States Senate spent over $1 million, including what may be the Senate's first $6 million man, Jesse Helms (Rep.) of North Carolina (who actually spent $6.7 million to retain his seat in North Carolina, a little over eleven dollars per vote received). Senator John Tower (Rep.) spent more than $3 million to eke out a narrow victory in Texas.

The costs of individual races are attracting increasing attention. In 1978 there were a number of expensive races at all levels that caught the public eye. Illinois Governor James "Big Jim" Thompson spent $2.5 million on a reelection bid against a weak opponent (Thompson won easily with 60 percent of the vote cast). One reason for Thompson's expenditure was his desire to become a creditable candidate for the Republican party's presidential nomination.

Thompson's opponent spent $1.2 million and, in the same state, Charles Percy spent $2.4 million in his successful bid to retain his Senate seat. His challenger's budget came to about $1 million.

In California, a state noted for its media politics and the high cost of its campaigns, Governor Jerry Brown (also harboring presidential ambitions) spent $4 million in his reelection campaign and his Republican opponent, California Attorney General Evelle Younger, about $3 million. Tobacco interests and the prosmoking lobby invested $5.5 million in California in the successful campaign to defeat Proposition 5, a proposal to ban smoking in public places.

An estimated total of $20 million was recorded for the 1978 races in Texas, another state known for lavish spending and one in which the races of the two Senate candidates alone came to over $5 million. Reportedly, the gubernatorial races in Texas and Florida ran into the millions of dollars. The Democratic nominee in Florida (Graham) budgeted $5 million for his race against Jack M. Eckerd, a Republican millionaire drugstore owner and a former head of the General Services Administration. Eckerd was known for his high-cost campaigns in previous efforts at elective office.

In Texas, the winner and first Republican to hold the governorship in 105 years, Bill Clements, used a $6 million campaign budget to squeak out a 20,000 vote margin from the over 2.29 million votes cast. His opponent spent half of what Clements did, a still respectable $3 million.

In all, reports indicate that about nineteen candidates among the sixty-nine seeking Senate offices (including two who were unopposed) had campaign budgets in the vicinity of $1 million or more. There are no accurate estimates on the gubernatorial contests, which are not monitored with the consistency of congressional races, but the expenditures would probably equal or exceed those for seats in the Congress.

WHERE THE MONEY COMES FROM: THE CANDIDATES

Figures such as these have led commentators to question whether candidates "should be allowed to buy public office" and whether a plutocracy has not begun to control elective offices in this country. Columnist David Broder referred to Texas's Clements as using his wealth for "political self aggrandizement."[4] The practice is not uncommon. Clements's Democratic predecessor, Dolph Briscoe, overcame his considerable political shortcomings through his personal wealth. In 1978 alone, over a dozen candidates made personal loans valued in the hundreds of thousands of dollars to their own campaigns. Some lost: Robert Short in Minnesota, Alex Seith in Illinois, Jane Eskind in Tennessee, Luther Hodges, Jr., in North Carolina, Philip Power in Michigan, Dolph Briscoe in his renomination try in Texas, and three in Virginia, Clive DuVal, Carrington Williams, and Rufus C. Williams. However, other candidates won. Clements is a prime example. Bill Bradley of New Jersey, John W. Warner of Virginia, Alan K. Simpson of Wyoming, and Nancy Landon Kassebaum of Kansas all were elected to the United States Senate with considerable help from personal funds lent (so that they might be reimbursed) to their own campaigns.

Anthony Lewis, writing in *The New York Times,* calls the rich candidate financing his own campaign "an outstanding phenomenon of American politics these days."[5] For example, Short of Minnesota, who upset Congressman Donald Fraser, the state party's nominee for the United States Senate nomination, spent $1,421,000, of which

[4] David Broder, "Buying Public Office," *Chicago Sun-Times*, November 19, 1978, Views, p. 6.
[5] Anthony Lewis, "The Rise of the Plutocracy," *The New York Times*, November 13, .978, p. A23.

$1,280,000 was his own money. John Warner "lent" (to be repaid by others investing in the campaign) his primary campaign $616,000, two-thirds of his total expenditures. Seith lent $600,000 to his Senate campaign; about four-fifths of his total came from his own pocket.

Eskind, the Democrat who opposed Senate Minority Leader Howard Baker, Jr., in Tennessee, gave or lent her own campaign virtually its entire budget (over $625,000). Bill Bradley lent some of his money from his professional basketball days with the New York Knicks (about $175,000) to his own campaign. Alan K. Simpson of Wyoming ($100,000), Larry Williams of Montana ($92,777) and Nancy Landon Kassebaum of Kansas ($90,000) also invested heavily in their own campaigns. In one New York congressional district (the Eighteenth, or "silk-stocking" district of the fashionable upper east side), the losing Democrat, Carter Burden, put over $675,000 of his own money into his campaign, virtually its entire budget. The winning Republican candidate, William Green, supplied about half of his campaign's $400,000 from his own pocket. In this race for a congressional seat, the total expenditures came to $1 million. Even in today's inflationary market, that is high for a job that pays $57,500.

Spending by individuals on this scale does affect the political process. Short, for example, was able to unseat Congressman Donald Fraser, the favorite and the state party's nominee in the primary. The Democrats lost both Senate seats, the governorship, and an unusually high number of state legislative districts. The Short candidacy introduced discord into Democratic party ranks, and Short's 35 percent of the vote in the general election did not help the party's ticket.

Charles Percy is a millionaire. His money has allowed him to become a force in national politics. He first served as the chairman of a Republican issues group in the late 1950s and later as the chairman of the platform committee of the 1960 Republican National Convention. He ran for governor in Illinois and lost in 1964. Nonetheless he had the funds to run for Senator two years later, and he won. He ran for reelection in 1972 and won handily. His campaign spent $1.4 million to his opponent's $335,000. In 1978, Percy spent heavily and won, in part, because when the election became close in the final weeks, Percy could dip into his bank account for the $400,000 to $600,000 needed to finance a last-minute television blitz.

As discussed earlier, Alex Seith gave Percy an unexpectedly close challenge. In large part, it was because Seith could finance his own campaign and could invest heavily in media. This was the first time since Percy entered the Senate that an opponent had recourse to such personal wealth.

Jack Eckerd has been a candidate for several major offices in Florida. Win or lose, his ability to personally fund his campaigns has made him a continuing threat in elections. Personal wealth permits this. Eckerd is not alone (Milton Shapp and Howard Metzenbaum are among the many others, as was Nelson Rockefeller).[6] Wealth allows an individual to come from obscurity to fund, and often win, competitive races. H. John Heinz III of Pennsylvania (mentioned earlier) is an example. He lent his campaign for the United States Senate $2.6 million (none of it repaid by 1978) in 1976. Heinz won. Clements, Warner, Eskind, and others could become competitive because of their formidable economic situation. Clements was a successful businessman but a political novice. Warner, a millionaire from his first wife's money, had never run for political office. Bradley, a millionaire, defeated the Democratic governor's choice for the Senate nomination. Bradley, in his thirties, had never held public office. Kassebaum had previously served on a local school board before winning the Republican nomination and the Kansas Senate seat. Winners such as Bradley, Kassebaum, and Warner join a body, the United States Senate, that already boasts forty millionaires.

There are other examples. The Democratic nominee for governor in 1978, and the eventual winner in Alabama, was Forrest (Fob) James. He had left the Democratic party in 1972 and had been prominent in Alabama's Republican affairs. James had served on the state party's executive committee and he had a reputation as one of the Republican party's best fund raisers. Nonetheless, James decided he had no chance for the governorship as a Republican, so he switched back to the Democratic party. A year before the primary he began campaigning.

James had a number of things going for him. He was a former football star at Auburn University. He was also wealthy. He was the inventor and marketer of plastic dumbbell sets that along with other business ventures made him a millionaire.[7] He had the time and personal wealth to invest in his campaign. James emphasized the media,

[6] See Crotty, *Political Behavior*, pp. 126–30.

[7] Christopher Buchanan, "Party Crashers: A Growing Force in Politics," *Congressional Quarterly*, October 28, 1978, p. 3107.

and put $1.5 million into a heavy television advertising campaign. He won the Democratic nomination (tantamount to victory in the general election), defeating in the process a former governor, lieutenant governor, and attorney general. The Democratic party was upset enough to withhold its endorsement, pending James's appearance before them to convince them of his party regularity. It did not really matter; James captured 72 percent of the general election vote. He had won, through judicious use of his wealth, what he wanted.

Personal fortunes appear to be becoming an increasingly important consideration for entering public office. To curb this, and in the effort to better equalize resources, the 1974 Campaign Reform Act limited to $25,000 (for House campaigns) and $35,000 (for Senate campaigns) the amount of money a candidate could spend of his own or his family's money in seeking federal office. On January 30, 1976, the Supreme Court threw the restriction out as an infringement of free speech (which it equated with the ability to spend a person's own funds). It is rare that a group of incumbent congressmen, with proven access to money and often wealthy in their own rights, pass legislation to limit campaign expenditures (whether theirs or anyone else's) or to improve the chances of their opponents' election. It is likely that the present trend toward higher and higher expenditures in congressional and state campaigns will continue and that those with personal wealth will maintain a decided advantage.

WHERE THE MONEY COMES FROM: THE PACs

Increasingly, the funds for political races are coming from Political Action Committees (PACs). There were 516 of these groups — business, labor, trade associations, and ideological groups — in 1974, the first year they were legally authorized under the new campaign laws.[8] They contributed $12 million to political campaigns. By the time of the 1978 election, the number of PACs had risen to 1938 and their

[8] Alexander, *Financing Politics*, pp. 131–68; Crotty, *Political Behavior*, pp. 168–90; and Freed, "Political Money."

financial contributions to federal campaigns had swollen to $35.1 million. This total compares with $6.4 million spent directly and $4.4 million indirectly in support of their candidates by the Democratic and Republican parties. PACs have become the dominant source of funding for political campaigns.

A survey of PACs' political activity for the most recent election (1978) shows that 75 percent of the registered PACs were active in the off-year elections. The majority of the funds invested by the PACs (56.9 percent) went to incumbents. The largest number of PACs (821) are affiliated with corporations (Table 6.3). Second in number are the Trade/Membership/Health groups (543). Third, and well behind the leaders in numbers, are the most publicized of PACs traditionally, the labor unions. The unions do, however, invest in campaigns second only to the trade and health interest groups, although the latter, added to the corporate PACs, doubled labor's contributions.

Among the top political contributors were the American Medical Association, the Realtors Political Action Committee, the Automobile and Truck Dealers Election Action Committee, and PACs representing the United Automobile Workers, the AFL-CIO, and the United Steelworkers.

WHERE DOES THE MONEY GO?

Most PAC funds were invested in incumbents sympathetic to a corporation's or union's political interests. Only 22 percent of the total went to challengers in contested races. Also, and not surprisingly, the candidate with the greatest access to funds won the overwhelming majority of races. Congress Watch, a Ralph Nader organization, reported that in twenty-eight of thirty-three contested Senate races in 1978, the candidate with the most money won. Furthermore, the winners outspent their rivals by a ratio of 4 to 1 (Table 6.4).[9]

The PACs did not neglect House races. In many respects, it could be argued that a relatively modest contribution to a House race (and

[9]"Nader Study Links Spending and Success in Senate Campaigns" (Washington: A Report Released by Congress Watch, November 16, 1979).

TABLE 6.3
Contributions of Political Action Committees (PACs) to Candidates in the 1978 Election, by Category (PAC Summary Financial Information)

(Figures in MILLIONS of dollars)

Committee Type	No. of Committees Active in 1977–78	Adjusted Receipts	Adjusted Disbursements	Latest Cash on Hand	Contributions to Federal Candidates	No. of Committees Making Contributions to Federal Candidates
Corporations	821	17.7	15.3	3.9	9.8	697
Labor Organizations	281	19.8	18.9	4.8	10.3	211
Independent Organizations	254	15.4	16.8	.9	2.5	120
Trade/Membership/Health	543	25.2	24.4	3.6	11.5	399
Cooperatives	12	2.0	2.0	1.4	.9	11
Corporations Without Stock	27	.4	.4	.06	.1	21
Totals	1938	80.5	77.8	14.7	35.1	1459

Source: Federal Election Commission.

TABLE 6.4

The Largest Discrepancies in Spending Between Candidates in United States Senate Races, 1978 (Winners and Losers)

When the Bigger Spender Won	*When the Lower Spender Won*
1. Sen. Ted Stevens (R-Alaska) $297,000 vs. Donald Hobbs (D) $2,000 Winner Spent 14800% of Loser's Total	1. Gordon Humphrey (R-NH) $112,000 vs. Sen. Thomas McIntyre (D) $124,000 Winner Spent 90% of Loser's Total
2. Sen. Sam Nunn, Jr. (D-Ga) $480,000 vs. John Stokes (R) $5,000 Winner Spent 9600% of Loser's Total	2. Roger Jepsen (R-Ia) $521,000 vs. Sen. Dick Clark (D) $738,000 Winner Spent 71% of Loser's Total
3. Gov. David Pryor (D-Ark) $779,000 vs. William Kelly (R) $11,000 Winner Spent 7081% of Loser's Total	3. Rep. Paul Tsongas (D-Mass) $538,000 vs. Sen. Edward Brooke (R) $1,020,000 Winner Spent 53% of Loser's Total
4. Sen. Jesse Helms (R-NC) $6,351,000 vs. John Ingram (D) $217,000 Winner Spent 2927% of Loser's Total	4. Carl Levin (D-Mich) $647,000 vs. Sen. Robert Griffin (R) $1,290,000 Winner Spent 50% of Loser's Total
5. Sen. Mark Hatfield (R-Ore) $179,000 vs. Vern Cook (D) $22,000 Winner Spent 814% of Loser's Total	5. David Durenberger (R-Minn) $811,000 vs. Robert Short (D) $1,810,000 Winner Spent 45% of Loser's Total
6. Sen. James McClure (R-Id) $369,000 vs. Dwight Jensen (D) $51,000 Winner Spent 724% of Loser's Total	
7. Sen. Pete Domenici (R-NM) $826,000 vs. Toney Anaya (D) $128,000 Winner Spent 645% of Loser's Total	
8. Sen. Walter D. Huddleston (D-Ky) $361,000 vs. Louis Guenthner (R) $65,000 Winner Spent 555% of Loser's Total	
9. Sen. Claiborne Pell (D-RI) $310,000 vs. James Reynolds (R) $69,000 Winner Spent 449% of Loser's Total	
10. Alan Simpson (R-Wy) $330,000 vs. Raymond Whitaker (D) $110,000 Winner Spent 300% of Loser's Total	
11. Rep. Larry Pressler (R-SD) $347,000 vs. Don Barnett (D) $131,000 Winner Spent 265% of Loser's Total	
12. Donald Stewart (D-Ala) $600,000 vs. James Martin (R) $241,000 Winner Spent 249% of Loser's Total	
13. Sen. Joseph Biden (D-Del) $372,000 vs. James Baxter (R) $150,000 Winner Spent 248% of Loser's Total	
14. John Warner (R-Va) $1,236,000 vs. Andrew Miller (D) $535,000 Winner Spent 231% of Loser's Total	

(Continued)

TABLE 6.4 *(continued)*

When the Bigger Spender Won	*When the Lower Spender Won*
15. Rep. Max Baucus (D-Mont) $552,000 vs. Larry Williams (R) $270,000 Winner Spent 204% of Loser's Total	
16. Rep. William Cohen (R-Me) $532,000 vs. Sen. William Hathaway (D) $337,000 Winner Spent 197% of Loser's Total	
17. Sen. Howard Baker (R-Tenn) $1,645,000 vs. Jane Eskind (D) $859,000 Winner Spent 192% of Loser's Total	
18. Sen. John Tower (R-Tex) $3,586,000 vs. Rep. Robert Krueger (D) $1,946,000 Winner Spent 184% of Loser's Total	
19. Sen. Strom Thurmond (R-NC) $1,765,000 vs. Charles "Pug" Ravenel (D) $992,000 Winner Spent 178% of Loser's Total	
20. Bill Bradley (D-NJ) $1,400,000 vs. Jeffrey Bell (R) $814,000 Winner Spent 172% of Loser's Total	

Source: From "Nader Study Links Spending and Success in Senate Campaigns." Washington, D.C.: A Report Released by Congress Watch, November 16, 1978. The last 8 races in the Congress Watch list of bigger spending winners have been omitted here. Reprinted by permission.

each PAC is permitted to give up to $5000 to any one candidate for federal office) can constitute a larger proportion of the officeholder's total budget and thus ensure a greater sense of obligation on the part of the recipient. The freshman class in the 1978 House elections (those elected to Congress for the first time) won their seats with the help of $3.3 million in special interest money. New members receive *on the average* $43,000 each in PAC contributions. Four incoming freshmen had campaign funds of over $500,000 available to them in their races; eight had special interest contributions totaling between $70,000 and $120,000. A Common Cause official made the obvious point: "Newcomers to the House are becoming heavily indebted to interest group PACs, even before they are sworn into office."[10]

[10]"Political Groups Reportedly Give $3.3 Million to New Congressmen," *The New York Times,* May 20, 1979, p. 49.

House and Senate committee chairmen rank among the most powerful people on Capitol Hill. As a result, their reelection campaigns are among the most lavishly financed. Only two Senate chairmen, Claiborne Pell of Rhode Island and Jennings Randolph of West Virginia, were up for reelection in 1978. Pell received $74,900 from special interest groups, or 23 percent of his total campaign expenses of $310,000. He won 75 percent of the vote. Randolph received $200,000 in PAC contributions, 30 percent of his campaign budget of $709,000. It may have made the difference in a close race.

Among the twenty-eight House Democratic chairmen, only three were in close races, receiving less than 55 percent of the vote. The balance of chairmen won handily. The average chairman in the House spent $80,000 on his reelection race in 1978. For his campaign he received $45,000 in special interest funding (up from an average of $21,700 in 1976).

Most House committee chairmen had funds left over after their reelection contests. These averaged $9300 per chairman. The money could be spent for any lawful purpose the chairman chose. The easy availability of funds from one campaign to another (if an officeholder chooses to use them in this manner) exacerbates the problem of equalizing campaign resources. In one respect favored candidates have a perpetual budget for campaigning (plus the media and communications advantage of incumbency) that helps remove them from the normal checks of their constituents.

A new development may be coming out of all of this. One House member, Henry Waxman (D — Calif.) gave $24,000 of his funds to ten members of the House Interstate and Commerce Committee. Apparently grateful, the members of the committee chose Waxman to head its important subcommittee on Health and Environment. Waxman explained that he had given funds ($21,000) to thirty other candidates for House or Senate seats because he did not need them. He also claimed that committee chairmen regularly made such donations from their own large war chests (which is true).[11] These are functions that House campaign committees of the two parties were supposed to fulfill.

The Waxman incident, and others like it, have direct policy implications. Waxman's assumption of the subcommittee chairmanship kept

[11] B. Drummond Ayres, Jr., "House Panel Elects a Chairman Who Gave Funds to Colleagues," *The New York Times*, January 31, 1979, p. A11.

from the position a more senior southern colleague with personal and family ties to the pharmaceutical industry, an area that fell under the subcommittee's jurisdiction. Whatever the merits of the case and the political persuasions of the donor, more of this career self-promotion through contributions to colleagues' campaigns is likely to be the norm. It represents — with the help of special interest funds — a new way of accumulating power in Congress.

A subcommittee on communications of the House Commerce Committee was scheduled to begin reassessing in the 1978 postelection period the 1934 Communications Act which regulated, in particular, radio and television. There was much at stake in the review, and rumors were that the Congress might be favorably inclined toward decreasing the federal controls over the electronic media. Not unexpectedly, all but one member of the subcommittee received contributions from the communications industry. Such names as AT&T, MGM, NBC, CBS, Western Union, Time Inc., Cox Broadcasting, Westinghouse, and the Motion Picture Association of America, all with a stake in how the act would be rewritten, began appearing as substantial contributors to subcommittee members' campaigns from New York to California. "The situation speaks for itself," said David Cohen, the president of Common Cause. "The lesson to be learned is that special interests only offer money to congressmen involved in their area of interest. It is a rare occasion that a candidate won't accept that money."[12]

The pattern of PAC giving can be illustrated by the Percy-Seith campaign. Seith spent $1 million, 90 percent contributed by himself. Percy, the incumbent, spent $2.4 million and he was far more successful in attracting donations from a wide range of special interest PACs (Table 6.5).

The power PACs can exercise over congressional actions is enormous. As their contributions to campaigns increase, as both incumbent and newcomer become indebted to special interest funds for election, their influence should grow. At present, there is no end in sight. Incidents such as the following will occur with regularity.

In a little-publicized action, the Senate Judiciary Committee voted out by a close 9 to 8 vote a bill to overturn a Supreme Court decision.

[12] Lorie J. Barzano, "Communication Giants Know Where to Give," *Chicago Sun-Times*, November 12, 1978, p. 38.

TABLE 6.5
Selective Contributors to the 1978 Reelection Campaign of Charles H. Percy (by Category)

Category	Contributors
Transportation	Pan American World Airways ($400), United Airlines ($2,000), Eastern Air Lines ($300), Trans World Airlines ($500), Chicago & North Western Ry. ($4,000), and Lockheed ($500).
Communication	AT&T ($1,000), 20th Century-Fox Film Corp. ($500), Reader's Digest ($250), and Templex-Eastern/Timex Inc. ($100).
Oil	Standard Oil of Indiana ($5,000), Standard Oil of Ohio ($1,000), Standard Oil of California ($300), Union Oil Co. ($1,000), and Texaco Inc. ($100).
Heavy Industry	Gould Inc. ($10,500), Kaiser Aluminum & Chemical Corp. ($400), International Harvester ($2,500), Republic Steel Corp. ($500), United States Steel Corp. ($1,000), FMC Corp. ($1,000), and many others.
Finance	Harris Trust & Savings Bank ($500), First Federal of Chicago Savings & Loan ($500), the American Bankers Assn. ($3,100), Household Finance Corp. ($250), the United States League of Savings Associations ($3,000), and the Northern Trust Co. ($3,500).
Labor	United Auto Workers ($10,000), United Steel Workers ($3,000), Communications Workers of America ($2,500), Railway Clerks ($100), and Carpenters and Joiners of America ($1,000).
Health	American Medical Assn. ($10,000), American Dental Assn. ($200), and Pfizer Inc. ($2,500).

Source: Federal Election Commission.

The issue was called "Illinois Brick," after the company involved in the original litigation, and concerned an effort by Senate liberals to expand those eligible to collect penalties from antitrust violators by permitting parties to a contract who are not direct purchasers from a company to collect damages if the company is convicted by an antitrust act. The key vote was cast by a Republican moderate, Senator Charles Mathias of Maryland, and, in fact, it was Mathias's bill that the committee finally reported out. Mathias took the lead in the legislative battle after reporting that a business PAC had threatened to withhold contributions for his reelection campaign in 1980 if he did not vote against the bill. The PAC involved, allegedly, represented the pharmaceutical firm of Bristol-Myers.

This particular PAC is not a heavy donor to individual campaigns (its biggest contribution in 1978 was $900 to Strom Thurmond). Yet its threat was taken seriously by Mathias.[13] A number of these business PACs linked in a common bond can seriously cripple (or, alternatively, aggressively promote) a candidate's chance for election.

When Mathias publicized the incident, it received virtually no media attention. A similar case in the 1950s was widely discussed and was treated as a serious scandal. It led to the direct defeat of a natural gas bill favored by the company threatening to withhold campaign funds from a senator. What was controversial a few decades ago is legal, ethical, and apparently condoned today.[14]

[13] Rowland Evans and Robert Novak, "Hardball in Washington," *Chicago Sun-Times*, May 23, 1979, p. 64.

[14] The incident is discussed in Crotty, *Political Behavior*, p. 171.

7
Single-Issue and Ideological PACs

Observers from Walter Cronkite to John Gardner, founder of Common Cause, have begun to comment on the "fragmentation" of American politics and the increasing, in Gardner's words, "paralysis in national policymaking."[1] Many have blamed the development on the rise of single-issue groups. Representatives are judged on their stand on one highly charged issue by groups and voters with the resources and motivation to punish (or reward) their elected officials based on their response to this one concern. Accentuated by the rise of PACs, with ample funding, with an emphasis on media campaigning, and fed by the weakness of the political parties, groups of single-issue voters can often prove decisive in low-turnout primary and general elections. The result is "single-issue government." In such a politically charged and balkanized political atmosphere "no coalition of interests is strong enough to set priorities for the overall public good, to effect reforms that have wide public support, to root out inefficiency and corruption in government programs, and to inspire confidence in political leadership."[2]

[1] John Herbers, "Deep Government Disunity Alarms Many U.S. Leaders," *The New York Times*, November 12, 1978, p. 1.
[2] *Ibid.*

117

The problem has been compounded in recent years by the proliferation of the PACs and the use of a diversity of single-issue lobbies whipsawing legislators. The strength and electoral success of these groups is recent (since the advent of the PACs in 1974). Among the most notable of the single-issue groups in the last several elections have been (roughly in order of political prominence) consumer, environmental, gun (and antigun) control, tax, and abortion groups. Tied in with these developments, and especially with the tax revolt, has been the rise of the "New Right." One of the more vocal of single-interest lobbies, the antiabortionists, feels confident enough to have laid the groundwork for what it hopes will be a new single-interest political party.

CONSUMER GROUPS

The groups with the greatest unrealized political potential are those representing the consumer. Every voter is a consumer, and in an era of high inflation and a decreasing standard of living, consumer consciousness should be at its peak. If so, it should be a relatively easy matter to translate this type of concern into political action.

Such has not been the case. Despite a decade of national concern with consumerism, born in the administration of Lyndon Johnson, and despite the well-publicized appointments of consumer representatives by recent presidents, the gains have been limited. Most states and cities now have some form of consumer complaint agency and state's attorney generals, and more significantly, private citizens have begun to use the courts more aggressively in pursuing consumer protection issues. These range from cases involving overpricing to efforts to penalize General Motors for substituting inferior Chevrolet engines in higher-priced GM cars. The federal government likes to boast that it has thirty-five separate agencies that deal with the concerns of consumers.

If anything, this diversity reflects the weaknesses of the consumer movement. It has proven itself largely incapable of concerted political action to achieve specific and important policy goals. Most of what has occurred in the last decade, though an improvement over the lack of concern that characterized previous years, represents marginal changes with a modest impact.

A 1979 Louis Harris Poll claimed that seven out of ten Americans are potential consumerists. Harris's figures are based on results that excluded those who thought of themselves first as businessmen, farmers, union members, or minority group members.[3] This figure is impressive. Yet in the one battle of the last decade with national political implications, the consumers came in second. For years consumer groups have been attempting to have Congress pass a bill establishing a Federal Consumer Protection Agency. The public supported the idea (58 percent to 28 percent, according to the Harris Poll) and the Carter administration backed the proposal. But the bill was weakened in the Congress. First its enforcement powers were removed (it became a "Consumer Representation" rather than a "Consumer Protection" Agency) and then in its weakened form it was voted down.

The battle had both practical and symbolic importance. Its practical dimensions are obvious. For the first time, consumers — like farmers, labor, business, and most other politically powerful groups — could count on a government agency to protect and advance their interests at the national level. In symbolic terms, the failure of the consumer groups to mobilize support for such an obviously appealing issue indicated to politicians the weakness of the movement. Few politicians will extend themselves for groups who cannot hold them accountable at the polls.

The Business Roundtable, a group representing the leaders of nationally powerful corporations, the National Association of Manufacturers, and the Chamber of Commerce beat such consumer organizations as the Consumer Federation of America, Consumer Union, and the Ralph Nader groups easily in the climactic battle over the consumer agency. Ironically, they did it by mobilizing grassroots support for their position by playing on public fears over more government regulation and higher taxes.

Consumer issues have since been paid lip service by politicians, including, many feel, the Carter administration. It is a popular issue for campaigners with no penalty for failure to deliver on promises. Until consumer leaders can effectively mobilize their clientele and specifically focus their political muscle on carefully selected, well-publicized congressional (and other) races, the movement's gains will continue to

[3] Arthur Woodstone, "The Consumer Army: Rebels With a Cause," *Parade*, November 12, 1978, p. 10.

be limited. After the defeat of the federal consumer agency, "we need to regroup," said Esther Peterson, consumer adviser to both Johnson and Carter.[4] "We have to go back to step one—the voting booth," volunteered the executive director of the Consumer Federation of America, an umbrella organization representing 30 million consumers.[5] They are right. At present, the movement is in disarray, its potential far from being realized.

ENVIRONMENTAL GROUPS

The environmentalists are well ahead of the consumerists in many regards. Spearheaded by such groups as Environmental Action and the League of Conservation Voters, they have attempted to defeat legislators whose policy stands they have found the most offensive. Environmental Action, for example, biennially names a "Dirty Dozen" congressional incumbents it then works to depose. It mobilizes nationwide publicity against its targeted legislators and funnels funds and workers into their primary and general election campaigns. Some years it has enjoyed major successes, winning in two-thirds of its targeted contests, and in others (1978, for example) it has enjoyed more limited gains (two wins, ten losses). Since beginning its lists in 1970, the group has defeated twenty-four of those in Congress who have appeared on its Dirty Dozen lists. Since lists are chosen on the basis of the individual's voting record on limited matters and his influence within Congress, many of the defeats have involved prominent antienvironmental legislators, including committee chairmen.

The League of Conservation Voters pursues a similar strategy. It concentrates more on supporting candidates it believes sympathetic to environmental protection and it focuses more on competitive races. In 1978 its major financial contribution was $9500 to James Weaver, an Oregon Democrat, who won a House seat despite opposition from lumber and utility interests. Overall, it contributed $80,000 to campaigns in 1978, and its scorecard in the gubernatorial and congressional races in which it endorsed nominees was fourteen wins and ten losses.

[4] Ralph Blumenthal, "Consumer Leaders, in Reappraisal, Seek New Initiatives," *The New York Times*, February 15, 1978, p. A21.
   [5] *Ibid*.

The environmental groups have done a good job in publicizing their concerns and in attracting media attention. The Sierra Club and other groups have attempted to educate the public to the need for wilderness conservation and the protection of the natural environment. Other groups have fought for stricter water and air pollution standards, restrictions on industrial waste, and controls on automobile emissions. Among recent concerns have been the fight against nuclear reactors and on behalf of the safer shipment and disposal of radioactive wastes. The "Clamshell Alliance," which protested the nuclear reactors being built in Seabrook, New Hampshire, in 1977, and the successful effort to suspend the opening of a giant dam in Tennessee in order to preserve the three-inch snail darter constitute some of the better-publicized environmental campaigns of recent years. Incidents such as the radioactive clouds let loose by the Three Mile Island nuclear reactor in Pennsylvania and the favorable reception given the movie *The China Syndrome* help keep public attention focused on environmental concerns.

One consequence has been a different type of political offensive, the use of initiative and referenda (later copied by tax revolt groups) to advance environmental causes. Such an approach has its costs. It assumes a public concern of sufficient strength to motivate people to familiarize themselves with an issue and to vote to support the position favored by the environmentalists. It also demands a good deal of funding and well-developed, short-term organizations. Despite its liabilities, environmental groups continue to realize some limited successes from this approach. In the 1978 off-year elections their gains were mixed. Proposals were on the ballots in twelve states. Among those passed were proposals in Hawaii and Montana to limit the construction of nuclear plants. In Hawaii a number of restrictions were placed on the construction of such facilities, including a provision that legislation authorizing such plants had to receive a two-thirds vote in both houses. In Montana, the construction of nuclear plants would be subject to a popular vote of the state's residents.

Environmentally-supported "bottle laws," mandating a deposit on all bottles to encourage their return, were defeated in both Nevada and Alaska. In the most publicized contest, a California initiative to ban smoking in all public and work places was voted down. The stakes in such referenda battles can be high; the tobacco industry reportedly spent $5 million to defeat the nonsmoking proposal in California.

THE GUN LOBBY

One of the perennially most successful political groups is the gun lobby. Led by the National Rifle Association (NRA), the gun lobby has been able to avoid serious restrictions on the use or manufacture of guns. The accomplishment is put in perspective when a number of factors are taken into consideration. First are the deaths by assassination since 1963 of John Kennedy, Martin Luther King, Jr., and Robert Kennedy; the disablement of then presidential candidate George Wallace; and the two attacks directed against Gerald Ford. No shade of the political spectrum has been immune from attack on the lives of its leaders.

Second, guns contribute directly to urban crime and are the principal weapon used in murders. Several states, though not outlawing guns, have tried to reduce the use of guns in crime by mandating strict automatic sentences (twenty-year minimum in one state) for those convicted of a crime with a gun. Third, the overwhelming majority of Americans favor handgun control — 80 percent by the most recent count.

These seem to be persuasive reasons for enacting gun controls. The political strength, persistence, and financial resources of the NRA have ensured, however, that no major legislation restricting access to guns has been enacted. The NRA accomplishes its ends by directly lobbying the Congress and by unremittingly opposing, in his own district, any legislator who supports gun control. The NRA and the progun lobby can be extremely aggressive in their election tactics. In the 1978 elections they played an impressive role. Progun PACs contributed a half million dollars to candidates in federal contests. Twenty-one candidates elected to the Senate and 142 elected to the House received contributions from progun PACs.

The NRA has strongly backed any opponent of Representative Abner Mikva, the chief proponent of gun control in the House. Its support can extend beyond the financial to encompass publicity through NRA organs against its opponents and on behalf of its friends. The NRA will also quietly open offices in a congressman's district and install such things as phone banks to work directly for or against a legislator's election. It did this in Mikva's case in the 1978 election, somewhat to the embarrassment of the congressman's opponent, who had not invited the NRA's help. The district favored gun control, although it was not the most important issue facing the voters, and the congressman's opponent did not want to be known as a progun candidate (although his stand was more compatible with the NRA's position than Mikva's was). In addition, to save money and resources, the NRA headquarters in the district linked the challenger to a number of candidates whom the NRA favored for state legislature seats (and with whom Mikva's opponent did not want to be associated). In a very close race this type of crude support probably hurt the Mikva challenger. Interest group backing can be a mixed blessing.

In opposing Congressman Donald Fraser's attempt to win the Democratic Senate nomination in Minnesota in 1978, the NRA, among other things, released thousands of balloons over the state with "Dump Fraser" on them. In a low turnout Fraser lost the nomination to Robert Short, a rich and conservative maverick Democrat. The NRA and other single-issue lobbies claimed credit for Short's victory.

Jimmy Carter ran as a gun control advocate. After two years of little success with the Congress, he abandoned his plans for legislation in the area. A spokesman for Handgun Control, Inc., claimed that "Jimmy Carter's advisers and strategists are afraid of the militant number of Americans who will stop at nothing in their misguided efforts to stop handgun control."[6] The White House admitted being impressed by, among other things, the Fraser loss.

Mikva won his reelection bid narrowly. Later, he was selected by President Carter for appointment to the federal bench. The NRA announced that it would strongly oppose his nomination. True to its word, the NRA generated a nationwide mailing to senators against approving the Mikva appointment (as Senator Robert Dole told Mikva in the confirmation hearings: "I didn't know so many people knew you in Kansas"[7]), and its representatives appeared before the Senate panel considering Mikva's nomination. The gun lobbyists labeled Mikva a "radical" and a "bigot" against firearms owners, and the executive director of the NRA's lobbying arm explained its opposition to Mikva as follows: "If you were a black and I were the imperial wizard of the Ku Klux Klan, then how you would feel about the nomination of the

[6] John Herbers, "Gun Limit Advocates Are Critical of Carter and Look to Kennedy," *The New York Times*, April 8, 1979, p. 1.

[7] "Mikva Under Fire for Anti-Gun Crusade," *Chicago Sun-Times*, July 22, 1979, p. 64.

imperial wizard of the Ku Klux Klan is how we feel about Abner Mikva being nominated as a federal judge."[8]

The gun lobby may not have won in the Mikva case, and its lobbying both before the Congress and in the home district may be obvious, but this type of unrelenting opposition causes most politicians to weigh the costs before they oppose the lobbyists' interests.

Mostly, however, the gun lobby has enjoyed substantial and continued successes. NRA opposition is credited during the Carter years for scuttling the nomination of Norval Morris, dean of the University of Chicago Law School, to head the Law Enforcement Administration. The NRA pressure also halted the Treasury Department from approving new, and more stringent, regulations concerning firearms.

In 1968, after the assassinations of King and Robert Kennedy, there was a strong national movement for effective gun control. The momentum had been building since 1963, and by 1968 restrictive gun legislation appeared to have the support of the majority of the public and the Congress; it was also backed by the Johnson administration. Nonetheless, after a long and frustrating national debate, the only legislation the antigun forces were able to enact was a weak ban on imported guns and restrictions on the sale of the "Saturday Night Special," a type of cheap handgun.

An indication of the NRA's legislative muscle is the law restricting the sale of Army surplus ammunition and weapons only to NRA members. These are sold at less than half their retail value. The program has been in existence for seventy-five years. The Army has 700,000 surplus M-1 rifles alone, but since the turmoil of 1968 has restricted the civilian sale of these. In 1978 the Army sold 1200 M-1s to NRA members and planned to halve the figure in 1979. The NRA and Congress were putting pressure on the armed services to expand the scope of their sales to NRA affiliates.

One rationale for the program was that NRA groups could form gun clubs and use the surplus weapons. Any individual, however, can join the NRA by paying fifteen dollars in annual dues. A group opposing the NRA announced a lawsuit in 1979 to challenge the law limiting the sales of Army guns to NRA members, a case it eventually won. Its intention was to weaken the attractiveness of NRA membership.

The proposed limitation of guns is an emotional one. Those supporting gun control point to murders and crime associated with guns.

---

[8]"Mikva Hit, Praised at Hearing," *Chicago Sun-Times*, July 13, 1979, p. 26.

Those opposing it believe it is a plot to restrict the freedom of gun owners, most of whom they argue are sportsmen and hunters. Some go further. They contend that proposals to register guns are efforts to deprive Americans of the right to defend themselves and their property against invaders or tyrants. They argue that the right to keep guns is guaranteed in the Constitution. The executive director of the NRA was asked before a House Judiciary Subcommittee on Crime if he and his organization "would rather allow those convicted felons, mentally deranged people, violently addicted to narcotics . . . to have guns, rather than to have the screening process for honest people like yourself. Is that correct?" "A price we pay for freedom," the NRA representative replied.[9] This pretty much sums up the opposing positions and the lack of common ground between them.

The gun control lobby is a classic example of effective lobbying. Although the majority of voters favor another position, opposition support is diffuse and unorganized. The single-interest gun groups are well organized and financed. Their members may hold a minority position, but they hold it strongly, and they are willing to vote against anyone who opposes them on this one issue.

THE ANTIABORTION LOBBY

"Aren't you glad your mother let you live?" "Babies are sisters, too." "All we are saying is, Give life a chance" (chants of the prolifers). "Not the church / Not the state / Women must decide / Our fate" (a cry of the "prochoicers"). These are among the less provocative slogans of the most emotion-laden issue of any of the single-issue groups: the abortion controversy. There is little common ground between the contenders on both sides. The communications of the National Abortion Rights Action League, a Washington-based proabortion group, convey the intensity of the feeling generated by the issue. They also are representative of the type of communication single-issue groups send out. For these reasons it is reproduced in full (see pages 126–128).[10]

[9]The quotation is contained in a memorandum (undated) sent out by Nelson T. Shields, III, Chairman of Handgun Control, Inc., p. 1.
[10]Fundraising letter (undated) of Karen Mulhause, Executive Director of the National Abortion Rights Action League.

NATIONAL ABORTION RIGHTS ACTION LEAGUE
825 15th Street, NW, Washington D. C. 20005
(202) 347-7774

Dear Friend,

　　January and February of 1978 were banner months for the anti-abortion fanatics.

　　They bombed, burned, vandalized or invaded dozens of different abortion clinics in locations as diverse as Anchorage, Alaska and Fairfax, Virginia.

　　With callous disregard for life and property, these attacks have been well-planned and seemingly well-coordinated -- many assaults on widely separated clinics occuring on the same day.

　　NARAL, the National Abortion Rights Action League, has compiled a report which shows that this wave of domestic violence has been raging for well over a year.

　　I have written you on behalf of NARAL in the sincere hope that you not only support women's right to choose abortion, but that you will decide to join us in our increasingly desperate struggle to preserve that right.

　　The nature of some of the recent assaults against clinics proves just how little is really meant by anti-abortion fanatics' pious mouthings about "right to life."

　　Numerous death threats have been issued against employees of a St. Paul, Minnesota clinic, and they have received warnings that their <u>children</u> will be kidnapped or murdered. Many of these clinic raids occurred while patients were being treated.

　　One Board member of this beleaguered clinic, which has been burned and shot at, had to remove her child from school because of chilling threats against the child's life.

　　Apparently these criminals reserve all their <u>concern for the unborn, but care little for the born</u>.

　　Why have these fanatics suddenly come out of the woodwork? Because, while they have been successful in intimidating some

(over, please)

Dedicated to Guaranteeing and Implementing a Woman's Constitutional Right to a Safe and Legal Abortion

-2-

politicians on abortion, the overwhelming weight of public support has slowed their efforts to return this country to the days of back alley butchery.

I underline politicians because every major opinion poll shows that the majority of the American public favors the continuance of safe, legal abortion.

But, in spite of the will of the majority, those who make the laws and those who administer them have dealt us such blows as --

-- passage of the Hyde Amendment, which denies federal funds to poor women seeking abortion;

-- calls for a Constitutional Convention by 12 state legislatures to pass an amendment which would forever outlaw all abortions;

-- adoption of a so-called "informed consent" law by the Akron, Ohio City Council which was intended not to inform but to intimidate patients and frustrate clinic procedures. This law requires parental consent for teenagers seeking abortion and forces patients to sign documents containing inaccurate information about fetal development and risks to their own lives;

-- the acquittal of six clinic disrupters in Fairfax, Virginia, by Judge Lewis Griffith on the grounds they believed they had to enter the clinics to save lives;

-- the release of four other Fairfax clinic disrupters when Judge Mason Grove declared that Virginia's abortion statute, which conforms with the U.S. Supreme Court's 1973 ruling, was unconstitutional;

-- Commonwealth Attorney Robert Horan's order to the Fairfax, Virginia police to ignore the clinic's calls for help since Judge Griffith and Judge Grove refused to prosecute these cases.

The last three points were virtually an open invitation for an anti-choice mob to run riot through the Fairfax clinic. Fortunately, a federal court issued a restraining order to temporarily halt these clearly illegal disruptions.

If the events described here and in the enclosed report shock you, if the very real possibility of a nationwide abortion ban appalls you,

(next page, please)

-3-

then I urge you to join me and thousands of other women and men as a member of NARAL, the National Abortion Rights Action League.

These acts of violence represent a further escalation of the anti-choice minority's campaign to intimidate our elected officials and to ensure the passage of more abusive legislation like the Akron ordinance and the federal cut-off of Medicaid funds for abortion. The only way to counter this intimidation is through persistent, astute political pressure in Congress and in the state and municipal governments across the country -- and NARAL is leading that political fight.

NARAL is the only national lobbying and membership organization devoted solely to maintaining safe, legal abortion, and your check for $15 or more will make you a member.

Your contribution will help us to continue to monitor clinic violence and to fight for the reinstatement of Medicaid funds for abortion for the poor and against measures which deny women their right to choose. In return for your contribution, I'll see to it that you are kept informed of our progress.

Just as important as your financial support, your membership itself will add weight to our voice when we lobby in Congress and the state legislatures to protect safe, legal abortion.

Because of the rise in anti-choice violence and because this is an election year, we need your help now more than ever. We must convince the politicians that pro-choice is the majority position in the only opinion poll they respect -- the vote.

A show of strength now could also help to send the anti-choice advocates of violence running for cover, and there is strength in numbers.

Won't you stand up and be counted today?

Sincerely,

Karen Mulhauser

Karen Mulhauser
Executive Director

P.S. Please don't put my letter aside with the intention of answering it later. The unselfish support of concerned individuals like you is all that makes our work possible.

The direct mail letter from the National Abortion Rights Action League's Executive Director was accompanied by a memo documenting incidents of "Violence against the Right to Choose" in communities across the United States; a pledge that the group was "Dedicated to Guaranteeing and Implementing a Woman's Constitutional Right to a Safe and Legal Abortion"; and a request to fill out a membership card and pledge a contribution of from $15 to $500 or better.

The slogan and tactics of the antiabortionists (or "prolife" groups) are at least as inflammatory as their prochoice opponents and considerably more politically effective. The National Right to Life antiabortion group claimed a membership of 11 million associated with its 1800 chapters in 1978. It expected a membership of 25 million by 1980.

The extreme emotional overtones associated with the issue were captured in the 1979 convention of the National Right to Life movement. To the applause of the delegates, one speaker compared abortions in America to the Nazis' extermination of the Jews in Germany in the 1940s. He felt that the news media in America played a role analagous to that in Hitler's Germany "in concealing the facts and the public's right to know."[11] Doctors who performed abortions were the "executioners"; bureaucrats who provided financial and support services were the "medical mercenaries"; and the Upjohn Company, a major pharmaceutical concern that manufactured abortion devices, the I. G. Farben of the proabortionists.[12] I. G. Farben, among other things, manufactured the chemicals used to exterminate the Jews in the death camps.

A rally, estimated by Washington police at 60,000, was held by a "new wave of prolife action" adults and children to mark the sixth anniversary of the Supreme Court decision striking down restrictive state laws on abortion. The march past the White House and to the Capitol has become an annual event. The movement's symbol is a rose and its slogan "the American Holocaust — Six Million Exterminated by Abortion." Speakers claimed that 1.3 million lives a year were lost to abortion.[13]

The abortion debate, though volatile enough on its own, touches on

[11] John Herbers, "Anger and Optimism Mixed at Parley of Abortion Foes," *The New York Times*, June 24, 1979, p. 16.

[12] *Ibid*.

[13] "Anti-Abortion March Hits 'American Holocaust,'" *Chicago Tribune*, January 23, 1979, Sec. 1, p. 2.

other concerns that have disturbed many Americans. These include gay rights and homosexuality; the pro- and anti-ERA debate; permissiveness in society; anticrime, anti-moral decay and profamily concerns; and the value and propriety of sex education in schools. To further inflame passions, there is an undercurrent of questions relating to church-state relations in the controversy. Specifically, the Catholic Church through the leadership of the National Conference of Catholic Bishops has been an active proponent of the prolife position. The Catholic bishops have created a lay lobby arm for its position, the National Committee for a Human Life [Constitutional] Amendment which it funds at approximately $300,000 a year. The contributions come from dioceses around the country. The Catholic Church itself has taken a direct role in making its position on abortion known to its communicants and in relating this to the political events of the late 1970s. Catholic clergy have actively represented the antiabortion position in public forums. For them and many others, it is a theological and moral issue as much as a political one. A priest writing in a Chicago newspaper, for example, in answering a pro-choice columnist exemplified the tendency. His letter indicated how deeply much of the clergy felt about the issue and its implications: "She [the columnist, Ellen Goodman] sees the Catholic Church as merely a political 'structure,' and not as the unequivocal defender of human life and dignity that it is and has always been. Its protective arm embraces those waiting to be born and the retarded, the deformed and the senile aged. To do any less would be an insult to Him who made us all."[14]

There has been a reaction among other religious groups to the Catholic Church's militant support of the antiabortion forces. A class action suit has been brought by the Women's Division of the United Methodist Church in cooperation with Planned Parenthood and a number of doctors and poor women, challenging the present restrictions on Medicaid abortions. The suit is supported by fifteen other national religious interest groups including the American Jewish Congress, the synagogue unions of Conservative and Reform Judaism, the United Presbyterian Church, the United Church of Christ, and the Disciples of Christ.

The case in question is called *McRae* v. *Califano*. It is presently in the federal courts, and may well end up in the Supreme Court. Basical-

[14] Father Arthur LaPorte in "Letters: Abortion So Important It Deserves 'One Issue' Victory," *Chicago Sun-Times*, June 29, 1979, p. 50.

ly, the plaintiffs argue that the present law (as refined by Congress in the Hyde Amendment of 1976) represents an unconstitutional "establishment of religion" because it implicitly accepts the teachings of one religious group (the Catholic Church) on abortion. The prochoice side argues that, practically speaking, Catholic dogma is advanced by federal law.[15] This is not quite accurate: the Catholic Church's views are far more restrictive than the present law. Nonetheless, supporters of abortion have argued that the Church's aggressive lobbying seriously impinges on religious freedom.[16]

A number of Catholics, in turn, many of whom do not support the Church's position, are alarmed by the reaction. They fear the beginning of an extremely serious challenge to the constitutional right of American Catholics comparable to the 1850s Nativist campaign.[17] Protestant groups, most notably the National Council of Churches, do not fault the attempt to make society responsive to ethical considerations, based on religious beliefs.[18] The introduction of such issues touches a sensitive strain in American history with roots that go well into the past.

Because of the emotionalism and the broad ramifications that surround the debate, compromise appears impossible. The president of the National Organization of Women (NOW), fearing that the "extreme climate of the crusade against abortion is taking on the overtones of a religious war," invited groups on both sides to a meeting in mid-February of 1979. The intention was "to seek ways to lessen the need for abortion, to reduce the incidence of unwanted pregnancy, and to end the polarization and violence that surround the abortion issue."[19] One congressman, a leader in the antiabortion movement, refused to sit down and negotiate "what respect for life means" until there was a moratorium on all abortions. The president of the March for Life organization responded: "I do not sit and negotiate with baby-killers."[20]

Nonetheless, the meeting was held, and it was attended by eight antiabortion and twenty proabortion groups. Three women interrupted the conference. They marched before the television cameras covering

[15] "Ecumenical War Over Abortion," *Time*, January 29, 1979, p. 62.
[16] *Ibid*.
[17] *Ibid*.
[18] *Ibid*., pp. 62–63.
[19] "Anti-Abortion March."
[20] *Ibid*.

the session and opened the blankets they carried, revealing two human fetuses.[21] The incident had the expected shock effects. It had been planned and carried out by the People Expressing a Concern for Everyone, an offshoot of the Right to Life Committee. Although many were appalled, the act was applauded by the National Right to Life Committee.[22] In such an atmosphere, little is likely to be accomplished.

Before discussing the political and other tactics of the prochoice and prolife single-issue groups, it is advisable to map the public attitudes on abortion. Most adults favor abortion in some form. According to the Gallup organization, 22 percent feel abortion should be "legal under all circumstances" and 19 percent believe it should be "illegal under all circumstances." These are the polar extremes. Most people fall somewhere in between in a complex mix of positions. The results of the Gallup Poll published in April 1979 on the issue are shown in Table 7.1. As shown, although the hierarchy of the Catholic Church has played a forceful role in fighting abortions, the position of most Catholics is close to that of Protestants. The position of the public on abortion parallels that found in the Gallup Polls of 1977 and 1975.

The tactics of the prolifers can be extreme (as the showing of the fetuses indicates). They do attract attention, and they do include everything from sit-ins and disruptions to political campaigning.

Many consider the antiabortionists the politically most successful single-issue group. Most of the groups that form the antiabortionist coalition were established between 1971 and 1973, the latter the date of the Supreme Court decision striking down many legislative restrictions on abortion. Since then, the prolife groups have moved from a position of little strength or visibility to one of remarkable achievements. The years since 1976 have been particularly fruitful for them.

In 1976 the antiabortionists decided to contest in primaries for the Democratic presidential nomination. Their candidate was Ellen McCormack, a fifty-year-old Long Island housewife and mother of four. McCormack entered presidential primaries in eighteen (of thirty) states — in itself an accomplishment of note. She received few votes however: only 238,027, or 1.5 percent of the total 16 million cast in the primary. From such a modest beginning, impressive results were to flow. First, McCormack generated a good deal of publicity and media

---

[21] "Birth Control Parley Shaken as Protesters Display Two Fetuses," *The New York Times*, February 16, 1979, p. B7.
[22] *Ibid*.

TABLE 7.1
Attitudes on Abortion, as Measured by the Gallup Poll (American Institute of Public Opinion), April 1979

I. *Abortion should be*

Legal under any circumstances	22%
Legal under certain circumstances	54
Illegal under all circumstances	19
No opinion	5

II. *Grounds for Abortion, by Time Period*

	First Trimester	Second Trimester	Third Trimester
When the woman's life is endangered	78%	66%	59%
When woman's mental health is endangered	42	31	22
When pregnancy results from rape or incest	59	32	19
When there is a chance baby will be born deformed	44	37	28
When woman may suffer severe physical health damage	52	46	33
If family cannot afford to have the child	15	6	4

III. *Protestant and Catholic Views on Abortion*

	Protestants	Catholics
Legal under any circumstances	20%	17%
Legal under certain circumstances	59	52
Illegal under all circumstances	17	25
No opinion	4	6

Source: American Institute of Public Opinion (Gallup Poll) release of April 22, 1979. Based on personal interviews with 1,534 adults, 18 and older, in 300 scientifically selected localities during the period February 23-26, 1979. Reprinted by permission.

133

attention. She was not a legitimate contender for the Democratic nomination. She ran simply to draw attention to the antiabortionists' position. This she succeeded very well in doing. The media exposure was free, which suggests an approach many single-issue groups with nationwide constituencies might follow in the future.

Second, she forced politicians generally, and the Democrats specifically, to deal seriously with the abortion issue. It became necessary for the presidential contenders to address the issue, and McCormack and the antiabortionists managed to bring it to the forefront of the nation's political agenda.

Third, her candidacy helped to unite the proliferating antiabortion groups and give them a common focus. Since 1973 the number of groups that have sprung up is enormous. As an example, in Illinois alone there are 162 antiabortion groups. Despite the political successes since 1976, one of the movement's chief weaknesses continues to be the diversity and independence of its many groups.

Fourth, despite McCormack's small-to-negligible vote (she averaged only slightly over 13,000 votes in the states where she contested), she and the prolifers demonstrated that there was a small, fiercely committed constituency who would vote solely on a candidate's stand on this particular issue. In a close race, such a highly motivated vote can make the difference. It is a small but potent constituency that a candidate cannot ignore. Also, siding with the antiabortionists invokes few risks. Although the majority of voters may favor the prochoice position, abortionist groups are not as well organized or as electorally sophisticated as their opponents. And, of course, the bulk of voters do not feel strongly on the issue and will not commit themselves to a candidate based on his abortion position alone. Five percent of the electorate in a CBS poll said they would vote for or against a candidate solely on the basis of their feelings against abortion.[23]

Finally, the success of McCormack has encouraged the antiabortionists to exploit this approach further. In 1978 another Long Island housewife and ally of McCormack's, Mary Jane Tobin, ran for governor of New York. She received few votes (120,000), but to the surprise of political experts she received more than one of the nation's longest established and most influential third parties, the Liberals, could deliv-

[23] Anthony Lewis, "A Singular Issue," *The New York Times*, November 16, 1978, p. A27.

er for the candidate they endorsed, Governor Hugh Carey. As a consequence, the antiabortionist Right to Life Party has won status as a regular party with an established line on the New York state ballot. As with its national counterpart in 1976, the purpose of the party is not to win office but to force all candidates, from tax assessor to governor, to take a public stand on abortion. "The issue is overriding," according to Tobin. "Disqualifying," is the way McCormack puts it.[24]

Morton Shawn Downey, Jr., son of singer Morton Downey and formerly a friend and associate of the Kennedys, announced to the national Right to Life convention in 1979 his intention to run in the Democratic primaries for that party's nomination for president in 1980. Downey is the head of the Life Amendment Political Action Committee, a successful, Washington-based lobbying arm of the prolife movement. He proposed to run primarily as a "right to life" candidate.

The antiabortionists (and, to a lesser extent up to the present, the proabortionists) have begun to employ a tactic favored by the environmentalists. Building on their successes from 1976, they entered the 1978 congressional races, supporting favored candidates with PAC funds and volunteers. To maximize the media value of their efforts, and to bring home their message to legislators, the prolifers have developed a "hit list" of candidates they feel it imperative to defeat. In 1978 their list included senators Dick Clark (D — Iowa), Floyd Haskell (D — Colo.), and Edward W. Brooke (R — Mass.) and Congressman Donald M. Fraser, then seeking the Democratic nomination for Senate from Minnesota. They also supported conservative Edward King in his efforts to unseat the incumbent governor, Michael Dukakis, in the race for the Democratic nomination in Massachusetts. Each of the candidates they opposed in these races lost, and the antiabortionists were quick to claim credit for the outcomes.

Without question, they were active in each of the races. In targeted states they invested funds and they established Pro-Life Action Councils, or their equivalent, to supervise and coordinate their campaign activities. The results are less persuasive than the antiabortionists would have us believe, however. Brooke suffered numerous personal problems involving a highly publicized divorce and the mishandling of personal funds, which invited continuing public, Senate, and court

[24] Maurice Carroll, "The Unlikely Beginning of the Right to Life Party," *The New York Times,* November 25, 1978, p. 25.

controversy. Undoubtedly, this was a factor in his loss. The winner in Massachusetts, Paul Tsongas, held a prochoice position close to Brooke's. Each of the other candidates lost for a variety of reasons, although the prolife vote appeared to be a factor. The latter seemed especially true in the Clark and Fraser races.

The Clark campaign provides a case study of the antiabortionists' role in a campaign. Clark had been selected by the national right to life organizations as their number one target. Clark was vulnerable; a Democrat, he had been elected in an upset six years earlier when his boss (then a congressman, and later senator, John Culver) refused to run in a contest he believed unwinnable. Clark had aroused the ire of the prolifers by voting for a bill permitting the federal government to support abortions for indigent women. He had also announced publicly that his conscience would not let him support a constitutional amendment to outlaw abortions.

The antiabortionists were already effectively organized in Iowa and had shown their political muscle by successfully working against a favored woman candidate who sought the Democratic nomination for lieutenant governor. The woman did not share the prolife views on abortion. The state contingent, "Iowans for Life," thus provided an experienced nucleus with which to oppose Clark. The senator was vulnerable regardless of what the antiabortionists did. He was the perfect target. He had voted wrong on abortion, and the antiabortionist opposition at the state level to his reelection was already organized.

It is the state group's contention that the national right to life groups made only marginal contributions to Clark's defeat. The state group, however, was very active on behalf of Clark's opponent, conservative Republican Roger Jepsen. Jepsen was a former lieutenant governor who took a strong antiabortion stand. Despite his liabilities, Clark was favored in the race and led in the polls by never less than 10 percentage points. Nonetheless, he lost in a close race to Jepsen by 26,000 votes. A poll by the *Des Moines Register* on election day found that 25,000 people voted for Jepsen on the abortion issue alone. This could be taken as evidence that the antiabortion vote put Jepsen over the top or that he would have won, barely, without it. The same voters, if they had swung in any numbers to Clark, would have made a difference in his behalf.

As in any other race, attributing the outcome solely to the prolife vote is simplistic. A number of factors were at work. Clark was a liberal (according to the *Congressional Quarterly's* computations, the most liberal senator in Congress in 1977), and Iowa is a conservative state. A number of single-issue groups — in addition to the antiabortionists — opposed his reelection. These included New Right opponents of the Panama Canal treaties, antilabor supporters of right-to-work laws, and the gun lobby. Also, and many thought this decisive, anger with the indecision and vagueness of the Carter administration's farm program alienated many farmers undergoing one of their periodic down cycles from the Democratic party.

The Republican party's candidate for governor, incumbent Robert Ray, was popular and won handsomely, eclipsing Jepsen's vote by 67,000. The Republican party was organized as well as it has been in its history and its leaders felt that its professionalized get-out-the-vote efforts made the difference in its campaigns. Republicans won both houses of the state legislature for the first time in four years. Clark's loss, in such circumstances, may not have been such an upset.

Nonetheless, analysts in Washington, the antiabortionists, and Clark himself seemed to believe that the opposition of the prolifers was critical in his loss. One particular tactic many believed to have swung the election: On the Sunday preceding the Tuesday vote, the antiabortionists distributed 300,000 pamphlets attacking the senator's stand on abortion. These were given out at churches, primarily in urban areas and principally (although not exclusively) to Catholics. The Clark forces could not answer these effectively in the short time remaining before election day. They believed this tipped the scales.

Finally, the entire effort cost the prolife groups only $10,000.[25] For this amount they defeated Clark, gained nationwide media exposure, and impressed congressmen with the potential costs of opposing them on legislation.

Right to life groups did not fare so well in House races. Their losses were not well publicized, but congressional candidates they opposed won in many states including New York (Ottinger) and Colorado (Schroeder). Incumbent Governor James Thompson retained his office convincingly in Illinois despite strong prolife opposition. And as cham-

[25] Douglas E. Kneeland, "Clark's Defeat in Iowa Laid to Single Issue," *The New York Times*, November 13, 1978, p. A18.

pion of the antiabortionists, Republican incumbent Senator Robert Griffin in Michigan lost to prochoice advocate Carl Levin. Again, though, a complex set of reasons accounted for the outcomes.

A *New York Times* editorial puts the matter in perspective:

> In a careful reading of the evidence, the foes of abortion do not appear to have won big this fall. They did, however, score an important psychological victory merely by winning small. For this is the first general election in which they have demonstrated even a modicum of strength at the ballot box. They have, thereby, tossed a challenge to the majority of voters in this country who, according to repeated polls, still favor free choice for abortion early in pregnancy.[26]

The appearance of victory is often more important than the reality. It is this that the antiabortionists counted on and are building from for the future. For 1980 they have announced a new "hit list." On it are senators Birch Bayh (D — Ind.), Robert W. Packwood (R — Ore.), Patrick J. Leahy (D — Vt.), George McGovern (D — S.D.), John C. Culver (D — Iowa), Frank Church (D — Idaho), and John Glenn (D — Ohio). The list was compiled by the Life Amendment Political Action Committee. In explaining its choices, its director maintained that all of its prime targets were participating in vulnerable races.[27] The antiabortion vote, however small, could make the difference.

The antiabortionists have been unusually effective in translating their demands into legislative successes. In fact, this is where the movement's greatest strength lies. Because of the relatively small numbers involved in the prolife movement, their success in the Congress says much for the potential influence of single-issue groups on the totality of American life. The policymaking process is particularly vulnerable to organized pressure of this nature.

Antiabortionists have used the Congress to limit the implications of the Supreme Court's 1973 decision. The assault began in earnest in 1976. In that year Representative Henry J. Hyde (R — Ill.) introduced what has come to be called the "Hyde Amendment." It resulted in the first successful legislative effort to limit the applicability of the Court's action. Hyde was able to attach to an appropriations bill fund-

---

[26] Soma Golden, "Abortion's Morning After," *The New York Times*, December 4, 1978, p. A20.

[27] "6 Senators Top Abortion Foes' Election 'Hit List,' " *Chicago Sun-Times*, December 3, 1978, p. 74.

ing the departments of Labor and Health, Education, and Welfare a prohibition against the use of any federal Medicaid money for abortions "except where the life of the mother would be endangered if the fetus were carried to term." In both 1977 and 1978 efforts were made to liberalize the provision. Modifications have been introduced, and the law presently reads that federal funds cannot be spent for Medicaid abortions except when the life of the mother is endangered or "for victims of rape or incest, where such rape or incest has been reported promptly to a law enforcement agency or public health service" or when "severe and long-lasting physical damage to the mother would result if the pregnancy were carried to term when so determined by two physicians."[28] Overall, the present prohibitions on the use of federal funds for abortions represent significant victories for the foes of abortion.

In the twenty-two states with restrictions on abortions similar to those contained in the Hyde Amendment, figures provided by the Alan Guttmacher Institute, the research arm of Planned Parenthood, show a decline in Medicaid abortions of between 96.8 and 99.2 percent. The director of the National Committee for a Human Life Amendment, the lobbying representative of the National Conference of Catholic Bishops, estimates, "We've been able to cut the public-funded abortions from 300,000 a year to 2800."[29]

In 1978 Congress adopted a provision that would apply the Hyde Amendment to the Defense Department, thus limiting public funding for military personnel and their dependents. There were 26,000 abortions that this provision could apply to in the fiscal year preceding its adoption. In addition, Congress in its pregnancy disability bill required private employers to include coverage of pregnancy in their health care plans. Abortion coverage was not required. Finally, Congress placed a restriction on the United States Civil Rights Commission, prohibiting it from studying or gathering any facts concerning abortion policies in this country.

The proabortionists are naturally disheartened. There have been some successes, but these have been mostly negative efforts — attempts to stop prolifers' actions. As of early 1978 there had been sixty-five attempts in the House and Senate to bring out an amendment

[28] Ellen Warren, "The Politics of Abortion — A Big Business," *Chicago Sun-Times*, November 27, 1978, p. 6.
[29] *Ibid.*

to the United States Constitution prohibiting abortion. The efforts have gotten nowhere because of the opposition of Bayh and Representative Don Edwards (D — Calif.) who head the respective subcommittees that must pass on the necessary legislation. Edwards has joined Bayh on the prolifers' "hit list" for obvious reasons.

Thirteen state legislatures have called for a constitutional convention to enact the antiabortion amendment to the Constitution. Twenty-one more states are needed; securing this backing is at best difficult and more than likely impossible.

If these are successes for the prochoice coalition, they do not discourage the antiabortionists. The prolifers believe that the actions of the states to date can be placed in a more favorable perspective. To their way of thinking, these actions place increased pressure on the Congress to seriously consider the human life amendment. Furthermore, they believe the battle on the state level is far from lost. In 1978 the antiabortionists turned their attention to state legislative races, investing $100,000 in these contests. That is not a large sum of money, but in poorly funded local races a little funding can mean the difference between victory and defeat.

In the immediate future the antiabortionists intend to continue contesting elections at all levels and to force candidates to take a stand on the abortion issue; to further restrict the availability of state and federal funds for abortions; to push the needed state legislatures to pass resolutions calling for a constitutional convention; and to force Congress to consider their demands for enacting a human life amendment to the Constitution. If anything, their visibility and success should increase over the next few years. The proabortionists, on the other hand, have yet to begin to effectively counter such initiatives.

THE NEW RIGHT, SINGLE-INTEREST POLITICS AND THE CONSERVATIVE REVIVAL

Many political observers believe the antiabortionists to be the most successful of the new single-issue groups, and without question they have accomplished much more than anyone would have predicted. Yet, despite the emotionalism involved, the media attention

given the movement and the significance of the concerns being debated, abortion is a relatively narrow issue that directly concerns few.
The rise of what has been called the "New Right" and the success of
conservatism in the late seventies involves a far greater number of
people. The New Right and its conservative policies on taxation, inflation, a balanced budget and cutbacks in government-sponsored social
services have far broader implications. The New Right is a label given
to a broad coalition of conservative groups that have assumed increasing importance in American elections. The development is new and
has grown since Watergate. It has been spurred by the new campaign
laws and it takes advantage of the new technology of politics. It makes
use of the issue politics of the contemporary period and it moves into
the void created by the decline of the political parties. The New Right
has benefited from the concern with single-issue politics and, in fact,
attempts to build coalitions in elections of groups from anti-ERA'ers to
those protesting taxes. The strategy has been successful. Its goals are
nothing less than the capture and redirection of the entire American
policymaking apparatus. The media dubbed the election of 1978 a test
of the New Right conservatism, and most media observers would agree
that it enjoyed considerable success: government policy in the 1980s is
expected to reflect a shift in the perspective brought on by the developments of the late 1970s.

"We have the talent and resources to move in a bold, massive way,"
Richard Viguerie, a New Right spokesman told a reporter for the *Congressional Quarterly* prior to the 1978 election. He promised to "move
against Congress in 1978 in a way that's never been conceived of."[30]
The threats were not idle rhetoric.

A number of factors have favored the New Right's surge. These
range from a spiritual exhaustion of both traditional liberalism and
conservatism to a receptive political climate in the late 1970s. The New
Right has evolved to fill the vacuum created by the political decline and
intellectual bankruptcy of the old conservatism, associated for generations with the Republican party and with such issues as protection of
the free enterprise system, a balanced budget, New Deal opposition,
and a primitive economic competition of all against all. Interestingly,
the New Right does not reject these positions; it simply does not

[30] Christopher Buchanan, "New Right: 'Many Times More Effective' Now," *Congressional Quarterly,* December 24, 1977, p. 2649.

emphasize them. It is concerned with winning elections. The belief is that the old-fashioned Republican conservatives of the 1950s did not "understand the politics of the average person" and could not relate to his concerns. The old-time conservatives were left to argue their cause; they were a "stuffy, boring lot" with little concern for electoral victory, according to one New Right leader.[31]

Traditional liberalism is also in a period of confusion. In effect, it is a victim of its own success on domestic issues. The programs of government economic regulation and social services associated with the New Deal have been largely enacted. They are popular with voters, a point the New Right (unlike the traditional conservatives) accepts. With its domestic goals basically realized, traditional liberalism has fallen into disarray. The New Deal coalition was shaken by the Vietnam War. Now it is in a period of flux with no clear leadership, value assumptions, or policy positions. The New Right has been quick to take advantage of the vacuum.

The new conservatives want to win. This alone, they believe, distinguishes their approach from the electorally disastrous one of their predecessors. Perhaps more than anything else they want to win and force American politics to move along the lines they believe it should. Many (but not all) on the New Right would argue that a majority of Americans actually support their position. Their contention would be that this support has simply never been adequately focused on politics. The argument is not new. The supporters of Robert Taft in 1952 and Barry Goldwater in 1964 made the same points, with terrible electoral consequences. The difference is that the New Right of contemporary politics has had visible success in translating their potential support into political reality.

To win, the New Right attempts to build coalitions of primarily middle-class Americans into an effective political force. It is not concerned that the coalition agree on all (or even most) points; it is willing to tolerate diversity for the sake of winning. "The secret is to be able to put together the right kind of coalition that will supersede the point of view on other issues," as one New Right strategist has maintained.[32]

The coalitions are built from single-issue groups such as those supporting prolife, anti-ERA, and anti-gun control positions. They have

[31] Gary McMillan, "What is the New Right Up To?" *Boston Globe*, December 17, 1978, Section A, p. 1.
[32] *Ibid*.

benefited enormously from the economic issues of the late 1970s and the rise of single issue groups to contest property taxes, inflation, a decreasing standard of living, and the energy squeeze. As a leader of the Committee for the Survival of a Free Congress, a New Right group, described it, the coalition is held together by a concern with "family, right-to-life, schools, [and] neighborhoods."[33]

Overall, its policy positions fall somewhere between those of the neoconservatives, the disgruntled New Deal Democrats symbolized by Senator Daniel Moynihan and Ben Wattenberg, former campaign manager for Senator Henry Jackson's presidential bid and co-author (with Richard Scammon) of the influential *The Real Majority* (1970),[34] and the Far Right of anticommunist fanatics. On social issues, and in its choice of candidates to support, many moderates in the Republican party see it as close to, and possibly interchangeable with, the Far Right. It is by any measure, among the most conservative influences in American politics.

The New Right is also far more pragmatic than its conservative predecessors. It principally, but *not* exclusively, supports Republican candidates and the Republican party. But the New Right's primary commitment is to policy positions and to winning office. Consequently, the New Right makes a point of backing conservative Democrats who identify with its causes. It goes further than this. In an approach that has alienated other conservatives, the New Right will enter Republican nomination battles to back candidates it favors. It will even field its own candidates to run against incumbent Republican moderates. These efforts have infuriated Republican officeholders.

Strategy

The tactics of the New Right are modeled after those of the left. The inspiration for the single-issue groups of the late 1970s was the anti-Vietnam lobby of the 1960s. The electoral approach of the New Right was pioneered by the National Committee for an Effective Congress (NCEC), a bipartisan liberal group that channeled funds and campaign services to congressional candidates it supported, and Com-

---

[33] *Ibid*.
[34] Richard M. Scammon and Ben J. Wattenberg, *The Real Majority* (New York: Coward, McCann & Geoghegan, 1970).

mon Cause, a public citizen lobby concerned with securing the public financing of elections. Both the NCEC and Common Cause used direct mail techniques to acquire funds and to develop a following. They, like the Vietnam lobby, employed the media as best they could to publicize their cause and develop a public awareness of their concerns. Common Cause has been successful. It has a membership of 15 million nationwide and it has been instrumental in the congressional adoption of presidential funding and campaign ethics bills. The NCEC is a more modest operation. Although it has been operating for three decades, it has a small staff, centered on an executive director, and a low overhead. Its only concern is with congressional races. In 1978 it backed thirty-five candidates supported fully through funding or in-kind campaign services, and it endorsed another thirty. Its projected budget ran to $1 million. These objectives represent an expansion of NCEC activities, but they hardly compare with those of the New Right.

The major New Right groups are: the National Conservative Political Action Committee (NCPAC), the most generous funder of conservative candidates; the Committee for the Survival of a Free Congress (CSFC); Citizens for the Republic (CFTR), begun by Ronald Reagan with a $1 million surplus from his 1976 presidential campaign and focusing on candidates and causes Reagan approved; the Fund for a Conservative Majority (FCM), an outgrowth of the Young Americans for Freedom, an extremely conservative youth group within the Republican party; Gun Owners of America (GOA); Committee for a Responsible Youth Politics (CRYP); the Conservative Victory Fund (CVF), affiliated with the American Conservative Union; and the Conservative Caucus, headed by Howard Phillips. President Nixon appointed Phillips to head the Office of Economic Opportunity with the explicit charge of dismantling this symbol of the Johnson era's commitment to social programs. Phillips left the Nixon administration in 1973 because he felt it was not conservative enough.

The chairman of the American Conservative Union, Congressman Philip Crane (R — Ill.), was an early candidate for president. Along with the expected candidacy of Ronald Reagan, this gave this small grouping of rightist groups two contenders for the Republican nomination. In addition, they felt comfortable with other potential nominees like Senator Robert Dole of Kansas, John Connally of Texas, and Representative Jack Kemp of upstate New York.

The New Right groups had better than seven times the amount of funds available to the liberal National Committee for an Effective Congress entering the 1978 elections. Most of it had been raised by direct mail solicitations and approximately two-thirds by four groups (NCPAC, CSFC, GOA and CRYP) directly associated with one of the technological gurus of the New Right, Richard Viguerie. Direct mail solicitation has proved a bonanza for right-wing groups, and Viguerie has mastered this art of fund raising. To avoid the $5000 limitation PACs can contribute to a candidate for each primary or general election race, Viguerie also hires out to individual conservative candidates (a reported thirty in 1978) to institute direct fund raising for them that is not subject to the PAC limitations.

Viguerie also claims to have direct mail lists estimated to contain from between 0.5 or 2 million up to 15 million names (hyperbole is not uncommon in the business) of proven contributors to conservative causes (compared to the NCEC's 80,000). Viguerie has proven to be a prodigious fund raiser, but the cost of his services comes high. In 1976, ninety-one cents of every dollar collected went to in-house costs. Only nine cents from the dollar reached the candidate. Other conservative groups, all of whom depend on direct mail, claim costs as low as forty to fifty cents on the dollar (and NCPAC claimed it could reduce its 1976 costs of forty-six cents per dollar by twenty cents in 1978). The liberal NCEC says its costs are less than thirty-two cents on the dollar with the remainder going directly to candidates.[35]

In 1978 Viguerie claimed he had pruned his lists and, devoid of startup expenses which he blamed on the initial poor showing, had reduced the direct mail costs to about 50 cents per dollar. Viguerie helped raise almost $7 million for Senator Jesse Helms's reelection campaign in North Carolina. Yet only 11 percent of what he raised actually went to Helms's campaign to spend (although, of course, Viguerie's costs count against the campaign's total costs). Viguerie has become a multimillionaire through his work on behalf of conservative causes.

Viguerie does make a point that is well taken. He argues that direct mail techniques publicize causes and candidates as well as raise funds; that these are an excellent way of reaching the voter, and thus in themselves are a form of campaigning. "Direct mail is an unbelievably

---

[35] Buchanan, "New Right," p. 2652.

successful advertising medium when properly used," he claims.[36] He is right.

Direct mail not only can publicize a cause; it also can motivate a large number of people to directly involve themselves in an issue. Their willingness to contribute funds to a campaign is one gauge. Another is the massive letter-writing campaigns these conservative groups have been able to institute to influence the Congress on legislation they favor. For example, the NCPAC claims it stimulated a million letters to Congress in 1977 when it was considering the Carter administration's bill to allow unregistered voters to enroll at the polls. Republicans feared most of the unregistered voters would be Democrats. They moved to kill the bill, and the New Right was happy to help. NCPAC claimed a major part of the credit for the results. The New Right also points out that the direct mail strategies of opposition they employ have been refined by Common Cause, the moderately liberal "citizens' lobby."

It is not difficult to understand the ability of direct mail letters to motivate recipients. First, the refined lists contain the names of people sympathetic to the cause being promoted. Second, the messages tend to be extreme; they present the worst possible case; and they aim to polarize and anger their audience. For example, NCPAC sent out a letter in the fall of 1977 asking recipients to "send $5 or $10 contributions today to help defeat liberal senators who want to give our Panama Canal away."[37] The solicitation was marked "Urgent" in red letters and went on to identify sixteen Democratic and Republican senators who "will decide if a Marxist dictator will take both our canal and our money, and then open the canal to Russian warships — while our Navy is blocked from going through."[38] Such exaggeration is not unusual. When the national chairman of the Democratic National Committee attacked the New Right for its "shrillness, stridency and superficiality," the leader of the FCM countered: "In some cases, the shriller you are the more success you have in raising funds."[39] This does appear to be the case. Nonetheless, some conservatives are concerned. The editor of *Policy Review*, a conservative journal, fears that "the New

[36] *Ibid.*, p. 2651.
[37] *Ibid.*
[38] *Ibid.*
[39] *Ibid.*

Right will position conservatives too far out."[40] If so, and despite its present position as the one reasonably cohesive political and intellectual force in American politics, it will destroy its credibility and with it that of conservatives generally.

Increasingly, the New Right is moving beyond the funding of selected candidates to provide a variety of campaign services. The larger New Right groups, particularly NCPAC and CSFC, believe that by providing campaign consultants, media advice, polls, voter targeting services and precinct organizers they can be both more effective and exercise more control over the candidates and campaigns they fund. Consequently, these groups (like the NCEC) have begun to take a more direct role in campaigns. The CSFC, as an example, will provide the salary of one full-time precinct organizer. If the organizer undertakes anything other than the precinct voter mobilization plan the CSFC believes so central to electoral success, his salary will be discontinued. As the director says, "If they want our help, they do it our way."[41]

NCPAC runs training seminars for candidates and prospective campaign organizers on ways to set up a campaign structure, to use telephone banks and mail contacts, to follow up on prospective voters, and to take polls. The successful campaign of Senator Gordon Humphrey of New Hampshire was built around trainees from these seminars.

There is a problem, however. Many conservative groups teach not only standard campaign techniques but the election strategy they favor and want implemented. First, they dictate the organizational arrangement. Second, they insist on developing special interest coalitions. The anti-ERAers, antiabortionists, and so on are cultivated. "Very seldom does a candidate win in his own right. More often he gets votes from those dissatisfied with the status quo," according to the director of the Conservative Caucus.[42] Finally, the candidate must present a clear conservative (New Right) alternative to his opponent. "Victories don't count unless you can influence public policy."[43] Both the left and right could probably agree on this. Those in the middle, where practicing politicians tend to be, feel the pressure.

[40] McMillan, "What is the New Right Up To?"
[41] Ibid.
[42] Ibid.
[43] Ibid.

There are a number of difficulties with the approach. One is that the candidate may have very little control over his own campaign. This appears to occur. If the candidate is totally in sympathy with the groups dictating his strategy (and the Humphrey campaign seemed to fit this description), problems are minimal. If not, the candidate may have a campaign direction and a set of legislative commitments he did not bargain on.

The New Right has gone one step beyond dictating campaign strategy. It has entered its own candidates into prenomination races to contest incumbents of whom it disapproves. Avi Nelson, a young, conservative talk-show host in Massachusetts, ran against incumbent Edward W. Brooke for the Republican Senate nomination in 1978. He lost. Another young conservative, Jeff Bell, a former aide to Ronald Reagan and former political director of a conservative group, proved more successful. He moved to New Jersey explicitly to qualify for the race against incumbent Senator Clifford Case. In a stunning upset, Bell defeated Case in a low-turnout primary election. A low-turnout election maximizes the influence of special interest groups, since the highly committed partisans can have their maximum effect. Bell went on to lose to another young newcomer, Bill Bradley, the Democratic nominee in the general election. Bradley was the Democratic nominee, in part at least, because other Democrats refused to face Case, whom they believed unbeatable. Bell lost the general election, but he did defeat Case; without him, it is unlikely Bradley would be in the Senate.

On the House side, conservatives had long been disillusioned with the moderate policies of Representative John Anderson of Illinois, the third-ranking Republican leader in the House. In 1978 they decided to challenge him. The Committee for the Survival of a Free Congress recruited a fundamentalist minister, the Reverend Don Lyon, to make the race. The CSFC, the Conservative Victory Fund (representing the American Conservative Union), and the Gun Owners of America sent funds and workers into the district. They instigated an active media campaign and managed to give Anderson what he considered to be his closest race. In a high-turnout race (70 percent voted in the district's primary), the congressman won with 58 percent of the vote. Anderson was, nonetheless, upset over the closeness of the vote: "There is a real danger that they [the New Right] can so totally focus on relatively narrow issues and dominate the political dialogue. There is an entirely legitimate conservative force, but I don't want to see it contaminated by a virulent anti-right that will provoke a backlash in other directions."[44] In 1980 Anderson gave up any chance for reelection to risk a long-shot bid for the Republican party's presidential nomination.

The influence of the New Right is probably overstated. These groups cultivate publicity, as do all single-issue groups, and their claims of success are often exaggerated. They do receive a good deal of political attention, and they can be effective. There are no cohesive, well-funded alternatives on the left, and the political parties offer little in the way of competition. The Republicans collected $8 million during the campaign year of 1978 and the Democrats $2.5 million. Most of these funds went into internal housekeeping, although the Republicans, unlike the Democrats, made some effort to invest in state legislative and congressional races. Such a vacuum invites attention for the New Right and increases the odds of their success.

Still, in the actual number of races won, the results are, at best, indicative of what might occur in the future. Approximately three to six House races contested in 1978 were won by candidates strongly backed by the New Right. In Senate races, Humphrey won in New Hampshire (over incumbent Thomas McIntyre); Jepsen won over incumbent Dick Clark in Iowa; and Republican William Armstrong won over incumbent Democrat Floyd Haskell in Colorado. The New Right claimed these as their victories. Case was denied renomination in New Jersey, although the New Right could not put their own candidate into the Senate. Brooke won renomination over a New Right candidate in Massachusetts, but lost the general election to a Democrat. The role of the New Right in this election is problematical — Brooke had many problems — but their opposition certainly did not help his failing candidacy. The New Right did claim others such as Mississippi's first Republican senator (Thad Cochran) since Civil War days as victories ("Don't worry, he'll vote like a rightwing extremist when we need him"),[45] although it attempted to play down its role in these contests during the campaign in the interests of electoral success.

The threat of the New Right may be as effective as its actual clout. An infuriated Senator Charles Mathias of Maryland, and eight other targets of the New Right, complained to Republican National Chair-

[44] Ibid.

[45] Adam Clymer, "Moderation is the Message for New Right Campaigners," The New York Times, November 26, 1978, p. 4E.

man Bill Brock about the movement's funding of extremely conservative candidates to contest incumbent Republicans. It "is not the kind of healthy competition we should encourage within the Republican party. It is cannibalism."[46] Such complaints, of course, have done nothing to deter New Right opposition. Its activists have even expanded their operations to include supporting candidates for Republican leadership positions in the Congress. These included pushing Senator Orrin Hatch of Utah, for example, to take control of the Republican Senate Campaign Committee from the less conservative John Heinz of Pennsylvania and creating a small, but politically astute, unofficial steering committee to guide strategy in Senate legislative tests.

Issue Tests of the New Right

It does appear that these single-issue tests of a candidate will continue in greater number. It was estimated that there were 1360 single issue groups in 1978. Not all are politically active or influential. The phenomenon is new and the numbers are still growing. The impact of just a few of these groups can be substantial. In the 1978 election, New Right groups spent lavishly. Reagan's Citizens for the Republic spent an incredible $4.5 million on the 1978 election, more than enough to fund a presidential campaign a generation ago. Reagan's CFTR ranked as the biggest campaign spender among all the PACs. NCPAC ranked second, investing $3 million in candidates, and the CSFC third with expenditures of $2 million. These are impressive figures. Such outlays are likely to grow as the years pass. The conservative to right-wing PACs should exercise a command of American politics far beyond the numbers sharing their political sympathies would warrant.

The emergence of conservative single-issue groups in the late 1970s was aided substantially by the faltering economy. High interest rates, increasing taxes, exploding gasoline costs, and ineffective governmental responses led to a frustration and anger that helped the New Right. It fed such battles as the one over Proposition 13 in California, a proposal to cut property taxes by 57 percent; startled officeholders; and

[46] Buchanan, "New Right," p. 2650.

demonstrated the political potency of an aroused citizenry. The National Tax Limitation Committee, headed by a former aide to Ronald Reagan, helped coordinate the 1978 effort to pass tax restriction initiatives in a number of states (Michigan, Hawaii, Arizona, Texas and Illinois) and the broader campaign for a national convention to amend the Constitution to force a balanced federal budget. Other groups, such as the National Taxpayers Union, "the Spirit of 13," headed by Paul Gann, the coauthor of Proposition 13, and the American Tax Reduction Movement, created by the other coauthor of Proposition 13, Howard Jarvis, have all been active in congressional campaigns during the 1978 election. Jarvis's group raised $750,000 in national appeals for funds. Jarvis then telegrammed all candidates for House and Senate and offered to back their campaigns if they pledged to sign up in support of his plan to cut $100 million in federal spending from the budget. "If you support the plan," he wrote, "my office will contact you with respect to possible financial assistance in your campaign from the American Tax Reduction Movement-PAC as well as direct mail, radio, TV and newspaper endorsements, which will be available to our supporters."[47] The appeal was highly publicized.

The move was resented. The chairman of the House Democrats' congressional campaign committee called it "a blatant effort to coerce candidates to succumb to bribery."[48] If so, 138 House and Senate candidates did. Ironically, as it turned out Jarvis gave only $100 contributions to all but three of the candidates whom he pledged to support. Of the three remaining, one received $1000 and lost and two incumbents who had attempted to enact the Jarvis proposition in the Congress prior to the election were given $250 apiece. Of those endorsed, sixty-one (of 106) House Republicans and seventeen (of twenty-five) House Democrats and three of seven Senate candidates (J. Bennett Johnson, D — La.; Strom Thurmond, R — S.C.; and Armstrong, R — Colo.) won.

For a minimal expenditure, with a clever use of the media and playing on the fears of the public, a group with no political muscle prior to the election had eighty-one members of Congress publicly pledged

[47] Adam Clymer, "Jarvis Gave to 138 in Congress Races," *The New York Times*, November 16, 1978, p. A13.
[48] *Ibid.*

to support its position. It is a textbook case of what a single-interest group can do in a very short period of time in the absence of effective opposition and under the right conditions.[49]

Overall, thirteen states voted in the 1978 election on some form of tax or spending limitation proposal that had legislative authority. Despite the hoopla and the high visibility of the issues during a troubled economic time, the results were mixed. Alabama, Arizona, Hawaii, Idaho, Nevada, North Dakota, South Dakota, and Texas passed some form of spending limitation referendum. Arkansas, Colorado, Nebraska, and Oregon (on two measures) rejected similar referenda. The people of Michigan may represent a good indicator of the national mood. Michigan voters overwhelmingly rejected measures to cut property taxes by almost half and to replace the property tax as the basis for school funding while accepting narrowly (52.5 percent to 47.5 percent) a proposal to restrict increases in the property taxes and the amount of money the state could spend. The public appears more ambivalent and discerning than media accounts of its views would indicate.

The ability of the policymaking institutions to respond to the broad demands made on it and to act in the best interests of the public-at-large is in question. A strong and cohesive party system could build broad coalitions and advance the policy concerns of the major groups in its coalition. It could also command a degree of loyalty to ensure that the programs it advanced were given serious legislative attention. The American party system has had difficulty in executing its responsibilities in these regards and, in comparison with those in other democracies, has appeared weak and disorganized.[50] Nonetheless, the old party system, if it can be called this, was considerably better than the single-issue, polarized politics of the present sick party era. The real problems may just be beginning. The ideological and single-issue PACs are new.

---

[49] For different accounts of these developments, see: Alan Berlow, "Group Wants to Balance Nation's Checkbook," *Congressional Quarterly*, February 17, 1979, pp. 277–79; Adam Clymer, "Co-Author Says Proposition 13 Is No Panacea for Rest of Nation," *The New York Times*, November 19, 1978, p. 26; Thomas Oliphant, "The Balance-the-Budget Myth," *Boston Globe*, March 25, 1979, p. 83; and Warren Weaver, Jr., "Budget Convention Drive Appears to be Faltering," *The New York Times*, March 11, 1979, p. 26.

[50] Kenneth Janda, *Comparative Political Parties: A Cross-National Survey* (New York: Free Press, forthcoming); and Janda, "A Comparative Analysis of Party Organizations: the United States, Europe, and the World," in William Crotty (ed.), *The Party Symbol* (San Francisco: W. H. Freeman, 1980).

They have been just feeling their way. As Jepsen, Iowa's new senator and a symbol of the New Right's success, has said: "They ain't seen nothing yet."[51] He just may be right.

CAMPAIGN REFORM

There is a movement afoot to correct some of the worst abuses in the electoral process. It is not popular in Congress, it is opposed by the PACs that fund political races, and it has aroused little media or public attention. Quite simply, it is the movement to equalize resources for elective office and to remove some of the worst abuses of the single-issue, corporate and labor PACs through the public funding of Senate and House campaigns.

There are a number of proposals before the Congress. One of those most favored by reformers in the House would be voluntary (candidates could opt in or out). For those accepting public financing, there would be a spending limit of $150,000 in general election campaigns, plus an additional $30,000 allowed for fund raising and $15,000 for one mailing within the district. A cost-of-living escalator has been proposed, but its specific provisions have yet to be worked out. Candidates would have individual contributions to their campaigns of $100 or less matched in $10,000 increments up to $60,000. Also, the amount an officeholder could contribute to his own campaign would be limited to $25,000.

Problems confront the House bill. At present its provisions apply only to general elections. When opponents, in a legislative maneuver designed to weaken its support, managed to expand it to include primaries, the bill was killed in committee. Others want (1) to increase awards made directly to the national parties, having the parties in turn distribute the funds to prospective candidates; (2) to reduce or eliminate altogether the role of the Federal Election Commission in administering the bill's regulations; and (3) to raise the threshold of funds needed to qualify for the program from the presently specified $1000 to $10,000 to make public funding more selective.

[51] Warren Weaver, Jr., "Conservatives Find Reason for Elation," *The New York Times*, February 10, 1979, p. 7.

There is a danger, as some opponents argue, that the spending ceilings may be too low to allow a challenger a real opportunity to unseat an incumbent and that the program may be too restrictive in its qualifying procedures (thus discouraging competition). Also the potential cost of the public financing of congressional elections in a period of economic uncertainty has been criticized. The House bill would cost between $22.2 million and $29.7 million according to the most recent estimates of the Federal Election Commission.[52] The bill is open to compromise, and its final form has yet to be decided.

The Senate public financing proposal would also be voluntary and would apply only to general elections. For those who accepted public money, a spending ceiling of $250,000 plus ten cents for every voting-age citizen of their state would be instituted. Population projections for 1980 indicate that the ceilings for individual states would range from $275,000 in Alaska to $1.8 million in California. To qualify for federal funds, candidates would first have to raise $100,000 or 10 percent of their state's spending quota, whichever was lower. They would be required to do this in contributions of $100 or less.

The Senate has traditionally proven to be more receptive than the House on matters of public financing. But overall, politicians, and especially the incumbents that must vote such bills out, prefer to retain a system heavily weighted to their advantage. The Republican party has been consistent in its opposition to such measures, and the corporate, single-issue, and ideological PACs strongly oppose any effort to undermine their influence. Nonetheless, there is a precedent for such a program. Public financing of presidential prenomination and general election races was introduced in 1976 and it has worked well. It was passed by the Congress in the backlash created by the revelations of Watergate and under heavy public pressure. Conservatives, centrists, and liberals all appear pleased with the program, and there is no effort presently underway to rescind it.

The cost of congressional campaigns increased by 50 percent (from $100 million to $150 million) between 1976 and 1978 alone. A major contributing factor to the escalation has been the abundance of funds made available by PACs. The public, at least, seems disillusioned. A majority of the American people (57 percent), as reported by a Gallup poll in 1979, favor the public funding of congressional races. Support is

[52] "New Numbers on Public Financing," *Congressional Quarterly*, April 28, 1979, p. 779.

strong among Democrats (57 percent), Republicans (54 percent) and independents (60 percent).[53]

The case for public funding has been well put by Vice-President Walter Mondale. The vice-president warned that the dependence of congressional candidates on massive amounts of financing, supplied in increasing abundance by the PACs, has reached "extremely dangerous proportions." He cautioned, "This nation is not for sale. It belongs to our people, . . . We should have a new system of comprehensive public financing."[54] It should not require another Watergate to bring about a needed reform.

[53] American Institute of Public Opinion (Gallup Poll), "Federal Campaign Funding Has Strong Support," *Chicago Sun-Times,* April 1, 1979, p. 24.

[54] Jon Margolis, "Mondale Urges Public Financing to Elect Congress," *Chicago Tribune,* December 9, 1978, p. 2.

8

The Parties Respond

The changes documented in the earlier sections of this part (and others) have threatened the operations and very existence of the political parties. Both political parties are aware, in varying degrees, of their problems. And both have made efforts to correct them and better prepare themselves for the demands of the late twentieth century. Most notable in these regards have been the reform movements of the last decade.

The Democrats were forced to reform after their unhappy experiences in 1968. The Democratic National Convention of that year, held in Chicago, turned out to be a bloody and bitter confrontation, the most violent in either party's history. It capped a debilitating series of battles between insurgents, backing Eugene McCarthy and Robert Kennedy (assassinated on the night of the California primary), and regulars, supporting Vice-President Hubert Humphrey. The nominating rules of each of the state parties were found to be antiquated and, in most cases, not open to influence from grassroots party members. The unruly Chicago convention with its volatile confrontations among party leaders, delegates, city officials, the media, street demonstrators, and the police ensured that something of consequence would have to be done about the abuses encountered in party procedures. The eventual result however was unexpected — a decade of reform that transformed the Democratic party.[1]

PRESIDENTIAL NOMINATIONS

The tone of the new reform movement was set by the first and most aggressive of the reform committees, the McGovern-Fraser Commission. The commission was created to assess the party's nominating practices (its most important duty) and to recommend changes. It held nationwide hearings, allowing both insurgents and regulars to voice their feelings. The hearings generated substantial media coverage and helped create a broad constituency for change. At the end of its first year of operation, the commission formulated seventeen "guidelines" intended to ensure "all Democratic voters . . . a full, meaningful and timely opportunity to participate" in the selection of national convention delegates, in influencing convention deliberations, and ultimately in choosing the party's presidential nominee.[2]

The commission made its position, and the intent of its proposals, clear: "We believe that popular control of the Democratic Party is

---

[1] Accounts of the process can be found in: William Crotty, *Decision for the Democrats* (Baltimore: Johns Hopkins Press, 1978); Austin Ranney, *Curbing the Mischiefs of Faction* (Berkeley: University of California Press, 1975); William Crotty, *Political Reform and the American Electorate* (New York: Crowell, 1977); Austin Ranney, "The Democratic Party's Delegate Selection Reforms, 1968–1976," in Allan P. Sindler (ed.), *America in the Seventies: Problems, Policies, and Politics* (Boston: Little, Brown, 1977), pp. 160–206; Austin Ranney, "The Political Parties: Reform and Decline," in Anthony King (ed.), *The New American Political System* (Washington, D.C.: American Enterprise Institute, 1978), pp. 213–47; Robert T. Nakamura and Denis G. Sullivan, "Party Democracy and Democratic Control," in Walter Dean Burnham and Martha Wagner Weinberg (eds.), *American Politics and Public Policy* (Cambridge: MIT Press, 1978), pp. 26–40; Kenneth Janda, "Primrose Paths to Political Reform: 'Reforming' v. Strengthening American Parties," in W. Crotty (ed.), *Paths to Political Reform* (Lexington, Mass.: D. C. Heath-Lexington, 1980); and William Crotty, "Assessing a Decade of Reform" (Washington, D.C.: A Paper Presented at the 1979 Annual Meeting of the American Political Science Association).

[2] Crotty, *Decision*, pp. 59–103.

necessary for its survival."[3] It did not find that popular control evident in the party procedures it examined. Its seventeen guidelines were meant to ensure such responsiveness in presidential nominations. Later reform commissions, most notably the Sanford, or Party Charter Commission (1972–74), attempted to extend the same concerns and safeguards to all aspects of party affairs.[4]

The McGovern-Fraser Commission made other notable contributions to the reform effort. In fact, without it, reform would have remained unrealized. After adopting its guidelines, it went on to *require* the state parties to enact them. It is this last point that reshaped the face of American party politics. Prior to this, national party committees were considered advisory: they had few sanctions over state parties and no real power to force a transformation of state party practices on the scale advocated by the McGovern-Fraser Commission. Nonetheless, through a clever use of the political resources available to it, with the backing of many groups influential in party deliberations and feeding on the public mood of discontent, the commission was able to force the individual state parties to conform to its standards. By the 1972 Democratic National Convention, the reformers could claim a 97 percent compliance with its guidelines.[5]

In effect, the reform battle was won here. There were later (successful) attempts to refine the guidelines to make them more accommodating to the interests of party regulars (while still preserving their integrity) and to expand the reform initiatives into other areas of party operations (beyond presidential nominations). National convention procedures were modernized, and a party charter, roughly analogous to the federal Constitution, was adopted to ensure fair and open party procedures.[6] By 1978, with the expiration of the last of the reform

---

[3]Commission on Party Structure and Delegate Selection, *Mandate for Reform* (Washington, D.C.: Democratic National Committee, 1970), p. 49; and Crotty, "Building a 'Philosophy,' " p. 24.

[4]Crotty, *Decision*, pp. 240–50; and Crotty, *Political Reform*, pp. 247–55.

[5]Crotty, *Decision*, pp. 104–47. There were substantial costs, however. See William Crotty, "Anatomy of a Challenge: The Chicago Delegation to the Democratic National Convention," in R. Peabody (ed.), *Cases in American Politics* (New York: Praeger, 1976), pp. 111–58.

[6]Crotty, *Political Reform*, pp. 252–55; Charles Longley, "Party Nationalization in America," in Crotty, *Paths;* and Denis G. Sullivan, Jeffrey L. Pressman, and F. Christopher Arterton, *Explorations in Convention Decision Making* (San Francisco: W. H. Freeman, 1976).

commissions (and actually by the presidential election of 1976), reform had largely run its course.

The results were impressive. Reform had fundamentally reshaped party politics, especially presidential nominating practices. Presidential nominations (and, to a lesser extent, all party agencies) had been opened to greater popular participation. Dominant influence within party circles had shifted from the elites and interest group leaders that had decided presidential nominations prior to 1972 to the individual party members who chose to participate in the local caucuses and primaries. As a consequence, more people than ever before have participated in party decision making. Party nominations had become more competitive within both major parties, and more contenders, representing all shades of political opinion, were competing for their party's nomination.[7] All of these had been objectives of the reform movement.

REFORMING THE PARTY STRUCTURE

Reform of the national party organization was intended to be part of the overall reform thrust after 1968. The earlier reform commissions, however, devoted all of their time and energies to restructuring the presidential nominating system and to modernizing national conventions. Little energy was left over for attacking the problems associated with the manner in which the national party operated or the representativeness of its institutions. As a consequence the 1972 Democratic National Convention created the Party Charter Commission, to deal with this area of concern. The new commission was led by Duke University president and former North Carolina governor, Terry Sanford. A moderate, Sanford was acceptable to all party factions.

The commission was the last of the creative reform exercises. Its report of 1974 attempted to spell out new directions that the party could follow. It attempted to institutionalize the party structure, open it to influence from Democrats at all levels, and provide party members with the basic procedural safeguards implicit in presidential

[7] Crotty, "Assessing a Decade."

selection (as a result of the McGovern-Fraser Commission's work). The new party charter was intended to govern all aspects of party affairs.

Some aspects of the party charter were clearly visionary: a judicial council, resembling the Supreme Court, to resolve all intraparty disputes, and a National Education and Training Council, intended to expand the party's influence to new areas of social concern. As adopted in December of 1974, the party charter:[8]

Requested the national party to take stands on policy issues that represented the views of its rank and file.

Recognized the national convention as the party's supreme governing body and asked the state parties "to take provable positive steps" to adjust their forms and policies to the national party and party charter requirements.

Reaffirmed the new (McGovern-Fraser and succeeding reform commissions') delegate selection rules for national conventions.

Enlarged the national committee to 350 members.

Made the national committee's executive committee more responsive to and dependent on the national committee's membership.

Allowed for midterm conferences to be held.

Established a judicial council to arbitrate party disputes.

Created a national finance council to fund national party operations.

Provided for a National Education and Training Council to conduct "education and training programs for the Democratic Party."

Banned discrimination and supported affirmative action programs in party affairs.

Encouraged "full participation by all Democrats, with particular concern for minority groups, native Americans, women and youth" in all party activities.

Required that all meetings of the national committee, its executive committee and those of all party commissions be open to the public and that all votes be public.

Required an annual report of the national party, to include an accounting of its finances.

Required written rules of all state parties for the conduct of all party business.

Because of the lax organizational structure that characterized the Democratic party, the party charter signified a potentially evolving

---

[8] See Crotty, *Political Reform*, pp. 247–55; and Crotty, "Assessing a Decade."

interest in developing a cohesive organizational style. A restructured and more democratically representative party could result in an organization more responsive to contemporary political and social concerns.

One of the more significant steps in this direction was the introduction of a midterm conference to consider policy alternatives and update the party's platform. The main objective of the first midterm convention was the debate over, and ratification of, the party charter. With a few modifications, party regulars found it acceptable and they and the reformers combined to pass it.

The 1978 midterm convention faced many restrictions on topics for debate imposed by a Democratic administration fearful of being embarrassed over its policy stands. Delegate selection (as in 1974) was tightly controlled. The midterm conference's agenda and delegate selection procedures were determined by the national chairman in consultation with the White House. In addition, the national chairman and a select committee of the national committee served as gatekeepers for the convention. Virtually all proposals for discussion had to be cleared in advance with them.

The midterm conferences as operated in 1974 and 1978 represented a considerable departure from what the reformers had envisioned. Nonetheless, the midterm conference has considerable potential for members to debate policy issues and address the concerns of the party's grassroots constituency. Party regulars appear to be increasingly comfortable with the idea, although any future Democratic administration is likely to react much the same as the Carter administration did. The midterm convention, if handled properly, could provide an instrument for evolving a policy-oriented party, in touch with contemporary concerns, much as the reformers had wanted.

Beyond the introduction of the midterm conference, the party charter has had a limited impact on the party. The national committee was tripled in membership, in an effort to make it more inclusive and reflective of the party's rank and file. As Charles Longley has shown, the changes have had negligible consequences. The national committee can be slightly more independent of a national chairperson, but its composition has not been greatly affected by the reforms.[9] The role of the national committee in American politics is as undistinguished now

[9] Charles Longley, "Party Nationalization in America," in William Crotty (ed.), *Paths to Political Reform* (Lexington, Mass.: D. C. Heath-Lexington, 1980).

as it was before the reform movement.[10] It would be hard to distinguish, in any positive sense, national committee operations in the post-1972 years from those of the 1960s. Overall, to this point the party charter's impact has not been notable.

REFORM IN THE REPUBLICAN PARTY

The Republican party has also attempted reform. It created two reform commissions, the Delegates and Organization (DO) Commission in the period 1969–72 and the Rule 29 Commission during 1972–74. These groups were intended to deal with the type of issue that occupied the McGovern-Fraser Commission, in particular: a recasting of the party's presidential nominating procedures to make them more equitable, open, and reflective of the party's grass-roots base; and the problem of adequate minority group representation in party processes. Both commissions came up with a series of broad recommendations, generally reminiscent of those put forward by the McGovern-Fraser Commission. However, where the McGovern-Fraser Commission's guidelines revolutionized the Democratic party's presidential nominating practices, the corresponding proposals advanced within the Republican party have had little impact.[11]

The reasons for this are many. First, there was little support for fundamental change within the Republican party. In effect, reform had no constituency. Despite their problems, Republicans are well satisfied with their party, whom it represents, and the way in which it operates. Second, the national Republican party perceives itself as a coordinating and servicing agent for fifty basically independent state parties. It takes what could be called a "states' rights" approach to party affairs. It prefers emphasizing how little power it has to force its state affiliates to follow any course of action specified by the national party. As a consequence, Republican reform proposals — or those which

[10] William Crotty, "The National Committees as Grassroots Vehicles of Representation," in William Crotty (ed.), *The Party Symbol* (San Francisco: W. H. Freeman, 1980).

[11] On Republican reform, see Crotty, *Political Reform*, pp. 255–60; and Charles Longley, "Party Reform and the Republican Party" (New York: A Paper Presented at the 1978 Annual Meeting of the American Political Science Association).

were finally endorsed by the national committee and the national convention, a process that adds years to the consideration of reform questions — are essentially advisory. They are exhortations to the states to allow for greater participation but they carry few penalties. Such an approach is guaranteed to produce little change.

Republican reform efforts did not proceed beyond presidential nominating processes. There was not, for example, any equivalent of the party charter or any effort to recast and make more representative such bodies as the national committee. Again, there was no significant group within the Republican coalition that felt such change was needed to ensure a party more responsive to its contemporary political environment.

Nonetheless, some change has come to the Republican party nationally. In an important work, Cornelius P. Cotter and John F. Bibby have traced the evolution of national party operations in broad historical perspective. It is their argument that, in comparison with the past, the national parties, "are more heavily engaged in rule enforcement, campaign and organizational services, and administrative activities. In addition, they are exerting greater discipline over their respective state and local organizations and influencing those organizations through the services provided by the national party."[12]

Cotter and Bibby's analysis has particular applicability for the Republican party. They make the point that Republican reform has not followed the participant-oriented, structural-change path taken within the Democratic party. Rather, the Republican party has emphasized increased nationalization and institutionalization of the party by, in effect, making the national party more relevant in politically traditional ways: providing new services and support.

The authors' intensive examination of the operations of the Republican National Committee lends substance to their point. For example, the Republican National Committee's 1978 budget of $9.7 million is quantum leaps above its 1965 budget of $125,000. Its budget supported a paid staff of 220 (in 1977) and a series of activities from public relations promotions to candidate recruitment and campaign counseling that was impressive (and that contrasted markedly with those

[12]Cornelius P. Cotter and John F. Bibby, "The Impact of Reform on the National Party Organizations: The Long-Term Determinants of Party Reform" (Washington, D.C.: A Paper Presented at the 1979 Annual Meeting of the American Political Science Association), p. 5.

provided by the far smaller Democratic National Committee with its limited budget and staff).[13]

The Republican party then has experienced changes. The national party has expanded its activities and services. The party's presidential nominating procedures have also been affected (perhaps against its will) by the reform spirit. When one party in the American two-party system changes extensively, it cannot help but affect the other. The emphasis on the increasing number of primaries and the shifting in the balance of national convention from caucus selection to primary election has taken place in both parties. In part, it results from modifications in state party laws for both parties. In part also, it is a concession to a changing age and the emphasis on media coverage that primaries encourage.

The spirit of competition over presidential nominations has also influenced both parties. An incumbent president is no longer guaranteed renomination. Serious intraparty opposition to the renomination of a party's incumbent president is a recent occurrence, dating back to 1968. Since that year the Democrats have had two incumbents — Lyndon Johnson and Jimmy Carter — challenged from within their own ranks. The Republican party has not escaped the changing mood. Gerald Ford, a sitting president in 1976, was barely able to withstand the challenge of Ronald Reagan for his party's nomination.

There have been changes then in both parties in form and approach and, in many respects, they are formidable. The party system of the 1980s is not the party system of the 1960s or even the 1970s.

CONCLUSION

The question remaining is, Has enough been accomplished? The McGovern-Fraser Commission, the most influential of the reform bodies, put the matter bluntly:

> If we are not an open party; if we do not represent the demands of change, then the danger is not that people will go to the Republican Party; it is that there will no longer be a way for people committed to

[13] *Ibid.*, pp. 17–19.

orderly change to fulfill their needs and desires within our traditional political system. It is that they will turn to third or fourth party politics or the anti-politics of the street.[14]

Party reform is just a beginning. Where the parties will go from here is, at the moment, uncertain. In broad terms, political parties have adjusted poorly to the political and social demands of the last quarter of the twentieth century. They have found themselves in a changing, and basically hostile, climate. To date they have not made the new technologies and the evolving political climate work to their advantage. Change has been resisted and adaption to change is (as, for example in the reform efforts) often bitterly opposed.

[14] Commission on Party Structure, *Mandate*, p. 49.

III
THE DECLINE OF PARTY
IN THE CONGRESS

Introduction

On October 5, 1978, the United States House of Representatives sustained President Carter's veto of a $10.2 billion public works bill. The vote on the motion to override the veto was 223 to 190, far short of the required two-thirds of voting House members (276 in this case). It was duly reported as an important victory for the Carter administration.

And it was. But it was more than that. The opposition to a Democratic president's veto was led by Speaker of the House Thomas P. O'Neill and Majority Leader Jim Wright. They were supported by Republican Minority Leader John J. Rhodes. Leaders of both parties treated it as a question of congressional prerogative: Congress, not the president, had the traditional right to determine what public works projects were to be financed and constructed. But their followers were not convinced; 46 percent of each party's members voted to sustain the veto.

Within the Democratic majority, different "generations" showed strikingly different voting patterns. Most freshman (first-term) and sophomore (second-term) Democrats supported the veto; only 28 of 74 (38 percent) voted to override. The more senior Democrats voted with the party's leaders; 104 of 158 (66 percent) voted to override.[1]

Although the White House worked hard to convince members to sustain the president's veto, few, if any, did so out of mere loyalty to

[1] *Congressional Quarterly Weekly Report* 36 (October 7, 1978): 2722.

President Carter. The same members had not hesitated to oppose his proposals on other occasions. Most had their eyes on the upcoming 1978 election. The dominant issue seemed to be taxes; it could easily be linked to "wasteful" government spending. Recently elected Democrats in particular felt compelled to prove that they were sufficiently frugal with tax dollars. The public works veto provided an opportunity. That individual "pork barrel" projects for members' districts might henceforth be subject to presidential approval was less alarming than the threat of being labeled a big spender.

The public works veto and its resolution, though not in themselves typical, exemplify the confusing mix of conflict and cooperation that now occurs between the president and Congress, between the president and his party in Congress, and between congressional party leaders and followers. It is not unusual, historically, for the president and Congress to be at odds or for party discipline in Congress to dissolve on a particular issue. What is unusual is the degree to which this has become the norm. President Carter's well-publicized troubles with the Ninety-fifth Congress (1977–78) stemmed in part from the circumstances of his election. But the roots of the problem reach far deeper than one president or one election. They are found in broad, long-term changes in American society as well as in specific events of recent political history. Put most simply, party and presidential leadership suffers from the effects of more than a decade of intense social and political strain. But other, less obvious forces have also been at work.

Our aim in this part is to explore how the congressional parties — and the task of leading them — have evolved in response to broad changes in the political climate and to specific political events. Chapter 9 focuses on electoral politics. In an important sense, the loosening of party ties in Congress is no more than a natural consequence of the decline in party loyalty among citizens. In this and other ways, relations between members and constituents have been developing in directions that increasingly limit the relevance of parties to both.

The consequences for congressional party leadership are traced out in Chapter 10. Adjustments within the congressional parties to the changing needs and perspectives of members have substantially altered many aspects of congressional organization and procedure. A few have strengthened the hand of party leaders; most have had the opposite effect. As will be apparent, these conflicting tendencies arise from the contrary demands of electoral and legislative performance.

Since every president depends to some degree on party leaders to enact his legislative programs, any important change in their capacity to lead bears implications for presidential power. President Carter in particular relies heavily on his party's leaders in Congress, so their problems are frequently his also. But Carter's difficulties have been compounded by the acts of his recent predecessors, congressional responses to them, and his own approach to politics. In Chapter 11 we will consider how the Carter administration has fared in dealings with the parties and party leaders in the House and Senate. In a final chapter we will then present some speculation about the future of the congressional parties and of party and presidential leadership.

9
Parties in Congressional Elections

THE ELECTORAL INCENTIVE

Perhaps the simplest way to begin untangling the complex combination of circumstances that has progressively undermined the authority of party leaders is to consider the motives and goals of individual members of Congress. Nearly all of them want to be effective legislators. They seek to win influence and respect in Washington and to put their imprint on public policy. But this means winning election and reelection. And the demands of effective policy making and of winning elections may pull members in opposite directions. When they do, party loyalty suffers.

Parties are most valuable to members of Congress when those members act as legislators, writing and passing laws. Legislating is a collective activity. At minimum, majority coalitions must be arranged at various stages of the legislative process. Normally, much more than this minimum cooperation is necessary. The party is the basic mechanism for arranging cooperative action in pursuit of legislative goals. The details of how the congressional parties do this will be taken up later.

172

Insofar as members are concerned with writing and passing effective legislation — and in gaining influence and respect through that achievement — the importance of parties is enhanced.

But for most members, winning elections comes first. Logically, of course, winning office is only a means to the achievement of other goals. The real point is not to get elected, but to do the things getting elected allows you to do. But you have to be in Congress to pursue a congressional career. So the need to get elected takes precedence. "All members of Congress," said a former congressman, "have a primary interest in being reelected. Some members have no other interest."[2] Although the electoral incentive is not the only one, it is so prevalent that David R. Mayhew, a political scientist, could make a convincing case that most of what goes on in Congress is best explained by the simple assumption that its members are "single-minded seekers of reelection."[3]

According to this argument, party loyalty, deference to the wishes of a president, or conscientious attention to legislative work will prevail only if they do not hinder reelection. In recent years, a growing number of members have evidently decided that they do. And they may well be right. The crucial question is: how do members win and hold congressional seats? And, in particular, what difference do parties and partisanship make in this endeavor?

PARTY ORGANIZATIONS IN CONGRESSIONAL ELECTIONS

As *campaign organizations,* parties have been relatively unimportant to congressional candidates for many years. Even in localities where party organizations have remained comparatively robust and active, congressional candidates are hardly the main attraction. Local party activists are much more interested in state and local offices — and in the patronage they bring. Often House districts do not coincide with the locally more important divisions, the counties or cities;

---

[2] Quoted in David R. Mayhew, *Congress: The Electoral Connection* (New Haven: Yale University Press, 1974), p. 16.
[3] Mayhew, *Congress,* p. 5.

congressional campaigns therefore do not fit neatly into the party's regular campaign operations. Congressional candidates fall, as it were,
between two or more organizational stools. Of necessity, they therefore put together their own campaigns. "If we depended on the party
organizations to get elected," observed one congressman in the late
1950s, "none of us would be here."[4]

The general irrelevance of local party organizations is apparent from
Richard Fenno's recent study of how eighteen different House members work to retain their seats. According to Professor Fenno,

> Only two of the eighteen members studied were originally recruited by
> the local party organization. And eight began their careers by challeng-
> ing the party organization. Most of the eighteen coexist with the party —
> because of party indifference to the congressional office or because the
> party leaders value the proven independent strength of the congressman
> as a resource. Most primary constituencies consist of people whose loyal-
> ties are to the congressman rather than to the party. And in only two or
> three cases is there an integrated working relationship between the
> congressman's personal organization and the local party organization.
> That is exactly the way most of our House members want it — separate
> organizations pursuing separate tasks. The task of the congressman's
> personal organization is to keep him in Congress. The task of the local
> party organization is to keep the party in control of local offices.[5]

FINANCING CONGRESSIONAL ELECTIONS

Furthermore, party organizations have never provided much
financial assistance to congressional candidates. On occasion, the parties have even expected contributions *from* the candidates.[6] The problem of financing campaigns has become more formidable over the past
two decades with the growth in campaign costs. Campaigning has
become more and more costly in part because party organizations have
decayed; they provided little help before; they provide even less now.

[4] Quoted in Charles L. Clapp, *The Congressman: His Work as He Sees It* (Washington, D.C.: Brookings Institution, 1963), p. 397.

[5] Richard F. Fenno, Jr., *Home Style: House Members in Their Districts* (Boston:
Little, Brown and Company, 1978), p. 113.

[6] Clapp, *The Congressman*, pp. 398–99.

Individual campaigning is naturally more expensive. The economies to scale that parties could supply by combining several campaigns are lost. And, apart from other changes, the development of new kinds of campaign technology has driven up the cost of campaigning quite dramatically. Congressional candidates must now be prepared to wage *expensive* individual campaigns.

The most obvious change in campaign technology has been the advent of television as a campaign medium, but it is by no means the only one. In many places, professional campaign managers have supplanted parties as conductors of campaigns. The professionals rely on modern techniques of advertising (especially broadcast advertising), market research, and personnel management. They employ professionally conducted polls, individualized direct mail advertising, and computerized data processing as part of the campaign arsenal. Campaign expenses have as a consequence increased sharply. The entire package of campaign techniques — not just television — is expensive.[7]

Congressional candidates who wish to run competitive races — challengers trying to unseat incumbents, incumbents facing attractive and well-heeled challengers, candidates scrambling for open seats — normally have to raise a great deal of money. And how much they raise and spend clearly does make a difference in the outcome. The vote won by nonincumbent candidates — challengers to incumbents or candidates for open seats — depends directly on how much they spend on the campaign. The more they spend, if other things are equal, the larger their share of the vote. This is not true of incumbent members of Congress, however. The more they spend, the *smaller* their share of the vote. The paradox is only apparent. Campaign expenditures do not cost them votes. What happens is that incumbents feel compelled to raise and spend more money when they face a serious challenge, and a serious challenge *does* cost them votes. The result is that close, competitive congressional elections are characterized by heavy spending by *both* candidates.[8]

A conservative estimate would place the cost of a competitive House campaign at close to $200,000; Senate campaigns are even more expen-

[7] For an extended account of these developments, see Robert Agranoff (ed.), *The New Style in Election Campaigns* (Boston: Holbrook Press, 1972).

[8] See Gary C. Jacobson, "The Effects of Campaign Spending in Congressional Elections," *American Political Science Review* 72 (June 1978): 469–91.

sive. Candidates with weak, underfinanced opponents may get by with much less than this amount. Indeed, wise incumbents work to discourage strong opponents; we will see more on that later. But serious opposition requires a major financial effort. Candidates who wish to enter and remain in Congress must therefore be able to raise large campaign kitties. And so they are likely to be sensitive to the wishes, interests, and expectations of those who supply campaign funds.

It is important to recognize, then, that parties normally supply a conspicuously *small* proportion of the needed campaign funds. And this proportion has been decreasing over the last few elections. In 1972 and 1976 was 87 percent. PAC contributions as a percentage of all candidates came from local and national party sources; by 1976, the figure was down to 6 percent. Republicans do receive a larger share of their funds from the party, but in 1976 this still amounted to less than 10 percent of the total. The greatest share of campaign money — about two-thirds — comes from donations by private individuals. The second most important source of funds is nonparty political action committees (PACs). Political parties now supply much less money than either of these sources.

As shown in Chapter 7, PACs represent a variety of economic and ideological interests. Some are organized by individual firms and labor unions. Others represent industries (banking or shipbuilding, for example), occupational interests (doctors, lawyers, teachers), or agricultural sectors (milk producers, tobacco growers). Collectively, they supply a growing share of congressional campaign funds. In 1972, nonparty committees gave $8.9 million to congressional candidates; in 1974, the total was $12.5 million; in 1976, it was $22.6 million. Taking inflation into account, the real-dollar increase between 1972 and 1976 was 87 percent. PAC contributions as a percentage of all contributions grew from 14.3 percent to 17.0 percent to 19.6 percent over these years.[9]

If members of Congress are at all attuned to the concerns of those who finance their campaigns — or who might, if aroused, finance their opponents' campaigns — they will be more attentive to individual

[9]The 1972 figure is calculated from data in "Common Cause Releases Study of 1972 Congressional Campaign Finances" (news release from Common Cause, September 13, 1973), Table 1; the 1974 and 1976 figures are from Common Cause data reported in Michael J. Malbin, "Labor, Business, and Money — A Post Election Analysis," *National Journal* 9 (March 19, 1977): 416.

donors and to organized interests than to their parties. They will be most sensitive to the wishes of individual donors *if* they can determine what these are. But this is often doubtful. People give money to candidates for a great variety of reasons, many of them irrelevant to what the candidate does in office. Although personal services and attention to the financial "constituency" are obviously prudent, it may well be impossible for a member to estimate the collective preferences of individual contributors on policy questions. They therefore can hardly circumscribe his actions.

With political action committees it is quite otherwise. As the second most important source of campaign funds, they cannot lightly be ignored. And they often have strong and conspicuous preferences on legislation and other matters before Congress. This does not imply that members must invariably dance to the tunes called by groups that help finance their campaigns. It does mean that their preferences will be taken into account as members decide what to do. This is the minimal payoff that contributing groups expect.

MOTIVES AND STRATEGIES OF PACs

A closer inspection of the motives and strategies of organized campaign contributors will provide some insights into how current campaign finance practices weaken the bonds of party loyalty in Congress. Many PACs openly contribute most heavily to members who are in a position to do them the most good — or harm — regardless of party. Dairy industry committees, for example, give most of their money to incumbents of both parties who sit on congressional committees dealing with agriculture. They give seven dollars to incumbents to every dollar they give to challengers, but they do not shrink from giving to *both* candidates if each has a chance to win. And they are entirely indifferent to whether or not the candidate actually needs the money; even unopposed candidates may get contributions. Although their declared intention is "to keep our friends in office and elect those who are our friends,"[10] it is perhaps more accurate to say that they aim to make certain that those in office remain friendly.

[10] *Congressional Quarterly Weekly Report* 31 (March 17, 1973): 569.

Similarly, the American Medical Association's AMPAC gives money disproportionately to sponsors of the AMA's health care proposals and to agreeable members of committees dealing with health policy; party is scarcely a factor.[11] The banking industry's BankPAC funds campaigns of members of committees handling banking legislation.[12] And maritime industry groups give mainly to members who support laws that would require American ships and crews to be used for the delivery of various products.[13]

For many groups, the strategy of contributing to members of Congress who are best situated to help or harm their interests is simply good business. When the Congress's decisions have a substantial impact on profits and losses, it is a sound business policy to deploy financial resources to promote the friendliest possible relations with its members. Campaign contributions are one approach among many. It should come as no surprise, then, that business associations contribute almost as much to Democrats as to Republicans, despite the ideological differences that continue to exist between the business community and the Democratic party. In 1976, for instance, 46.5 percent of the $10.7 million contributed by business and professional committees went to Democratic congressional candidates.[14] Democrats will continue to enjoy a sizable share of business' bounty as long as they control the Congress.

Other economic interests are more definitely partisan. The leaders of organized labor have traditionally claimed independence from any party, preferring to "reward friends and punish enemies" wherever they are found. But in fact labor has become the major organizational source of funds for Democratic congressional candidates. In 1976, for example, the Committees on Political Education of the AFL-CIO contributed to 250 Democratic House candidates but only four Republicans — one of whom switched to the Democratic party shortly after the election.[15] More than 95 percent of the money given by labor groups in 1972, 1974, and 1976 went to Democrats. Friendly Republi-

---

[11] *Congressional Quarterly Weekly Report* 30 (October 21, 1972): 2720–21; *Congressional Quarterly Weekly Report* 31 (March 17, 1973): 570.

[12] *Congressional Quarterly Weekly Report* 31 (March 17, 1973): 570.

[13] *Dollar Politics*, vol. 2 (Washington, D.C.: Congressional Quarterly, October 1974), p. 54.

[14] *Congressional Quarterly Weekly Report* 36 (January 21, 1978): 119.

[15] *Ibid*.

cans are more often helped by labor's lack of support for their opponents than by any direct assistance.

Recently, labor has been less than delighted by the return on its political investments. Almost every major item on labor's agenda for the Ninety-fifth Congress failed to pass. Most galling must have been the antilabor votes of many Democrats who had received large labor contributions in the 1976 campaigns. The alternative sources of funds—including business PACs—readily accessible to agreeable incumbents are no doubt partly to blame. But there are other, stronger reasons, as we shall see. The inability of organized labor, traditional mainstay of the Democratic party, to get its way with a Congress two-thirds Democratic and a Democrat in the White House is by itself a clear signal that parties are not what they used to be.

DISCOURAGING CHALLENGERS

Shrewd incumbents are as sensitive to the effects of their actions on potential challengers (and their financial backers) as they are to the effects on their own supporters. The reason is that the ease with which they can win reelection depends on the vigor of the challenge they face. If the opponent is an inexperienced campaigner who conducts a modest, shoestring campaign, the incumbent is certain to win. An experienced, amply funded opponent means a much harder campaign. More time and energy must be invested, and more money must be raised. Members may sometimes enjoy campaigning, but by all accounts they hate raising money. The late Senator Hubert Humphrey once called it a "disgusting, degrading, demeaning experience,"[16] to which the great majority of his colleagues would reply, "Amen."

Even though they raise and spend large sums of money and mount full-scale campaigns, members suffer their closest calls — and defeats — when opposed by attractive, well-financed challengers. It is much safer to discourage vigorous opposition before the campaign

[16] Quoted in David Adamany and George E. Agree, *Political Money: A Strategy for Campaign Finance in America* (Baltimore and London: Johns Hopkins University Press, 1975), p. 8.

starts. Indeed, because of the way money works in congressional elections — helping nonincumbents much more than incumbents — it is more important for members to prevent campaign resources from being mobilized against them than it is to mobilize their own campaign resources. Members serve themselves best by denying their potential opponents financial support. This has the complementary benefit of keeping more experienced and ambitious politicians from making the challenge. They recognize that without adequate resources, the chance of winning is slight.[17]

Members of Congress therefore have a real incentive to avoid actions that might excite opposition from groups not already actively committed against them. Among other things, they are likely to be conscious of the potential reactions of groups, such as the gun lobby or the antiabortionists or the environmentalists, which specifically target prominent "enemies" for electoral attack. They are also well advised to keep in visible touch with their districts. A high profile back home prevents any impression from developing that a member is losing his grip on the district and is therefore vulnerable.

MEMBERS AND THEIR CONSTITUENTS

Congressional candidates run individual, personal campaigns in part because they must; party resources are much too thin to carry them. But they also do so because this approach to campaigning pays off on election day. Members of the House must run for reelection every two years. Their campaigns never really end. They pursue reelection throughout the term, so their campaign strategy is visible in all their dealings with constituents. It is important to emphasize, then, that within their constituencies, members typically cultivate personal images surprisingly empty of partisan or even programmatic content. They present themselves to people in the district as trustworthy, hardworking individuals who merit support on the basis of personal qualities rather than political beliefs or goals.

[17] See Gary C. Jacobson, "Money in Congressional Elections" (New Haven: Yale University Press, 1980), pp. 106–107.

Richard Fenno, who traveled extensively with eighteen House members as they made the rounds of their districts, found that each member projected a personal "home style" that defined his relationship to the groups he relied on for political support. Home styles varied among members according to the character of the district and the personality of the individual member. But in one way or another, all members basically sought to inspire *trust* among their constituents.[18] They did this by emphasizing their personal qualifications, including moral character, by identifying with their constituents ("I am one of you," they implied, "so you can trust me to make the right decisions"), and by working to develop bonds of empathy with the groups and individuals they met.

For most of them, issues, policy, and partisanship were *not* prominent objects of discussion with constituents and were not used to elicit support. Even members who did display an issue-oriented home style used issues primarily to cement ties of trust: "Issues are not as important as the treatment of issues."[19] Members used issues to present themselves as the kind of people constituents would want in Washington; the issues themselves were secondary.

Fenno's House members agreed that representation could basically be defined as accessibility. Constituents were continually reminded that the lines of communication were open, that they had access to the member whenever they needed it. And this was done most effectively through a steady flow of services to the district.

> Many activities can be incorporated under the rubric of "district service," or "constituency service," but the core activity is providing help to individuals, groups, and localities in coping with the federal government. Individuals need someone to intercede with the bureaucracies handling veterans benefits, social security checks, military status, civil service pensions, immigration proceedings, and the like. Private groups and local governments need assistance in pursuing federal funds, for water and sewer projects, highways, dams, buildings, planning, research and development, small business loans, and so forth.[20]

[18] Fenno, *Home Style*, p. 55.
[19] *Ibid.*, p. 241.
[20] *Ibid.*, p. 101.

VOTING IN CONGRESSIONAL ELECTIONS

Members of Congress believe that their personal standing, maintained through individual attention to constituents and emphasis on district services, is what discourages opposition, wins votes, and keeps them in office. Studies of the congressional electorate indicate that they are right, even though, paradoxically, most voters base their voting decision on the candidate's party. One veteran House member recently complained that "party loyalty has really withered away. It shouldn't be that way. They didn't get elected on their own. A lot of these guys wouldn't have been elected if they didn't have Democrat behind their name."[21] In a way, he is right. The basic determinant of voting in congressional elections is the party identification of the voter. Voters most often vote for the candidate of their preferred party. But, in a broader sense, he is quite wrong. Members do not win reelection on the basis of their loyalty to the party.

For one thing, there is no evidence that people who vote for members on the basis of party affiliation expect candidates to vote with their parties once they are in office. Voters' perceptions and evaluations of congressional candidates are almost empty of policy content. Only a tiny minority usually has any knowledge of how a member voted on any particular bill, let alone how loyal the member has been to party leaders. The basic reason so many voters use party cues in deciding how to vote is that they have no other information about the candidates. In a study made of the 1958 House elections, for example, Donald F. Stokes and Warren E. Miller found that 59 percent of the people they surveyed had neither read nor heard anything about either House candidate; fewer than one in five knew something about both candidates. Forty-six percent cast their ballots without having received any information about either candidate.[22] With no other information, voters simply go by their party preference.

When voters do have additional information about candidates, party loyalty is not nearly so automatic. The evidence for this is in Table 9.1. Table 9.1 shows the impact of one piece of information—the name of

---

[21] *Congressional Quarterly Weekly Report* 36 (May 27, 1978), p. 1302.
[22] Donald E. Stokes and Warren E. Miller, "Party Government and the Saliency of Congress," in *Elections and the Political Order* (New York: John Wiley and Sons, 1966), p. 204.

TABLE 9.1
The Effects of Candidate Recall on Partisan Defection in House and Senate Elections

Percentage Who Defected in:	*Voter Recalled Name of:*			
	Both Candidates	Own Candidate	Other Candidate	Neither Candidate
House Elections				
1958	17	2	40	8
	(196)[a]	(166)	(68)	(368)
1966	19	4	66	14
	(198)	(98)	(41)	(231)
1968	23	5	51	19
	(303)	(97)	(57)	(267)
1970	24	1	57	13
	(152)	(148)	(37)	(256)
1972	23	7	62	21
	(151)	(100)	(26)	(242)
1974	29	1	58	15
	(281)	(154)	(79)	(374)
Senate Elections				
1974	25	2	62	10
	(317)	(138)	(87)	(205)

Source: Information for the years 1958–1970, reprinted by permission from Robert B. Arsenau and Raymond E. Wolfinger, "Voting Behavior in Congressional Elections." Paper presented to the Annual Meeting of the American Political Science Association, New Orleans, Louisiana, September 4-8, 1973, p. 14; 1972 and 1974, CPS American National Election Studies.

[a]Number of cases from which percentages were computed. The 1974 sample is weighted.

the candidate — on party loyalty among congressional voters. Voters who remember the name of their own party's candidate only are the most consistent party line voters; they remain loyal in more than 90 percent of the cases. Voters who remember only the name of the other party's candidate have actually defected to the opposition in a majority of cases since 1966. Any recall of the other party's candidate increases the likelihood of partisan defection.

There is, to be sure, more to it than merely recalling the name of the candidate. Voters' *evaluations* of candidates are even more important. A survey of voters' attitudes toward 1974 Senate candidates found that about 80 percent of those who remembered a candidate's name could also remember something they liked or disliked about the candidate. Interestingly, about one-third of those who could *not* remember the candidate's name were still willing to offer evaluative comments. Most comments — 51 percent — referred to the candidate's personal qualities. Only 15 percent referred strictly to partisan characteristics. These were, not surprisingly, more common among voters who could not recall the candidate's name. The other 34 percent combined these and other miscellaneous criteria in specifying their likes and dislikes.[23]

Assessments of the candidates had a strong impact on how people voted. This is shown in Table 9.2. Partisan voters who evaluated the other party's candidate positively and their own negatively were most likely to defect to the opponent. Voters who had positive things to say about their own party's candidate and negative comments about the other party's candidate were most loyal.

Comparable studies of voting for House candidates support the same conclusions: personal judgments of candidates predominate, and they affect the vote.[24] Thomas E. Mann's research on the 1976 elections actually suggested that evaluations of House candidates were more important than party identification in determining how people voted that year. He carefully explored the connection between a candidate's familiarity to voters — measured by whether voters could either *recall* his name or *recognize* it once it was mentioned — and their evaluations and support. He discovered that "visibility does not insure popularity, but it is an essential prerequisite. Voters who fail to *recognize* a challenger's name . . . invariably move disproportionately into the incumbent's camp. . . . Among those who did not recognize them, the challengers lost an average of 38 percent of their own partisans."[25]

The importance of visibility explains why money works as it does in congressional elections. Incumbents are already known by voters at the beginning of the campaign; most have spent a good portion of the previous two years keeping constituents aware of them. Challengers are rarely as well known; victory is possible only if they can grab the attention of voters during the campaign. The campaign is crucial, and a

[23] Jacobson, "Effects of Campaign Spending," p. 488.

[24] See Stokes and Miller, "Party Government," pp. 205–07; Thomas E. Mann, *Unsafe at Any Margin: Interpreting Congressional Elections* (Washington, D.C.: American Enterprise Institute for Public Policy Research, 1978), pp. 60–74; Alan J. Abramowitz, "Name Familiarity, Reputation, and the Incumbency Effect in a Congressional Election," *Western Political Quarterly* 28 (1975): 678.

[25] Mann, *Unsafe at Any Margin*, p. 59.

TABLE 9.2
Evaluation of Senate Candidates and Partisan Voting Behavior in 1974
(Percentage of Partisan Voters Defecting)

Evaluation of Other Party's Candidate:	*Positive*	*Positive and Negative*	*Negative*	*Marginal Totals*
	Evaluation of Own Party's Candidate:			
Positive	28.6	77.1	77.1	65.9
	(21)[a]	(35)	(35)	(91)
Positive and Negative	4.5	31.1	56.0	16.3
	(139)	(45)	(25)	(209)
Negative	4.2	3.4	40.0	4.8
	(167)	(59)	(5)	(231)
Marginal Totals	5.8	30.9	66.2	19.8
	(327)	(139)	(65)	(531)
No Evaluation	16.5			
	(115)			

Source: 1974 CPS Survey.

[a] Number of cases from which percentages were computed. The sample is weighted.

vigorous campaign costs money. Challengers do better the more they spend because they become better known the more they spend.[26] Spending an ample amount of money does not guarantee them victory (any more than it would the incumbent). The kind of person who is presented by all that campaigning is by no means irrelevant. But without the money, even a very good candidate will not get very far. Voters will remain unaware of his virtues, and they will therefore ignore him on election day. This is why it is so valuable to incumbents to face obscure and poorly funded opponents.

THE DECLINE OF PARTISANSHIP IN CONGRESSIONAL ELECTIONS

Returning for a moment to the figures in Table 9.1, notice that partisan defections appear to be much more common in the 1960s and 1970s than they were in 1958. Other data show the trend away from

[26] Jacobson, "Effects of Campaign Spending," pp. 479–85.

TABLE 9.3
Party Line Voting in House Elections, 1956–76 (in percentages)

Year	Party Line Voters	Defectors	Independents	Total
1956	82	9	9	100
1958	84	11	5	100
1960	80	12	8	100
1962	83	12	5	100
1964	79	15	5	99
1966	76	16	8	100
1968	74	19	7	100
1970	76	16	8	100
1972	73	17	10	100
1974	74	18	8	100
1976	72	19	9	100

Source: Reprinted by permission from Thomas E. Mann, *Unsafe at Any Margin: Interpreting Congressional Elections* (Washington, D.C.: American Enterprise Institute for Public Policy Research, 1978), p. 14. Data are originally from SRC/CPS National Election Studies.

Note: Party line voters are those who voted for the party with which they identified. (Independents leaning toward a party are treated as partisans, not independents.) Defectors are those who voted for the party other than the one they claimed as their own. Data may not sum to 100 due to rounding.

party loyalty even more clearly. Table 9.3 lists the proportion of loyal, defecting, and independent voters in congressional electorates from 1956 through 1976. The proportion of voters casting ballots for candidates of the opposite party more than doubled between 1956 and 1976.

The decline in party line voting for Congress is part of a wider decrease in the electoral importance of party. Voting behavior at all levels has undergone significant changes in this direction since the early 1960s. Not only do an increasing number of voters refuse to identify themselves as Republicans or Democrats, preferring to be called independents, but even the self-designated partisans are less loyal to their party's candidates than they once were. And public attitudes toward the parties as institutions have grown increasingly negative.[27]

The weakening of party loyalty has had profound consequences for the electoral side of congressional politics. Partisan defections are by no means randomly distributed among candidates. Voters are much

[27] See Jack Dennis, "Trends in Public Support for the American Political Party System," paper presented at the Annual Meeting of the American Political Science Association, Chicago, Illinois, August 29–September 2, 1974.

TABLE 9.4
Partisan Defections to Incumbents and Challengers, 1958–74 (in percentages)

Year	Incumbent Partisans		Challenger Partisans	
1958	8.9	(406)[a]	16.2	(291)
1960	7.7	(534)	19.3	(394)
1962	—[b]		—[b]	
1964	10.9	(430)	25.1	(311)
1966	9.1	(296)	32.5	(200)
1968	13.5	(355)	32.5	(286)
1970	4.7	(253)	32.1	(190)
1972	5.9	(323)	56.0	(168)
1974	12.9	(255)	48.6	(181)

Source: From Albert D. Cover, "One Good Term Deserves Another: The Advantage of Incumbency in Congressional Elections," *American Journal of Political Science*, Vol. 21 (August 1977), p. 535, Table 4. Reprinted by permission of the publisher, The University of Texas Press.

[a] Number of cases from which percentages were computed.

[b] Data not available.

more likely to defect to *incumbents* than to nonincumbents of the opposing party. And the increase in defections is composed almost entirely of more frequent defections to incumbents. The figures in Table 9.4 make these points very clearly. Defection rates of voters identifying with the incumbent's party have fluctuated; no trend is apparent. In sharp contrast, voters of the challenger's party defect much more frequently in recent elections. Albert Cover, who collected these data, emphasizes the crucial point: "*Since 1972 about half of those identifying with the challenger's party have deserted their party's congressional candidate in contested elections involving an incumbent.*"[28]

THE ADVANTAGES OF INCUMBENCY

Why have voters consistently defected more often to incumbents than to challengers? And why do they now defect more frequently than in the past? The first question can be answered with relative confi-

[28] Albert D. Cover, "One Good Term Deserves Another: The Advantage of Incumbency in Congressional Elections," *American Journal of Political Science* 21 (1977): 535.

dence. Partisan defection is clearly related to the amount of information voters have about candidates. Table 9.1 established that point. And voters normally have much more information about incumbents than about nonincumbents. Using recall of the candidate's name as a simple indicator of information, Table 9.5 shows this to be the case. Incumbents are invariably recalled more frequently than nonincumbents; their advantage here is unmistakable. Its effect is even more telling — in light of the data in Table 9.1 — because when the contest is between an incumbent and a challenger and only one of the candidates is recalled (the two middle columns of Table 9.1), that candidate is almost always the incumbent. This is true in more than 96 percent of the cases in the 1972 and 1974 surveys, for example.

But the second question is not answered so easily. The information in Table 9.5 indicates that the relative advantage of incumbents in voter recall has *not* increased over the years during which defections to incumbents *have* increased. In fact, partisan voters are more likely to defect to incumbents even when they cannot recall their names.[29] This has led some scholars to conclude that the growing value of incumbency cannot be attributed to more successful self-promotion by officeholders (though more *extensive* self-promotion cannot be doubted; these efforts will be reviewed shortly). But name recall is not a perfect measure of candidate information. Voters need only recognize the name of the candidate when they see it (e.g., on a ballot in the voting booth) for the effects of candidate familiarity to operate. And name recognition is much more common than name recall.[30] If voters consistently preferred incumbents to challengers without recognizing *or* recalling either one, the phenomenon would defy rational explanation. So the question of whether or not incumbents are merely reaping the benefits of more extensive self-advertising is still open.

This and the other explanations that have been offered for the increase in voter support for incumbents more often reinforce than contradict one another, but clear differences at least in emphasis are evident. One straightforward explanation is that as voters have progressively detached themselves from party ties, they have merely replaced one simple voting cue — party — with another — incumbency. Incumbents are simply enjoying the windfall from the general decline in partisanship among voters.

[29] John A. Ferejohn, "On the Decline of Competition in Congressional Elections," *American Political Science Review* 71 (1977): 171.

[30] Mann, *Unsafe at Any Margin,* p. 32.

TABLE 9.5
Percentages of Voters Recalling Names of Candidates in Contested Congressional Elections

	Incumbents		Nonincumbents	
House Elections				
1958	57.6	(738)[a]	38.0	(947)
1964	63.0	(856)	39.8	(920)
1966	55.9	(583)	37.6	(703)
1968	63.7	(703)	46.5	(861)
1970	54.7	(548)	31.3	(630)
1972	50.0	(498)	30.9	(718)
1974	57.2	(856)	32.2	(1230)
Senate Elections				
1974	72.7	(595)	48.3	(1023)

Source: From John A. Ferejohn, "On the Decline of Competition in Congressional Elections," *American Political Science Review* 77 (1977), p. 170. Reprinted by permission.

[a] Number of cases from which percentages were computed.

An alternative view is that members of Congress are responsible for their own increased electoral success. Although they have always worked hard to win reelection, they now have access to — and exploit — vastly greater resources for keeping themselves in office. The quantity, variety, and dollar-value of the resources available to members of Congress through their offices have grown dramatically since 1960. Recent estimates place the value of salary, staff, travel, communications, and office allowances at about $400,000 *per year* for a United States representative[31]; even more is provided to senators, with the amount scaled to the size of the state. Staff allowances alone may come to more than $900,000.[32]

Back in 1960, each member of the House could hire up to nine staff employees; today, the number is eighteen. House members were permitted three reimbursed round-trips to the district in the early 1960s. The number was subsequently increased to five (1966), twelve (1968), eighteen (1973), twenty-six (1975), and finally to thirty-two (1977).[33]

And the growth of other official resources has kept pace. The most important congressional prerequisite is no doubt the franking privilege—the right of members to use the mails free of charge for

[31] Cover, "One Good Term," p. 537.
[32] *Congressional Quarterly Weekly Report* 34 (July 3, 1976): 1700.
[33] Morris P. Fiorina, *Congress: Keystone of the Washington Establishment* (New Haven: Yale University Press, 1977), p. 61.

"official business," which is broadly interpreted to include most kinds of communications to constituents. Franked mail increased by more than 600 percent between 1954 and 1970. A recent estimate put the total cost of congressional mail for a twelve-month period (1976–77) at $62,736,438, which averages out to more than $117,000 per member.[34] Other media have not been ignored. Facilities for preparing radio and television tapes and films are available to members free of charge. And in 1977, members voted themselves an unlimited WATS line for long distance telephone calls.[35]

The centrality of the electoral incentive guarantees that members will use whatever resources their office provides to pursue reelection. And the uses to which this growing array of assets have been put are instructive. Self-promotion through publicity and communication directly to constituents is only one important example. Morris P. Fiorina has published some equally revealing data about congressional staffing. They are presented in Table 9.6. Notice that in 1960, 14 percent of congressional staff personnel were assigned to district offices; by 1974, when staff sizes had doubled, 34 percent worked in district offices. The percentage of congressmen whose district offices close when they are not in town has fallen to nearly zero. And almost half the members now maintain more than one district office. A disproportionate share of the additional personnel available to members has been used to augment their capacity to provide services to constituents.

Fiorina contends that this is the basic source of greater incumbent security. His argument is subtle. Decisions taken by the Congress have increased the size of the federal government and the scope of federal authority tremendously. This, in turn, has greatly increased the demands for help from members to cope with the bureaucratic maze or to take advantage of federal programs. Members have, at the same time, continually added to their capacity to deliver services. The greater demand for such services generates more opportunities for building credit with constituents, and "the nice thing about case work is that it is mostly profit; one makes many more friends than enemies."[36]

[34] *Hartford Courant*, March 28, 1977, p. 6.
[35] Lewis Perdue, "The Million Dollar Advantage of Incumbency," *Washington Monthly* 9 (March 1977): 51.
[36] Morris P. Fiorina, "The Case of the Vanishing Marginals: The Bureaucracy Did It," *American Political Science Review* 71 (1977): 180.

TABLE 9.6
Growth of Personal Staffs of Congressmen, 1960–74

	1960	1967	1974
Total Staff	2344	3276	5109
Percentage of total staff assigned to district offices	14	26	34
Percentage of congressmen whose district offices open only when congressman is home or after adjournment	29	11	2
Percentage of congressmen listing multiple district offices	4	18	47

Source: From Morris P. Fiorina, *Congress: Keystone of the Washington Establishment*, p. 58. Copyright © 1977 by Yale University. Reprinted by permission of Yale University Press.

It is also nonpartisan. The party of the member delivering the service — or of the constituent receiving it — is beside the point. What matters is a member's ability to deliver services, which increases with his tenure in Washington and his consequent seniority and mastery of the administrative apparatus. It therefore makes perfect sense for voters to prefer candidates on the basis of their incumbency rather than on their party or policy stands. And it makes equally perfect sense for incumbent members to focus on providing services rather than on making national policy as a means for staying in office.

Fiorina's theory admittedly rests more on reason than on evidence at this point, but there is little question that attention to constituency services commands a greatly enlarged share of members' and their staffs' time. And there is no question that incumbents have become more secure. By this argument, voting behavior has changed in response to changes in the behavior of members of Congress. But the causal link might just as well work in the opposite direction: members may have exploited the weakening of party ties to solidify their position by more intense cultivation of the district. When voters vote as partisans, attention to the district makes little difference; incumbents may still be swept out by national tides favoring one party or the other. They may still be punished for the perceived failings of their party or its leaders. But if voters are detached from parties, members will be able to ride out contrary political tides on the cushion of their personal esteem and popularity. It then makes good strategic sense to cultivate a highly personal connection with the district.

THE DISAPPEARING MARGINALS

Whatever its true causes, an obvious consequence of this change in congressional voting behavior is that incumbent members are winning reelection more easily than in the past. They are not winning any more *frequently*, however; their success rate was already so high that it left little room for improvement. In House elections from 1956 through 1978, over 90 percent of the candidates running were incumbents. Of these, a mere 1.7 percent lost primary election contests; only 6.0 percent were defeated in general elections; 92.4 percent won reelection. The smallest percentage of incumbent victories in general elections in any of these years was 86.9 percent; the largest was 96.8 percent.[37] By the criterion of reelection, House incumbents have been quite safe for years.

But by another standard — the ease with which they are reelected — incumbents have enjoyed a measurable increase in security since the mid-1960s. Political scientists designate congressional seats that are won with less than a specific percentage of the two-party vote "marginal" seats. By either of the usual thresholds, 55 or 60 percent, the number of close elections, and hence marginal seats, has fallen off significantly. In the decade prior to 1966, about two-thirds of incumbent House candidates won with more than 60 percent of the vote. Since 1966, 75 percent have won by at least this margin. In contrast, elections for open seats, when neither candidate is an incumbent, remain thoroughly competitive and fall frequently into the marginal range.[38]

[37] William J. Keefe, *Parties, Politics, and Public Policy in America*, 2nd ed. (Hinsdale, Ill.: Dryden Press, 1976), p. 39; *Congressional Quarterly Weekly Report* 34 (November 6, 1976): 3119–22.

[38] Albert D. Cover and David R. Mayhew, "Congressional Dynamics and the Decline of Competitive Congressional Elections," in Lawrence C. Dodd and Bruce I. Oppenheimer (eds.), *Congress Reconsidered* (New York: Praeger, 1977), pp. 55–56; David R. Mayhew, "Congressional Elections: The Case of the Vanishing Marginals," *Polity* 6 (1974): 298–301.

Additional evidence of the enhanced electoral value of incumbency is found in data on elections involving first term incumbents and on elections in districts where incumbents have voluntarily retired. The average gain in the percentage of the vote between a member's first and second election (adjusted for national trends) was +2.7 percent from 1962 through 1966, +6.6 percent from 1968 through 1974. Similarly, the fall-off in the vote for a retiring incumbent's party averaged −2.2 percent in the earlier period, −7.7 percent more recently.[39] These data also indicate that House seats are safe for specific incumbents, not for their parties. When a safe incumbent retires, the seat is likely to become marginal — candidates of either party have a chance to win.

INCUMBENCY IN SENATE ELECTIONS

It is important to note that the sharp increase in incumbent security is confined largely to the House. Incumbent senators remain much more vulnerable. In the four decades between 1920 and 1960, from 75.0 to 78.6 of Senate incumbents contesting general elections won. In the 1960s, their success rate jumped to 92.2 percent; but for the 1970s, it fell back to 76.6 percent.[40] Senate seats are much more likely to be marginal. Most are won with less than 60 percent of the vote. Party loyalty has evidently declined as a force in Senate elections, too, relative to incumbency, but not to a point where incumbent senators are significantly more difficult to defeat.[41]

This difference between the two houses needs explaining. Senate elections have not been very thoroughly studied, but plausible explanations are not difficult to imagine. Senators are not nearly so well situated to build and maintain bipartisan support through personal services to their constituents. States are, with six exceptions, more populous than congressional districts, often very much so. The

[39] Cover and Mayhew, "Congressional Dynamics," p. 60.

[40] From data in *Congressional Quarterly's Guide to U.S. Elections* (Washington, D.C., 1975), pp. 457–509, and *Congressional Quarterly's Guide to the 1976 Elections: A Supplement to CQ's Guide to U.S. Elections* (Washington, D.C., 1977), pp. 36–44; the 1978 data were compiled by the author.

[41] Warren Lee Kostroski, "Party and Incumbency in Postwar Senate Elections: Trends, Patterns, and Models," *American Political Science Review* 67 (1973): 1213–34.

opportunities for personal contact with constituents and attention to individual problems are proportionately fewer. Even the larger Senate staffs cannot make up the difference.

Nor is it certain that voters expect senators to act as their ombudsmen and errand boys. They may expect senators to take more prominent policy stands, which are controversial and divisive in a way that district services are not. Action in the Senate is more visible; it has fewer members, and they are given more attention by the news media. And normally they must try to represent much more socially and politically diverse constituencies — whole states rather than congressional districts.

Senators also do not have the pressure of a two-year election cycle to keep them attuned to the folks back home. Electoral coalitions may fall out of repair, and a careless senator may discover that he must begin almost from scratch when reelection time rolls around. Senate incumbents are much more likely to face prominent, well-funded opponents; Senate races attract stronger candidates and larger amounts of campaign money than House races.

For whatever combination of reasons, incumbent senators remain twice as vulnerable as House members. The evident loosening of party ties has not benefitted them so directly. Yet incumbency is still to their advantage, and most incumbents win. The 1974 survey found that partisan voters defected to Senate incumbents at a rate of 32.9 percent; the defection rate to challengers was only 12.2 percent. Recall from Table 9.3 that the comparable defection rates for House voters were 48.6 percent and 12.9 percent that year.

THE DECLINE OF PRESIDENTIAL COATTAILS

The growing security of incumbent members of Congress (at least those in the House) has, among other things, greatly diminished the electoral relevance of presidents and presidential candidates. Although the performance of presidents and presidential aspirants may influence the vote received by other candidates of their parties,[42] most incum-

[42] See Edward R. Tufte, "Determinants of the Outcomes of Midterm Congressional Elections," *American Political Science Review* 69 (1975): 812–26; Samuel Kernell, "Presidential Popularity and Negative Voting: An Alternative Explanation of the Midterm

TABLE 9.7
Proportion of Split Results: Congress and President, 1940–76

Year	Number of Districts Analyzed	Percentage of Split Results
1940	362	14.6
1944	367	11.2
1948	422	22.5
1952	435	19.3
1956	435	29.9
1960	437	26.1
1964	435	33.3
1968	435	31.7
1972	435	44.1
1976	435	28.5

Source: 1940–1972, from *The American Party Systems: Stages of Political Develop-ment*, Second Edition, by William Nisbet Chambers and Walter Dean Burnham. Copy-right © 1967, 1976 by Oxford University Press, Inc. Reprinted by permission. 1976 from Charles M. Tidmarch, "Congressmen and the Electorate, 1976: A Halt to the Onward March of Party Decomposition?" prepared for delivery at the Annual Meeting of the Northeastern Political Science Association, 1978. Used by permission.

bents now enjoy a sufficient electoral cushion to survive even in the face of a disaster at the top of the party ticket. Richard Nixon's landslide victory over George McGovern in 1972 (he won more than 60 percent of the vote) resulted in a Republican gain of only 13 seats in the House. Republicans suffered a net *loss* of two seats in the Senate. The aggre-gate vote for Republican candidates was very high by historical stan-dards. But the distribution of those votes, strongly affected by incum-bency, was such that they scarcely helped where it matters, in election victories.[43]

The detachment of presidential from congressional voting is most readily apparent in Walter Dean Burnham's data on the percentage of congressional districts that delivered split results — majorities for the congressional candidate of one party and the presidential candidate of the other. They are reported in Table 9.7. In 1972 no less than 44.1 percent of the House districts voted for a president and a congressman

Congressional Decline of the President's Party," *American Political Science Review* 71 (1977): 44–66; Gary C. Jacobson, "Presidential Coattails in 1972," *Public Opinion Quar-terly* 40 (1976): 194–200.

[43] Jacobson, "Coattails," pp. 197–99.

of opposite parties. Richard Nixon actually carried 77.4 percent of the districts that elected Democrats to the House in 1972.[44]

In 1976 the number of split results dropped back to 28.5 percent, but there is no evidence that Jimmy Carter's coattails had anything to do with it. Of the 292 Democrats elected to the House that year only 22 received a smaller share of the vote in the district than Carter. Few members of the Ninety-fifth Congress had reason to think that his performance in the election had anything to do with getting them elected.[45] Research has shown that members of Congress are more loyal to presidents who have run ahead of them in their districts, so this is not a trivial point.[46]

WINNING AGAINST THE TIDE

The 1974 and 1976 elections gave striking evidence of the capacity of incumbents to hold onto their jobs in the face of contrary electoral tides. And they reinforce another critical point: the value of incumbency does not appear magically or automatically; it depends on what the incumbent does with the resources available to him.

The 1974 election, following Watergate, Nixon's resignation and pardon by President Ford, and a period of distressful economic conditions, was generally a disaster for Republicans. The party took its worst electoral beating in many years; thirty-six of the Republican House incumbents were defeated. But Burnham made the surprising discovery that "first generation or 'new-incumbent' Republicans as a group actually *improved* their position very slightly in the face of an exceptionally large national shift towards the Democrats."[47] And in 1976, no fewer than forty-eight of the forty-nine Democrats elected to formerly

[44] Walter Dean Burnham, "Party Systems and the Political Process," in William Nisbet Chambers and Walter Dean Burnham (eds.), *The American Party Systems*, 2nd ed. (New York: Oxford University Press, 1975), p. 321.

[45] *Congressional Quarterly Weekly Report* 36 (April 22, 1978): 971–74.

[46] See George C. Edwards III, "Presidential Electoral Performance as a Source of Presidential Power," *American Journal of Political Science* 22 (1978): 152–68.

[47] Walter Dean Burnham, "Insulation and Responsiveness in Congressional Elections," *Political Science Quarterly* 90 (1975): 419.

Republican seats in 1974 won a second term; seventy-two of the total seventy-four freshman Democrats who sought reelection won.

In both instances, new members resisted a trend against their party more successfully than older members. The best explanation for this is that they behaved differently. Legislative activity and status and power accumulated in Congress through seniority had little to do with their success, obviously. Rather, they made energetic use of the perquisites of office to solidify their position back home. The younger Democrats in particular "exhibited great ingenuity and phenomenal tenacity in 'cultivating' their districts."[48]

The general point has been ably argued by Thomas E. Mann. He found that the district-level shifts in the vote from one election to the next show a much wider range of variation than could be accounted for by the national shifts from one party to the other. The difference from district to district depends largely on differences in the use incumbents make of their opportunities and resources. Members who use both to cultivate the district make themselves "safe." Those who do not can and will be successfully challenged.[49] This is the clear message of the last few elections. The lesson has been learned especially well by members first elected in the 1970s. Members who do not heed it are, indeed, likely to be weeded out by a sort of natural selection.

Constituency services and attention do pay off at the polls. But they may well detract from the job members do in Washington. The time, energy, and staff resources members use to pursue their separate reelection strategies back home in the district are taken from legislative chores on Capitol Hill. By concentrating on their individual electoral pursuits, members of Congress necessarily slight their collective policy-related activities. This naturally lessens the importance of the congressional parties. Another consequence is that the institutional performance of Congress declines as the electoral performance of its members improves. And this explains the otherwise surprising conjunction of strongly *negative* popular evaluations of Congress with quite *positive* assessments of individual members — and their monotonous reelection. As Fenno discovered, members appeal to constituents

---

[48] Charles M. Tidmarch, "The Second Time Around: Freshman Democratic House Members' 1976 Reelection Experiences," paper presented at the Annual Meeting of the American Political Science Association, Washington, D.C., September 1–4, 1977, p. 27.

[49] Mann, *Unsafe at Any Margin*, pp. 101–06.

by disassociating themselves from the institution; they run *for* Congress by running *against* Congress.[50] The implications of this pattern of activity for what goes on in the House and Senate, and particularly for the willingness of members to follow party and presidential leadership, are traced out in greater detail later.

THE CHANGING GENERATIONS

Since members of Congress have become harder to turn out of office since the mid-1960s, we might expect the turnover in congressional seats to be decreasing. Congress would be composed of an aging group of increasingly senior legislators. But that has not happened; quite the opposite. Although incumbents who run for reelection are winning more handily, fewer of them are choosing to run. Consider the data in Table 9.8. They are quite remarkable. The table lists the number of members retiring voluntarily from the House at the end of each session of Congress from 1966 through 1978. The increase in the number of voluntary retirees is striking. Of course some members "retire" to run for another office or to accept political appointment. But the proportion of "pure" retirements — members choosing to leave without aiming at another office — has remained steady at about 56 percent. Thus the number of pure retirements has gone up just as sharply.

The combination of greater electoral security and less inclination to seek reelection is only apparently paradoxical. They are actually explained by the same circumstances, for what has made incumbents more secure has also made the job less appealing to many members.

Constant cultivation of the district provides the margin of electoral safety. But it is an endless, time-consuming chore. Fenno points out that the trust members try to inspire in their constituents is not something that can be achieved once and for all. It must be built up, and *maintained*, by constant attention to the district. Service-oriented members must continue to deliver the services if they are to continue winning by comfortable margins.

But attention to the district detracts from work in Washington. Reelection is a means, not an end in itself, for most members. Congres-

[50] Fenno, *Home Style*, pp. 163–68.

TABLE 9.8
Voluntary Retirements from the House of Representatives, 1966–78

1966	(after Eighty-Ninth Congress)	12
1968	(after Ninetieth Congress)	13
1970	(after Ninety-first Congress)	7
1972	(after Ninety-second Congress)	28
1974	(after Ninety-third Congress)	30
1976	(after Ninety-fourth Congress)	47
1978	(after Ninety-fifth Congress)	49

Source: This table drawn from "Opting Out: Retirement from the House of Representatives 1966-1974," by Stephen E. Frantzich is reprinted from *American Politics Quarterly* Vol. 6 No. 3 (July 1978) pp. 251-273 by permission of the publisher, Sage Publications, Inc.; 1976 and 1978, *Congressional Quarterly Weekly Report*.

sional careers involve more than merely hanging on to the office. Success on the Hill means influencing policy, writing and passing legislation, and gaining the respect of one's colleagues. All of these things require attention to legislative and other duties that can only be given in Washington. The longer an individual is in Congress, the more opportunities open to pursue legislative and other policy-related goals. But they demand a different allocation of resources — of time, energy, and staff — than does the maximal pursuit of reelection. The contradictory demands of district and Washington service generate a tension that increases the longer a member remains in office.

Members are safe only as long as they continue to do what they have been doing. They may lose their security if they do not continue to use their resources to maintain constituency support. When, in time, they do more in Washington, less at home, they are likely to face increasingly serious electoral challenges. The campaign may become tougher and the struggle for reelection more arduous, if no less certain, statistically, rather than easier after the first few terms. An increasing number appear to be deciding that the game is not worth the candle.

These are not the only pressures retiring members mention. The pace and volume of work has grown enormously in recent years. Changes in rules and procedures intended to strengthen the legislative branch and to "reform" its operations (these will be discussed at length later) have made work on Capitol Hill more burdensome at the same time that constituency demands have grown. The issues Congress now faces are extraordinarily difficult and complex. The general public is in a surly mood, skeptical and suspicious of political institutions and politicians. And measures designed to bolster public confidence in members of Congress may have encouraged some to leave. The amount of money members may earn by outside activities is now limited to 15 percent of their salary; they are required to report yearly on their financial status and sources of income. Many can make much more money — with less work — elsewhere. And finally, more generous pensions enacted a few years ago may have made retirement more inviting than before.[51]

The growing number of retirements has meant a larger influx of new members into the most recent congresses. This trend was magnified among the Democrats by the Democratic sweep in the 1974 elections. The impact of this new generation of legislators has been extraordinary, for its members are by no means carbon copies of their predecessors.

Table 9.9 displays the trend toward an increasingly junior, inexperienced Democratic contingent in the House. Listed are the number of Democrats elected to the Ninetieth through Ninety-sixth Congresses and the proportion of each group composed of freshman and freshman and sophomore members. In the most recently completed congress, the Ninety-fifth, a full 43 percent of the Democrats were in their first or second term.

The average House member at the start of the Ninety-sixth Congress was 48.8 years old — the youngest since World War II.[52] A majority of all House members elected to the Ninety-sixth Congress in the fall of 1978 entered Congress no earlier than January 1975. The same is true of a majority of House Democrats; 152 of 277 were not in office when Richard Nixon was president. And the Senate is not immune from the same trend; forty-eight of its hundred members were serving their first term in the Ninety-sixth Congress.

The influx of new members is important because, to put it simply, they are quite different from their elders. This is hardly surprising. They are mostly people who came of political age during a decade of assassination, riot, protest, the Vietnam War, environmental crisis, energy shortages, political scandal, and a decline in respect for authority of all kinds — especially that of political institutions and leaders. If the Congress reflects, however imperfectly, American society, it would

---

[51] Richard E. Cohen, "Retiring from Congress — The Job Ain't What It Used to Be," *National Journal* 10 (March 11, 1978): 391–93.

[52] *Congressional Quarterly Weekly Report* 37 (January 27, 1979): 154.

TABLE 9.9
First- and Second-Term Democrats in the House of Representatives, 1967–79

Year and Congress	Number of Democrats	Percentage First Term	Percentage First and Second Term
1967 (90)	248	7	23
1969 (91)	243	7	16
1971 (92)	255	11	20
1973 (93)	248	10	20
1975 (94)	291	26	35
1977 (95)	290	16	43
1979 (96)	276	15	31

Source: After Table 4.5 (p. 82) in *Stability and Change in Congress* by Barbara Hinckley. Copyright © 1978 by Barbara Hinckley. Reprinted by permission of Harper & Row, Publishers, Inc.

be strange indeed if all this turmoil left the institution and its members unchanged. It has not.

The newer members tend to differ from their elders in political goals and strategies, expectations of themselves, standards of behavior, and attitudes toward parties, party leaders, and presidents. They have contributed heavily to transformations in the way Congress operates, with important consequences for the distribution of power among its members. Their aggressiveness and independence has, indeed, changed the entire tone of congressional life; retiring members often complain of it. The result has been new headaches — and new opportunities — for congressional party leaders. These developments are the subject of the next chapter.

10

The Congressional Parties:
Leaders and (Sometimes) Followers

PARTIES IN CONGRESS

The changing electoral environment — and the influx of new congressmen adept at carving out secure niches in it — has left few aspects of congressional life untouched. The impact on the congressional parties has been complex and profound. Any change that alters the effectiveness of the parties carries important institutional implications, for it is largely through the parties that Congress generates whatever *coherent* policy making it can muster. Parties are crucial to the collective legislative activities of Congress.

The House and Senate are highly decentralized bodies. Power and influence are widely distributed. Most important legislative activity and all administrative oversight — the major institutional functions of Congress — take place in separate committees or subcommittees.

Activity and authority in Congress are decentralized in order to allow *specialization*. The volume and complexity of matters that come before Congress require that members develop specialized knowledge of specific policy areas. This in turn requires a division of labor among members. Each needs to focus his legislative attention narrowly, since none has the time or energy to develop a thorough grasp of more than a few complex issues and questions. The alternative to developing specialized expertise in Congress is surrender of power to the experts in the White House, the administrative agencies, or the private sector. A decentralized system of standing committees with fixed jurisdictions is Congress's organizational strategy for survival as a significant policymaking institution. And largely because of its committee system, Congress has been able to maintain its authority far more successfully than most legislatures in other advanced democracies.

The decentralized and specialized committee system cannot work effectively without some regular means for coordinating the activities of the diverse parts. Although most important decisions are made in committee or subcommittee, bills and resolutions can be passed only by a majority of each house. The fragmented activity must be brought into some sort of harmony, the diverse membership welded together from time to time into majority coalitions, if Congress is to play its policymaking role. This is what the congressional parties are for. They operate to counteract the centrifugal tendencies of the committee system.

CONGRESSIONAL PARTY STRUCTURES

Members of Congress elect their own party leaders and run their own party organizations. The congressional parties are entirely their instruments and necessarily reflect their purposes. National party leaders, even presidents, are expected to keep their hands off, and they do. The main components of both parties in the House and Senate are quite similar, with one important exception. The head of the majority party in the House of Representatives is the Speaker, who is also the chief presiding officer of that body. Party leadership and House leadership are therefore formally united. The Speaker is assisted by the majority leader and the majority whip; these three run the party — and House — machinery on a day to day basis.

The Senate has no direct counterpart to the Speaker. The vice-president is its constitutionally designated presiding officer, and his duties, other than breaking tie votes, are largely ceremonial. So the majority leader is the head of the majority party in the Senate. He is also the principal leader of the whole Senate insofar as it ever allows itself to be led.

In both houses, the (currently Republican) minority is led by a minority leader, aided by the minority whip and his assistants. Each congressional party also maintains an organization composed of all members of the party as a body. The House Democrats call theirs a caucus; Senate Democrats and Republicans in both houses call it a conference. The elected chairman of the caucus (or conference) is also an important party leader (the majority leader retains this position in the Senate Democratic Conference). The business of these groups is often conducted by smaller executive committees, variously called policy, steering, or policy and steering committees, which normally work in tandem with the elected party leaders.

On paper, the caucus or conference has the final say in all party decisions, but their actual power varies from party to party, house to house, and time to time. Until a few years ago, they had been somnolent for a long time, content to ratify decisions made by party leaders. This is no longer true; the Democratic caucus has played a major part in bringing about far-reaching changes in House procedures, as we shall see.

MAJORITY PARTY LEADERSHIP IN THE HOUSE

Members of Congress have traditionally preferred party leaders who focus on the legislative process, giving little attention to the content of legislation. Party leaders of the majority in the House set the agenda, organize the distribution of work and plan and execute legislative strategy. They operate at the center of a network that gathers information on the progress of legislation through committees, schedules the workload (no small matter when so many members head for home, at government expense, every chance they get), and tries to keep count of the supporters and opponents of pending legislation. They are thus strategically situated to take a hand in the negotiations, compromises, bargains, and persuasive arguments through which legislative coalitions are pieced together.

The leaders are also well situated to put their own imprint on legislation, but they rarely exploit the opportunity. They are usually more interested in coming up with bills that can command majorities than with enacting specific measures. Party leaders normally formulate no independent "party policy" or "party program." If the president and the majority are of the same party, his proposals become the party program, and leaders take responsibility for passing the president's agenda (though rarely without modification). When the president's party is a minority in Congress, congressional majorities may enact alternatives to the president's proposals, but these are most often created in committee. The party program, such as it is, is merely a collection of measures churned out by the fragmented committee system.

Reflecting their role, party leaders are usually legislative pragmatists with moderate ideological commitments (within, of course, the context of their respective parties). But they are also party and institutional loyalists and consider the effectiveness of the party and the Congress as policymaking entities their responsibility. They therefore take pains to line up party (and opposition) support for the measures they adopt as the party's programs regardless of origin.

Congressional party leaders control some resources that help them to gather the support of party members, but not nearly enough to permit them to keep a tight rein on party members should they wish to do so. Control over the scheduling of legislation, for example, allows leaders to do favors for members. They may facilitate bills for members' pet projects or arrange for votes to be postponed when members are out of town. Such favors are useful bargaining chips for coalition building.

Party leaders are also influential in assigning members to committees. This is potentially the most valuable chip they hold. Committee assignments are very important to members. Many gravitate toward those committees which handle matters of interest to their constituents. Those representing farm areas want seats on Agriculture; westerners prefer Interior; members from coastal areas go after Merchant Marine and Fisheries. Appointment to the right committee can help ensure reelection by giving members additional means for serving their districts. Members also seek power over legislation and policy; this too is apportioned by the committee system. A good committee assignment can help where it counts in either case.

Traditional congressional wisdom held that control over committee assignments gave the party leaders special clout with junior members, who had yet to acquire choice committee seats. But this particular source of leadership influence has gradually dried up over the last two decades. Irwin Gertzog has shown that freshman committee assignments have become thoroughly routinized. They are much more automatic than discretionary and so not very amenable to manipulation by party leaders. His figures on freshman assignments to "semiexclusive" committees for three ten-year periods are presented in Table 10.1.[1] Between 1947 and 1955, only 38 percent of the House freshmen won seats on these relatively desirable committees. Between 1967 and 1975, the figure was 94 percent. Louis P. Westefield's work explains what has happened. Over the years, party leaders have increased the size of the desirable committees in order to control more rewards for encouraging loyalty and cooperation. They increased the supply of assignments to meet the demand. But scarcity determines the value of this as of any other currency. As the supply increases, scarcity decreases. In time, the currency loses its value. When nearly everyone can count on a desirable committee assignment, influence over committee assignments provides leaders little leverage.[2] Ironically, a potentially valuable resource for rewarding loyalty among junior members had withered away just as a horde of new members was entering the House.

THE DEMOCRATIC CAUCUS

Without question the most important party-related change to hit Congress in the 1970s was the emergence of the Democratic caucus as a powerful party agency. An increasingly assertive caucus has effected major changes in the way House business is conducted, and these have had a decisive impact on the distribution of power and influence in that body. House party leaders have both gained and lost power as a result,

[1] The distinction between "exclusive," "semiexclusive," and "nonexclusive" committees was made in the Legislative Reorganization Act of 1946. Exclusive committees are the most desirable; they are exclusive because House members who sit on them have no other committee assignments. Least desirable are the nonexclusive committees; semiexclusive committees are the best to which freshmen can aspire.

[2] Louis P. Westefield, "Majority Party Leadership and the Committee System in the House of Representatives," *American Political Science Review* 68 (1974): 1593–1604.

TABLE 10.1
Freshman Assignments to Semiexclusive Committees, 1947-75

Years	Congresses	Number	Percentage	Total Freshmen
1947–1955	80–84	143	38	378
1957–1965	85–89	227	69	329
1967–1975	90–94	289	94	306

Source: From Irwin N. Gertzog, "The Routinization of Committee Assignments in the House of Representatives," *American Journal of Political Science,* Vol. 20 (1976), p. 700. Reprinted by permission of the publisher, The University of Texas Press.

Note: These figures do not take into account transfers made during the first term. Moreover, if a freshman was initially assigned to two semiexclusive committees, both were included in these summary figures.

the net effect being important changes in the way leadership is exercised.

The revival of the Democratic caucus as a major party institution was inspired by the Democratic Study Group. The DSG was originally founded in 1959 by frustrated junior liberal Democrats. They hoped by pooling their numbers to provide a counterweight to the conservative southern Democrats who dominated the House leadership. The DSG has since grown to include more than two-thirds of all House Democrats, many of whom have now advanced through the seniority system to important committee and party leadership positions. It now constitutes the core of the Democratic party in the House. The DSG is chiefly responsible for all of the procedural reforms intended to "democratize" the workings of the House.

The DSG's first important success came in 1969 when it overrode Speaker John McCormack's objections to initiate regular meetings of the caucus. Before, meetings had been called at the Speaker's discretion, which meant rarely. Members were also accorded the right to place items on the agenda for the caucus to consider, which had also been the Speaker's prerogative. In 1971, the newly revived caucus enacted a rule that permitted debate on nominations made by the Committee on Committees. Up to that time, the caucus could only vote on them — a vote that was a mere formality. It passed another rule that forbade members to chair more than one subcommittee (though members already holding multiple chairmanships could keep them). This opened a number of subcommittee chairmanships to junior members.

Procedural reforms continued in 1973. The most important change was to make committee chairmen subject to election by secret ballot in the caucus if at least 20 percent of the caucus members requested it. This was a direct blow at the sacrosanct seniority system, through which members had been elevated to committee chairmanships — powerful positions in a body organized as the House is — by the criteria of reelection and longevity. The caucus also reduced the power of committee chairmen by giving the Democratic members on each committee the right to select subcommittee chairmen, set subcommittee budgets, guarantee each member a good subcommittee assignment, and set party ratios on subcommittees that reflected party ratios in the full House. Chairmen could no longer run their committees like independent despots.

The caucus reform movement reached its peak in 1975. The DSG contingent was bolstered by the votes of seventy-five freshmen Democrats, who gave nearly unanimous support to DSG-sponsored motions. Three committee chairmen who under the old rules would have held their positions automatically as senior Democrats in years of service on their committees were deposed. A fourth would have been voted out had he not voluntarily resigned his chairmanship. The formal authority to make committee assignments was taken away from the Democratic membership of the Ways and Means Committee and given to the caucus's own Steering and Policy Committee. The caucus also took over the right to determine the number and jurisdiction of subcommittees on each committee. And it transferred to the Speaker the power to nominate Democratic members of the powerful Rules Committee. Other minor changes aimed at opening choice subcommittee chairs to junior members were also adopted.

THE EFFECTS OF THE CAUCUS'S REFORMS

The effects of all these changes are not particularly difficult to assess. Committee chairmen lost a great deal of power. They are no longer the independent barons they once were, able to defy the party, the House, their committee's members, or just about anyone else. Most of their control over the committee has been absorbed by the caucus. And the caucus retains the ultimate sanction of deposition. Committee chairmen quickly recognized this and have adjusted their behavior accordingly. Richard P. Conlan, staff director of the DSG, summed up the consequences:

> The power of committee chairmen to punish members who oppose them has been sharply curtailed. Even if a chairman does have such power, he is less likely to use it because members can now retaliate when the chairman stands for reelection by secret ballot. . . . Thus chairmen who a few years ago expected members to be solicitous of them are solicitous of the members.[3]

The power lost by committee chairmen has been picked up by subcommittee chairmen, the Speaker, and the caucus. The effects on party authority have been contradictory. The Speaker's hand has been strengthened. He now controls the Rules Committee, which stands astride the flow of legislation coming out of committee to the floor of the House. He can now set up ad hoc committees to handle specific bills and choose their members. He also appoints eight of the twenty-three members of the caucus's Steering and Policy Committee which, among other powers, makes committee assignments. Plainly, the image of the Speaker dealing as the first among equals with the refractory committee barons is out of date. His power has grown while theirs has waned.

The invigoration of the caucus might also be interpreted as strengthening the congressional party. But if so, it must also be acknowledged that the caucus and the party leaders may frequently pull in opposite directions. The caucus is not easily led. One recent observer concluded,

> No one seems to control the caucus, or is able to lead all factions of the party. A majority, egalitarian body, the caucus is subject to direction by shifting factions and coalitions. Whether the Speaker or the Steering and Policy Committee has enough power to organize it and lead it over a sustained period of time is doubtful.[4]

A lingering source of conflict between the caucus and the senior party leaders is the question of what power the caucus ought to have

[3] Michael J. Malbin, "House Reforms — The Emphasis is on Productivity, Not Power," *National Journal* 8 (December 4, 1976): 1733.
[4] *Ibid.*, p. 1735.

over substantive policy. Its authority to decide procedural matters is not questioned. But its proper influence on legislation is a subject of much dispute. Both party and committee leaders reject the notion that they should bow to the wishes of the caucus majority on matters of substantive policy. Other members feel that the caucus should be heard on occasional important issues. And some younger members dream of the caucus taking a major legislative role as the voice of the majority party in the House.

The last is not a likely possibility, but the caucus has intervened in substantive matters on infrequent occasions. In 1975, heady after having ousted four committee chairmen, the caucus ordered the Rules Committee to let the House vote on a bill repealing the oil depletion allowance and passed a resolution opposing military aid to Vietnam and Cambodia. But, according to Representative Pete Stark, "that was about as much as some of the old fogeys could digest," and the protests of alarmed senior members put a temporary end to caucus votes on policy.[5]

Not until 1978 did the caucus again attempt to tell a committee what to do. Members worried about the upcoming election wanted to roll back a planned increase in the Social Security tax. They were resisted by the Ways and Means Committee, which would have sent such a bill to the floor, and were opposed by Speaker O'Neill, who supported the Carter administration's position against the rollback. But on April 5 the caucus voted 150 to 57 a nonbinding resolution urging the Ways and Means Committee to act on rollback legislation. A similar resolution was placed on the agenda of the caucus for January 1979.

The question of how much authority the caucus may legitimately exercise remains in doubt. Ironically, many of the strongest advocates of a policymaking caucus are junior members most prone to independence and least impressed by appeals to party loyalty. They want it both ways: independence plus effective policy control. The combination is not likely to come about. At present the caucus seems likely to avoid policy stances except on rare occasions. Were this to change it would be a major alteration in the role of the congressional party. In any case, it is clear that the caucus is as willing to resist party leaders as to follow them, and so if the congressional parties have been strengthened by the reforms of the 1970s, they have been strengthened in potentially conflicting directions.

[5] *Congressional Quarterly Weekly Report* 36 (April 15, 1978): 874.

SUBCOMMITTEE CHAIRMEN:
THE NEW BARONETS

A third consequence of the reforms, the enhanced power of sub-committees and subcommittee chairmen, has manifestly weakened the party and added to the difficulty of building party and House majorities. Subcommittee fiefdoms have replaced committee fiefdoms; at last count (in the Ninety-fifth Congress) there were 158 standing subcommittees. Once fragmented to the committee level, the House is now fragmented to the subcommittee level. Many more little bastions of power are distributed among many more individuals. This naturally pleases them, but it makes organizing the House for coherent policy making a more formidable chore than ever.

The devolution of power to subcommittees has the aspect of a revolt of youth against age. Younger members used the caucus, where their swollen numbers gave them the most strength, to wrest power from senior committee leaders. The powers absorbed by the caucus over the formation, appointment, and operation of subcommittees ensured the widest possible distribution of good subcommittee assignments and, most importantly, chairmanships.

So it is little wonder that junior members like the new system. It gives them an early opportunity to exercise real authority over legislation. Like other Americans of their generation, they are typically better educated, more independent of party, less awed by age and authority than were their predecessors. They seem to share the conviction that they were elected to lead, not follow. It is not surprising that they refused to wait around docilely until time, electoral security, and the seniority system elevated them to positions of power in the House. The new system they have fostered gives them a solid piece of the legislative turf early in their careers.

The wider distribution of subcommittee chairmanships also serves the electoral needs of junior members. Like full committees, subcommittees are frequently chosen for the opportunities they provide to serve district interests. Subcommittee chairmen are free to push legislation, pursue pet projects, or conduct investigations that generate favorable publicity back home.

Control of a subcommittee confers another valuable resource: subcommittee staff. Members have learned to rely on committee and subcommittee staffs to take over the legislative work that is slighted when personal staffs concentrate on serving constituents either in Washington or in district offices. "Right now," complained one member, "people want committees just so they can hire staff."[6]

The inevitable result of the demand for subcommittee chairmanships has been an increase in the supply, requiring, naturally, more subcommittees. The total number of subcommittees of all kinds grew, by one count, from 148 to 181 between 1974 and 1976. While serving the needs of individual members, the proliferation of subcommittees works against the collective policymaking effectiveness of the House as an institution. And it most clearly adds to the difficulty of exercising party leadership.

LEADING THE CONTEMPORARY HOUSE

The reforms of the 1970s have created an even more decentralized and fragmented power structure than existed in the heyday of the despotic chairmen. And this spells problems for anyone, party leader or president, who tries to lead the Congress. Coalition building is harder because there are so many more centers of power to deal with; it is no longer enough to win the support of a handful of prominent leaders. With more subcommittees, members face more meetings, more work with less time for it, more reasons to be away from the floor. Planning, scheduling, and coordinating the flow of legislation are therefore increasingly complicated and difficult tasks. And with junior members more assertive, independent, sensitive to constituency interests, and insistent on having a say in all manner of policy, leading Congress is a formidable job indeed.

Under the circumstances, the current Speaker, Thomas P. O'Neill, has been remarkably effective. Part of the reason is his own personal political style. "If the times demand a Speaker whose strong suits are persuasion and an ability to mediate disputes among warring factions of the House, O'Neill may be ideally suited."[7] One congressman "likened

---

[6]Quoted in Thomas E. Cavanagh, "The Two Arenas of Congress: Electoral and Institutional Incentives for Performance," paper presented at the 1978 Annual Meeting of the American Political Science Association, New York, N.Y., August 31–September 3, 1978, p. 32.

[7]Richard E. Cohen, "Tip O'Neill — He Gets By With a Little Help From His Friends," *National Journal* 10 (September 2, 1978): 1385.

O'Neill to a good parent with a lot of precocious but disagreeable children. 'He monitors the conflict until the parties work it out.' "[8]

O'Neill has also enlarged and extended the party's organizational apparatus to cope with the greater demands it now faces. The Democratic whip organization has been augmented. Party whips — the name comes from Britain, where the "whipper-in" keeps the hounds together during a fox hunt — form the essential information network that links party leaders and followers. They carry messages between leaders and party members, take straw polls, get members to the floor when their votes are needed, and help in the overall planning and execution of legislative strategy. Seven new whips were added by majority whip John Brademas when he took office in 1977. He now has a chief deputy whip, three deputy whips, ten at-large whips, and twenty-two zone whips. His 1979 budget of $416,800 for the whip organization was more than triple the 1970 budget. And there is little question that the larger whip operation is now necessary.[9]

The Speaker has also increasingly resorted to using special "task forces" to shepherd important bills through the House. Ad hoc groups of twenty-five or so Democratic members, frequently led by relatively junior Democrats, are put together to help the leaders carry out legislative plans. They count votes, persuade reluctant or wavering members to vote with the party, and let the Speaker know where his personal intervention would be effective. Task forces work closely with the whip organization, but "O'Neill has found the task forces to be useful supplements to the whip system because not all the assistant whips can be expected to support the leadership on each bill or be sufficiently familiar with all bills to lobby their colleagues."[10]

For especially important and sensitive legislative jobs, O'Neill sometimes exercises his right to appoint special legislative committees to supplement the work of the regular committees. They are most useful when important legislation falls under the jurisdiction of several standing committees. They also allow the Speaker to put bills in the hands of a committee whose members are chosen for their willingness to cooperate with the leadership. President Carter's welfare reform and energy proposals and the House's own earnings limitation and

[8]*Ibid.*, p. 1385.
[9]*Congressional Quarterly Weekly Report* 36 (May 27, 1978): 1302.
[10]Cohen, "Tip O'Neill," p. 1386.

financial disclosure measures were handled by ad hoc committees in the Ninety-fifth Congress.[11]

The measure of success for all of these party instruments is in their ability to persuade members to cooperate with the leaders. "Persuade" is the key term; leaders control few sanctions, and pleas for party or presidential loyalty are insufficient by themselves. O'Neill has often been persuasive, usually to the direct benefit of President Carter. The public works issue mentioned at the beginning of this chapter is exceptional in this regard. The Speaker is a staunch party loyalist. He regards Carter's programs — with few exceptions — as the party's programs, and the president's victories in the House (notable examples are the House's version of the administration's energy package and civil service reform) are largely traceable to his efforts. Party leadership in Congress is highly *personal;* it depends on the character and skills of individual leaders. O'Neill's abilities have prevented the full consequences of the changes in House rules and House membership from being felt.

MAJORITY PARTY LEADERSHIP IN THE SENATE

Although the most dramatic changes have taken place in the House, the Senate has not been immune to the same forces working there. Traditionally, party leaders in the Senate have been less powerful than their counterparts in the House. Individual Senate leaders — Lyndon Johnson is the best example — might accumulate a great deal of influence over the Senate, but it arises from personal rather than institutional characteristics. The Senate is a much smaller body than the House. The organizational imperatives that make the party's role so important in the House are much less compelling. Senators have a stronger tradition of independence and have always enjoyed greater opportunities for individual participation, influence, and obstruction. The difference now is that more members are taking advantage of them.

[11] *Ibid.*, pp. 1386–88.

Newer Senate members share the independent mood of young House members. But there, the tools available for exerting that independence are considerably more powerful.

Senate leaders must rely on custom and courtesy to keep debate restrained. But the informal checks have broken down in the last three years, and some more militant members have tied the Senate in procedural knots for days at a time.[12]

And not only newer members have freed themselves from procedural restraints. The late Senator James Allen, one of the most senior Democrats in the Senate, developed a variety of new obstructive tactics late in his career. Senate minorities have always enjoyed the right to filibuster — to talk legislation to death — because debate in the Senate is normally unlimited. Until the Ninety-fourth Congress, it took a two-thirds vote to invoke *cloture,* which shut off debate and allowed a vote to be taken. Filibusters became so common in the 1970s (more than half the cloture votes taken in the Senate's history have occurred since 1971[13]) that the rule was amended to require a three-fifths vote to pass a cloture motion. Senate Majority Leader Robert C. Byrd lamented in 1978 that "it used to be that it was resorted to only infrequently and on great national issues, mostly on civil rights. But anymore, it's just resorted to promiscuously, I think."[14]

Easier cloture has not solved the problem. Senator Allen pioneered the tactic of offering dozens of amendments to bills — each requiring some debate and a vote — after cloture has been invoked. And other obstructive techniques, such as withholding unanimous consent when it is needed to bypass time-consuming routines, have been exploited by single individuals seeking to kill or amend legislation. Senator Mike Gravel "went so far as to include the text of former President Nixon's memoirs within an amendment he offered and then invoke his right to require the reading of the entire amendment."[15]

Late in 1978 Majority Leader Byrd proposed changes in the rules which would allow the leadership to restrict postcloture filibuster-by-amendment and to limit other dilatory tactics, but it was not at all certain they would be accepted by the Senate. "One or two members

[12] *Congressional Quarterly Weekly Report* 36 (September 2, 1978): 2306.

[13] *Congressional Quarterly Weekly Report* 36 (March 1, 1978): 452.

[14] *Congressional Quarterly Weekly Report* 36 (September 2, 1978): 2307.

[15] Richard E. Cohen, "The 96th Congress Is in for an Overhaul," *National Journal* 10 (November 25, 1978): 1910.

can, when time is running out, resort to obstructionist tactics and endanger any bill they're opposed to," Byrd complained. "And while they're doing that they're also endangering passage of other measures which will be caught in the backlog."[16] Senators across a spectrum from liberal Democrats to conservative Republicans have been guilty, but few show signs of any remorse. They argue that they are simply using the rules to protect their interests and have a perfect right to do so. A consequence has been very tough going on controversial proposals backed by the administration and Senate party leaders. The president's energy package, which took two years to get through the Senate and emerged bearing very little resemblance to what Carter asked for, is the most conspicuous example.

SENATE COMMITTEES

The Senate has been slower in redistributing power downward to more junior members through the committee system. One reason is that junior Senators already enjoyed the kind of legislative influence coveted by young House members. A major reform of the Senate committee structure (reducing the number of standing committees, altering the jurisdictions of many) was carried out in 1977. A rule increasing the number of subcommittee chairmanships open to junior members, taking effect in 1979, was also passed. A senator who chairs a full committee may chair only one subcommittee of any major Senate committee plus one of a minor committee. Senators who are not committee chairmen may chair one subcommittee of every committee on which they sit. The effect is to reduce the number of subcommittees chaired by senior members, opening more positions to junior members.[17] Most senior Democrats voted against the proposal, but to no avail. Junior senators have the advantage of numbers and so are able, like their counterparts in the House, to force a redistribution of power in their favor. If results in the Senate match those in the House, more members will control a piece of the legislative action, fostering more fragmentation and more headaches for the leadership.

[16] *Congressional Quarterly Weekly Report* 36 (September 2, 1978): 2307.
[17] Richard E. Cohen, "Take Your Pick," *National Journal* 9 (September 17, 1977): 1457.

THE MINORITY PARTY IN CONGRESS

The Democratic party has controlled both houses of Congress for more than twenty years. Any study of the congressional parties and their impact on policy making therefore naturally focuses on Democrats and slights Republicans. But the Republican minority does merit some attention, if only because Republican votes are often essential to Democratic (and presidential) victories, and coalitions of Republicans and dissident Democrats are often fatal to them.

Minority members share equally in the abundant official resources useful for pleasing constituents and winning reelection. In that they are protected by what Mayhew calls "powerful norms of institutional universalism." The result, he says, is that "in a good many ways the interesting division in congressional politics is not between Democrats and Republicans, but between politicians in and out of office. Looked at from one angle, the cult of universalism has the appearance of a cross-party conspiracy among incumbents to keep their jobs."[18]

But universalism does not necessarily extend to universal participation in policy making. Democrats control the committees, their staffs, the schedule, and the agenda. Opportunities for the minority to have a creative impact on legislation depend on the good will of the majority. And in the Ninety-fifth Congress, the Democrats, at least in the House, have not been particularly gracious. "As far as interplay between the minority and the majority, there is very little because that is the way the majority wants it," said House Minority Leader John J. Rhodes in 1977. "Tip O'Neill used to say to me when he was majority leader, 'If you Republicans think you are going to have anything to do with legislation, forget it.' "[19]

Minority leadership in the House is rather a thankless task. With so few votes (146 of 435 in the Ninety-fifth Congress) the party cannot hope to enact any programs of its own. Any good ideas are adopted by the Democrats, who then take the credit. The leader may be hard pressed just to keep up the morale of his troops. And their frustrations are often taken out on the leader. Twice in the last twenty years House Republicans have deposed their leader. Charles Halleck unseated

[18] Mayhew, *Congress*, p. 105.
[19] Richard E. Cohen, "House Republicans Under Rhodes — Divided They Stand and Fret," *National Journal* 9 (October 29, 1977): 1686.

incumbent Minority Leader Joseph Martin in 1958, only to be defeated himself six years later by Gerald Ford. Each defeat followed drastic election setbacks. Republicans lost forty-seven House seats in 1958 and forty-eight in 1964. During the same period, the Democratic Speaker has rarely been challenged and never seriously threatened.[20]

During the Ninety-fifth Congress, House Republicans were again grumbling about their leaders. Congressman Mickey Edwards complained in a speech that "the Republican Party in Congress is nothing more than a custom, an old relative hanging around the party, with no purpose, no influence, and no power." His party, he said, was one

> without leadership, with a caucus that never meets, with no official party positions on any major piece of legislation before Congress, with few real alternatives on anything, with no regular spokesman on the House floor, with floor managers who look like, sound like, and vote like the floor managers for the Democrats.[21]

Complaints are heard mainly from junior Republican members who want their party to take stands on policy clearly distinct from those of the Democrats. They tend to be more conservative and more firmly attached to their ideological moorings than their seniors. As the Democratic party has extended its appeal to cover a broader spectrum of opinion, the shrinking Republican party has become increasingly narrow, and more conservative, in its range of views. This has made the party a more cohesive, if smaller, force in congressional politics. But it has troubled leaders like Rhodes who doubt that doctrinaire conservatism will lead to majority status for the party.

Despite criticisms directed at Rhodes during the Ninety-fifth Congress, he was not challenged for the minority leadership of the Ninety-sixth. And the Republican record for the Ninety-fifth Congress was not without significant legislative successes. Republicans managed to frustrate both the Democratic leadership and President Carter on occasions when the Democrats split and the Republicans stuck together. For example, House Republicans voted 129 to 14 against the common situs picketing bill, which would have changed the labor laws to permit unions fighting one subcontractor at a construction site to picket all of them. Enough Democrats deserted their party to kill the bill. Demo-

---

[20] Barbara Hinckley, *Stability and Change in Congress*, 2nd ed. (New York: Harper and Row, 1978), pp. 121–26.

[21] Cohen, "House Republicans," p. 1686.

cratic divisions give a united Republican party the opportunity at least to stop legislation they oppose even if they cannot initiate their own proposals.

Republicans do this even more effectively in the Senate, where their numbers are proportionately greater and where the rules allow minorities a great deal more room for maneuver. Republican Senate leadership is very loose; the minority leader is not even permitted to chair the conference or its Policy Committee. But effective opposition in the Senate does not depend much on organization.

Republican senators — and representatives, for that matter — have a long history of cooperation with conservative members of the Democratic party. The Democrats have been divided on ideological lines for years. The divisions are also usually, though not invariably, regional. Conservative southern Democrats regularly find they have things in common with their conservative Republican colleagues. The so-called "conservative coalition" that results has been a familiar element in congressional politics since the 1940s. And when the coalition is formed, it usually wins. *Congressional Quarterly* has kept track of all recorded House and Senate votes since the early 1950s. Its figures on the conservative coalition's frequency of appearance in recorded votes and its frequency of victory when it did appear from 1961 through 1977 are given in Table 10.2. These data show the coalition to be generally successful in both houses. And it was particularly successful in the Senate during Carter's first year in office. Conservatives won ten of thirteen votes in the Senate when they opposed Carter. In the House, the president won twelve of twenty-two of the votes that pitted him against the coalition.[22]

The conservative coalition is of course another problem for Democratic party leaders. It should not be overlooked simply because it is a familiar, rather than new, source of aggravation. It also splits the Republican party to some degree. In 1977, for example, House Republicans supported the coalition 76 percent of the time, southern Democrats 63 percent of the time, and northern Democrats 23 percent of the time. The corresponding figures for the Senate were 72 percent, 64 percent, and 23 percent. Some members have suggested making the coalition permanent and using it to organize the Congress. Representative Joe Waggoner made the following comment in 1973: "Don't be too

[22] *1977 Congressional Quarterly Almanac*, p. 16B.

TABLE 10.2
The Conservative Coalition in Congress, 1961–77

Year	Appearances[a]	Total	Victories: Senate	House
1961	28%	55%	48%	74%
1962	14	62	71	44
1963	17	50	44	67
1964	15	51	47	67
1965	24	33	39	25
1966	25	45	51	32
1967	20	63	54	73
1968	24	73	80	63
1969	27	68	67	71
1970	22	66	64	70
1971	30	83	86	79
1972	27	69	63	79
1973	23	61	54	67
1974	24	59	54	67
1975	28	50	48	52
1976	24	58	58	59
1977	26	68	74	60

Source: From *1977 Congressional Quarterly Almanac*, p. 16-B. Reprinted by permission of Congressional Quarterly, Inc.
[a] Percentage of recorded votes in which conservative coalition appeared.

surprised if eventually some efforts are made to take control of the majority in the House through a coalition that wouldn't require change in party registration." To conservative Democrats he said, "You wouldn't have left your old Democratic friends back home, you'd have brought them some more influence, instead."[23] The idea may have seemed less farfetched right after the 1972 election; that it could be suggested by a member of Congress is an indication of the forces that divide the congressional parties, especially the Democrats.

THE PERILS OF OPENNESS

The trend toward fragmentation and independence that challenges party leaders in Congress has been reinforced by other changes in congressional rules. Measures intended to open congressional activities to closer public scrutiny have had the unanticipated consequence

[23] Hinckley, *Stability and Change*, p. 137.

of making it harder for Congress to get its work done and for leaders to lead. A rule adopted in 1970 requires recorded teller votes when the House acts as a Committee of the Whole, which it often does to free itself from some of the constraints of its own rules. The growth in the number of House teller votes and of comparable Senate votes since then is apparent in Table 10.3. The number of House teller votes increased from 266 to 834 in eight years. Recorded Senate votes were fewer in 1977 and 1978, evidently because of the six weeks spent debating the Panama Canal treaties and the growing use of obstructive delaying tactics.

Recorded teller votes take time, about fifteen minutes each. The old unrecorded votes took about five minutes. Hence the time members must spend on the floor has increased without any matching increase in legislative productivity. The 834 teller votes in 1978 took over 200 hours of House floor time. Any twenty members could request a teller vote be taken, and the demand for recorded votes was sometimes used to obstruct action by using up the House's time.

Recorded votes have another effect. They make members' actions more visible, exposing them to more pressure from interest and constituency groups. Lobbyists have been quick to take advantage of this. A number of observers have remarked on the notable increase in the sophistication and effectiveness of lobbyists working in Washington during the Ninety-fifth Congress.

Business organizations, taking their cue from public affairs activists such as Common Cause and Ralph Nader, organized highly effective

TABLE 10.3
Roll Call Votes in Congress, 1971–78

Year	House	Senate	Total
1971	320	423	743
1972	329	532	861
1973	541	594	1135
1974	537	544	1081
1975	612	602	1214
1976	661	688	1349
1977	706	635	1341
1978	834	516	1350

Source: From *Congressional Quarterly Weekly Report,* October 21, 1978, p. 2999. Reprinted by permission of Congressional Quarterly, Inc.

grass-roots lobbying campaigns and were able, for example, to block enactment of legislation establishing a consumer protection agency.

The anti-abortion lobby was responsible for enactment of strict language prohibiting the government from paying for most abortions with Medicaid funds or military appropriations.

The women's lobby was surprisingly successful in persuading Congress to extend for 39 months the deadline for ratification of the Equal Rights Amendment.

The Health industry took on the administration on the question of mandatory ceilings on hospital rates and prevented one of the president's most significant bills from being enacted.[24]

Responsiveness to pressure groups is, of course, a natural companion of the electoral environment members confront. Politicians closely attuned to their constituencies are especially sensitive to interests that can work through the grass roots. And the system of campaign finance also encourages them to take the views of potential donors — to their own or their opponents' campaigns — into account when they cast their votes.

A growing number of committee and subcommittee meetings have also been opened to the public, and with similar results. Members recognize that what they do in committee will be monitored by interested pressure groups and constituents; their maneuverability is therefore constrained. In the past, party leaders were sometimes able to trade for crucial *secret* votes in committee from members who could not publicly support particular bills — southern Democrats with civil rights legislation, for example. Opening the process to public view makes such deals impossible.

PARTY UNITY IN CONGRESS

Both participants and observers unanimously agree that the most recently completed Congress, the Ninety-fifth, was stubbornly resistant to party and presidential leadership. Data on congressional voting lend empirical support to this view, but they probably underestimate

[24] *Congressional Quarterly Weekly Report* 36 (October 21, 1978): 3000.

the extent of disagreement within, particularly, the Democratic party. The *Congressional Quarterly* classifies any vote in which a majority of one party votes one way and a majority of the other party votes the other way as a party vote. Party unity scores for individuals and groups in Congress are then computed as the percentage of party votes in which they vote with their party's majority.

The proportion of votes classified as party votes fell from 46 percent in the 1950s to 43 percent in the 1960s and to 39 percent in the 1970s. Fewer votes now find majorities of both parties on opposite sides. Party unity has fallen, too. Among Democrats, it has gone from 69 percent to 66 percent to 64 percent across these decades. Among Republicans, it fell from 71 percent to 68 percent to 66 percent. The trend in these general figures has not been uniformly downward, however. Party unity was somewhat higher in the Ninety-fourth Congress and in the first session of the Ninety-fifth Congress than it had been in the previous five congresses. These figures plainly do not tell the whole story. They do not indicate how important a vote was, nor do they measure how much effort leaders had to put into rounding up members' votes. And they do not take into account the times when party leaders, after counting heads, decide against bringing a bill to the floor because they are likely to lose.

More detailed studies of voting in the Ninety-fifth Congress provide a clearer picture of what has been happening. The generation gap that develops on procedural issues also appears on substantive matters, but in a much more complicated way. *Northern* freshman and sophomore Democrats are significantly less supportive of the Democrat's traditional ally, organized labor. Ironically, these younger Democrats have received much more campaign money from labor groups than have their seniors. But votes are even more important than money. Their reluctance to support labor's proposals is directly connected to their electoral circumstances. A large proportion of them — almost half — were elected to seats that had previously been held by Republicans. And it is this group that diverges most strikingly from other Democrats in voting on labor-related issues.[25]

Generational differences appear on some other issues as well. The "Watergate" generation of House Democrats are more supportive of

[25] William Schneider and Gregory Schell, "The New Democrats," *Public Opinion* 1 (November/December, 1978): 7–13.

defense spending than are members with slightly more seniority. Indeed, they are more "conservative" in this regard than even the most senior group. Those members who entered the House while Vietnam was the dominant issue are still the most skeptical of defense spending and the most reluctant to commit American troops abroad. But on environmental issues, the class of 1974 remains more "liberal" than any other group of Democrats. Sixty percent of the northern Democrats in the class of 1976 voted to relax auto emissions standards, whereas only 41 percent of their colleagues from the previous class did so, for example. Members seem to carry the scars of whatever major issues predominated at the time they were first elected to Congress.[26]

Still, the most formidable barrier to party and presidential influence in Congress lies in the electoral connection. The extension of the Democratic party into districts once held by Republicans brought swollen Democratic majorities into Congress. But at the same time it broadened the ideological base of the party to include many views once represented by Republicans. Greater internal strain has been the inevitable consequence. The interests of old and new components of the Democratic coalition are not easily reconciled. And individual members find it prudent to work out their own separate solutions. Representative Floyd J. Fithian, first elected in 1974 to a district that had been held by a Republican as long as anyone could remember, put it this way:

> Subconsciously, I began to realize that being a Democrat from the 2nd District of Indiana is a high-risk game politically and that the Democratic leadership in the House and the president didn't elect me. If the 535,000 people of my district perceive me as standing up to the president on one vote and the Chamber of Commerce on the other, they react positively.[27]

Herein lies the principal source of President Carter's problems with Congress. But there are others, too, and they are the subject of the next chapter.

[26] Michael J. Malbin, "New Democrats Don't See Eye to Eye With Their Senior Colleagues," *National Journal* 9 (July 9, 1977): 1080–81.

[27] Quoted in Richard E. Cohen, "The Big Issue for November is the Voter's Pocketbook," *National Journal* 10 (August 12, 1978): 1275.

11

Congress and the President

EXPECTATIONS AND REALITY

A superficial glance at the results of the 1976 elections might have suggested that the United States was about to enter a period of amiable and effective cooperation between the president and Congress. Democrats took the White House for the first time in eight years and maintained large majorities in both houses of Congress. The new leader of the House Democrats, Speaker O'Neill, was a dedicated party loyalist, experienced in the ways of the House and committed to the concept that the president's program was the party's program. The Senate majority leader was also a skilled parliamentary expert who was generally committed to supporting the Democratic president. After nearly a decade of often grim conflict between the White House and Capitol Hill, a government united by the bonds of party loyalty appeared to be at hand.

It did not, of course, work out quite that way. For the first two years of President Carter's term in office, relations between the president and Congress were anything but easy. One reason is that the congressional party leaders' troubles are usually the president's troubles also.

The aggressive independence of the current crop of congressmen works against the president as well as the party. Bare appeals for loyalty to President Carter are no more effective than bare appeals for party loyalty.

But the problem has been magnified by both recent historical experiences and the performance of the Carter administration itself. Either would be a source of real difficulties; their combination has aggravated matters considerably.

THE BATTERED PRESIDENCY

Carter had the singular misfortune to assume the presidency at a time when it had been seriously damaged by the actions of his recent predecessors — and by congressional responses to them. The almost automatic bipartisan support postwar presidents had enjoyed in foreign affairs had disappeared under the impact of the Vietnam War. First President Johnson, then President Nixon faced growing resistance to their war policies in Congress. Congress never took decisive action hindering the war effort until nearly all of the American forces were out of Vietnam. But after the issue of "protecting our boys overseas" was eliminated, Congress enacted a number of measures designed to restrict the president's freedom of action beyond the United States borders.

The most prominent measure, the 1973 War Powers Act, is largely symbolic. It requires congressional review and, if military actions ordered by the president are to continue, congressional approval. Congress is not likely to withdraw support while Americans are fighting and the president is rallying people behind the "national interest," so it is not clear how much this act actually restricts presidential initiatives. More effective have been laws that forbid the president to use money appropriated by Congress to intervene in foreign conflicts. Congress forbade money to be spent on bombing Cambodia in 1973; other military operations in Vietnam were banned in 1975. In 1976, Congress effectively prohibited military aid to Angola by requiring that it first be approved by Congress. Congress seems most successful when it restricts presidential actions *before* they take place.

Other specific problems for the president arise from the widening connection between foreign and domestic affairs. Carter had to overcome stiff resistance organized by the small but effective Greek-American lobby to get Congress to lift the embargo on arms for Turkey, a NATO ally. He faced similar difficulties from the much larger pro-Israeli contingent when he moved to sell military aircraft to Egypt and Saudi Arabia. In both instances, strong Republican support was essential to the administration's success. Senate Democrats opposed the Mideast arms sale 33 to 28 and split 31 to 31 on the Turkey embargo. Republicans supported both, 26 to 11. More generally, the Arab oil boycott of 1973 and the consequent shortages of gasoline and heating oil forcefully focused public attention on the domestic ramifications of what went on overseas. Members of Congress recognize that the United States's economic interdependence with the rest of the world means that foreign events can have immediate and drastic domestic effects. They are therefore less inclined to follow any president's lead automatically without assessing the consequences for their own concerns.

In spite of these difficulties, Carter, like most presidents before him, has drawn more support from Congress for his foreign policy initiatives than for his domestic programs. But it is only a relative advantage. It took a massive effort by the White House and Majority Leader Byrd and his allies to persuade the Senate to ratify the Panama Canal treaties. His choice to negotiate a new strategic arms limitation agreement with the Soviet Union, Paul Warnke, had difficulty winning Senate confirmation and ultimately had to resign because hawkish senators from both parties would be biased against any treaty he negotiated.

Congressional assertiveness on foreign affairs is not confined to any single partisan or ideological faction. Conservatives as well as liberals have become accustomed to opposing the president's foreign policies when they see fit. The collective result is a Congress no longer willing to simply follow the administration's foreign policy lead. Support must be solicited by the usual means of political persuasion. And it is by no means certain that the administration will always win. The fragmenting of power in Congress and the stubborn independence of its members make the problem worse. Representative Lee H. Hamilton remarked,

> It used to be that the Secretary of State could call up Arthur Vandenburg [a senior Republican senator in the 1940s] and that was consultation

enough. No more. Now there is no single individual who can say what the mood of Congress is on a range of foreign policy issues. It is very hard, especially because many foreign policy issues don't come out of the Foreign Relations and International Relations Committees at all.[1]

BUDGET REFORM

It was in the area of domestic policy, however, that congressional habits of resistance rather than deference to presidential policy initiatives developed most fully. The lessons learned in the struggles between Democratic congressional majorities and Republican presidents have not been quickly forgotten. And institutional innovations designed to strengthen Congress's ability to make policy in confrontation with Republican presidents have not fallen into disuse with the election of a Democratic president.

The foundation of Congress's power as a political institution is its control of the budget. Money to do any and all of the things the federal government undertakes must be raised, authorized, and appropriated by acts of Congress. During the postwar years prior to the Nixon administration, Congress had been content to watch much of its budget-making authority slip away to the administration. This was partly a consequence of the way Congress operates. The decentralized committee/subcommittee system promotes fragmented decision making on financial as well as other matters. The aggregate fiscal effects of the balance of authorized expenditures and federal revenues raised by the mix of taxes imposed were systematically overlooked before Congress established its own budget office and budgetary process. Presidents do concern themselves with such comprehensive fiscal questions, and wisely so; the health of the economy is closely linked to their political fortunes. The Office of Management and Budget is the institutional embodiment of the president's intense interest in the federal budget.

Congress's instinct is to make citizens happy by (1) authorizing and funding as many programs as possible and (2) cutting taxes. The sepa-

[1] Quoted in William J. Lanouette, "Who's Setting Foreign Policy — Carter or Congress?" *National Journal* 10 (July 15, 1978): 1121.

rate interest of each member is in providing programs that please constituents without worrying about the collective impact on the budget of all of them doing the same thing. But the aggregate result is too much spending. That means either raising taxes or having too large a deficit, neither one politically desirable. For years the problem was solved by leaving it up to the president. The president, his eye on the deficit and its negative economic consequences, would "impound" — refuse to spend — some of the funds Congress authorized, saving the country (and the Congress) from the effects of congressional generosity. Members could happily claim credit for at least authorizing services without suffering the embarrassment of presenting a bill for them to the public.

This mechanism for controlling federal spending broke down during the Nixon administration. Nixon refused to play the game. He used impoundment to impose his own spending priorities on Congress and to subvert those of the Democratic majority. Even authorizations passed over his veto were impounded. The challenge to Congress as an institution was unmistakable, and Congress understandably responded. Language in existing laws that the Nixon administration used to justify impoundments was removed. Procedures were set up to keep Congress informed about impoundments and to compel the release of impounded funds if Congress chose to do so. Most importantly, Congress took steps to alter its own procedures so that impoundment would not be necessary to keep the gap between revenue and spending from becoming too wide. And these were *congressional,* not partisan Democratic moves; they had the overwhelming support of both parties in both houses.

The centerpiece of the legislation restricting presidential impoundment, the 1974 Congressional Budget and Impoundment Control Act, was the establishment of a Budget Committee in each house. The task of these committees is to help Congress keep its spending and revenue-raising policies in harmony. Each spring, the budget committees must report a budget resolution setting spending and revenue targets for the fiscal year beginning the following October. Once the budget resolution is adopted, the regular committees go to work on their segments of the budget as before. But they are now expected to abide by the constraints imposed by the budget resolution.

In the fall, when work has been completed on the appropriations and tax bills, the budget committees review the result. If the targets set in the spring have not been met, the budget committees can recommend reducing spending, raising taxes, or revising the original goals. Congress is thus forced to determine the size of the deficit. It must acknowledge the fiscal consequences of the myriad separate decisions that are made during the session.

It is still too early to judge whether or not the new budget process will give Congress the kind of control over the budget it desires. So far, the results are mixed. The system has occasionally bent (the Senate budget resolution has been ignored by some committees) but not broken under the pressure to do what is individually pleasant (providing services and projects) without paying the price (raising taxes). Members have even learned to use the budget resolution to appear generous and tight-fisted at the same time. They vote for all kinds of items that add to the budget, then vote against the higher deficit they would produce. "That's the beauty of the budget process," explained one House member. "You can vote for all your favorite programs, and then vote against the deficit."[2]

Least happy with the new budget process are the senior committee chairmen, especially those heading the important financial committees (Appropriations and Ways and Means in the House, Appropriations and Finance in the Senate). The weakened House chairmen are in no position to do much about it, but the chairman of the Senate Finance Committee, Russell Long, has fought, with a fair degree of success, to keep his committee's power intact.

Having cranked up the machinery to do their own budgeting with Republicans in the White House, congressional Democrats have not seen fit to let it rust away now that a Democrat lives at the other end of Pennsylvania Avenue. Congressional and presidential priorities inevitably clash, and Congress is in a much stronger position than it was a few years ago to hold its own in budgetary contests. "Congress," said Senator Henry Bellmon, "as I am hopeful the president will one day fully understand, now has its own budgetary process. It is a good budgetary process. It is working."[3] It is, but not necessarily for President Carter.

---

[2] Joel Havemann, "Budget Process Nearly Ambushed By Carter and By Congress," *National Journal* 9 (May 21, 1977): 787.

[3] Joel Havemann, "The Congressional Budget Committee — High Marks After the First Years," *National Journal* 8 (September 25, 1976): 1351.

AN "OUTSIDER" IN THE WHITE HOUSE

Congress now has more tools, and more inclination, to challenge presidents of whatever party. Any president elected in 1976 could expect some resistance to his programs and policies. But the circumstances of Jimmy Carter's election and the performance of his administration in its dealings with Congress during his first two years in office plainly aggravated the situation.

President Carter's difficulties with congressional Democrats are not surprising. He campaigned for the presidency as an "outsider" to both the regular Democratic party and the whole federal establishment in Washington of which, according to Fiorina, Congress is the keystone. He won the nomination through primary election victories without the help — and against the preferences — of regular party organizations, beating several senators and a representative in the process. His general election campaign was financed entirely by the federal government, not the old Democratic contributors and fund raisers. His stance as an outsider was no small part of his popular appeal. But a president who rides into office on a groundswell of public disaffection with national political institutions — the parties, the Congress, the federal bureaucracy — naturally faces a problem. He must work with and through those institutions when he turns to the task of governing the country.

The people Carter brought to Washington to help him govern were also "outsiders," most of them from Georgia. They were in the beginning less than adept at dealing with Congress. Members frequently complained of the inexperience and ineptitude of the administration, its failure to understand how Congress and the rest of the Washington establishment works. "The people at the top of the administration don't understand Congress and they don't show any desire to learn," remarked a House leadership aide early in 1978.[4]

The administration was criticized for not consulting congressional leaders while legislative proposals were being formulated. Leaders were brought to the White House for "consultation" *after* legislation had been drafted and submitted to Congress, hardly an effective way of building support. Another complaint was that the president did not

---

[4] Richard E. Cohen, "The Carter-Congress Rift — Who's Really to Blame?" *National Journal* 10 (April 22, 1978): 630.

support his supporters. For example, Carter had proposed a fifty-dollar tax rebate for all taxpayers to stimulate the economy. When the idea ran into trouble in Congress, he abruptly dropped it, arguing that it was no longer needed because the economy had improved. Members who had loyally defended the controversial measure were left to deal with their embarrassment as best they could. On another occasion, Carter and Vice-President Mondale helped to stop a filibuster that was organized to support the administration's own natural gas pricing policy, an important part of Carter's energy package.[5]

The main congressional complaint, however, was that the administration did not recognize that real political horse trading was an essential part of the game. "Washington is very much a city of 'You scratch my back, I'll scratch your back,' " observed Representative Norman Y. Mineta. But Carter "deals with issues on a vertical plane. He won't say to you 'I need your vote on Mideast arms sales and therefore I will give you the dam you want in your district.' "[6]

By his second year in office, Carter appeared to be learning how things were actually accomplished in Washington. "We had an overly optimistic impression that I could present a bill to the Congress which to me seemed patently in the best interest of our country and that the Congress would take it and pretty well pass it," he told an interviewer. "I have been disabused of that expectation."[7] Liaison with Congress was greatly improved; federal agencies became more responsive to requests from members. Consultation became somewhat more frequent. The administration worked hard to pass its proposals and was more willing to strike political bargains when necessary. By the end of the second session of the Ninety-fifth Congress the president had won some important legislative victories. But by then, many of the ambitious programs sent to Congress two years earlier were all but forgotten.

This had been another problem for the administration and for congressional party leaders. The president's long agenda of controversial bills had overloaded the system. Party leaders are most effective if they can focus on one important piece of legislation at a time. But they were asked to handle a series of complex and divisive measures on taxes,

[5] *1977 Congressional Quarterly Almanac*, pp. 65A–67A.
[6] *Congressional Quarterly Weekly Report* 36 (September 2, 1978): 2304.
[7] Joel Havemann, "Will Late-Session Successes Spoil Jimmy Carter?" *National Journal* 10 (December 2, 1978): 1943.

welfare, energy, hospital costs, civil service, labor regulation, consumer protection, and foreign policy in a single congress. Speaker O'Neill remarked early in 1978 that Carter had simply made too many promises during his campaign. "He finds himself in a dilemma," O'Neill said. It is "impossible to do everything, but we'll help him as much as we can."[8] And the Democratic leadership in Congress did work hard for most of the administration's legislative proposals. Without this effort, Carter's legislative record would have been much worse. In this sense, party bonds were by no means trivial.

RALLYING THE PEOPLE

Members of Congress of course criticize presidents from the biased perspective of the Hill. Thus not all of what they would call administration "mistakes" would be considered errors from the administration's point of view. The act in Carter's first year that most upset congressional Democrats (and Republicans, for that matter) was his unilateral decision to withdraw funds for eighteen water projects from the 1978 budget. No one in Congress was forewarned about the decision, which challenged Congress's traditional control over pork barrel projects. It is an article of faith among congressmen that such projects pay big reelection dividends. Congressional outrage forced Carter to back down somewhat, shortening the list of eliminated projects. Congress finally agreed to kill nine. But Carter revived his attack on the pork barrel with his veto of the public works bill. And he won. This was no mistake, based on a misunderstanding of Congress. It was a deliberate decision not to play by the old rules.

Carter's public works veto was sustained because enough members of Congress sensed that their constituents supported the idea. Many Republicans and junior Democrats ignored the pleas of their party leaders because they were worried about how voters would respond in the upcoming elections. The president was, in this instance, resorting to a tactic familiar to his predecessors: using public support — or the perception of it — to bend Congress to his will.

[8]Cohen, "Carter-Congress Rift," p. 632.

It is not a tactic the administration used frequently. Consider the president's energy program, for example. The energy package clearly had top priority. Carter announced it with a nationally televised speech in which he declared the energy crisis to be the "moral equivalent of war," implying that a wartime spirit of selflessness was called for. But when his package of proposals was predictably attacked, chopped up, and rearranged by various special interests and their congressional allies from oil- and gas-producing states, he did not counter with further appeals to a broader public, rallying support for the "national interest," but instead allowed his program to be reduced to a small holding operation. Nothing was done to reduce the ever-growing importation of foreign oil and its baneful effects on the balance of trade. Even the natural gas pricing legislation that was finally enacted after a long legislative struggle (which pitted the administration and the Democratic congressional leadership against both Democratic liberals and Democratic members from oil- and gas-producing states) was scarcely what Carter had requested.

In general, it makes a great deal of sense for presidents to rally public support for their measures as a complement to their political work in Washington. If members are as sensitive to grass-roots sentiment as they seem to be, the cooperation that can no longer be elicited by appeals to party loyalty may be acquired by showing members that constituents would appreciate it. But this approach works only if members are convinced that their constituents do support the president. And this was another source of Carter's difficulties with Congress: he lacked popular support.

President Carter's drop in the public opinion polls during his first two years in office was extraordinary. The Gallup organization reported that "only one other president in the last 50 years — Ford, right after he pardoned Nixon — was in such disfavor so soon in his presidency. All others had solid measures of approval in their second year in office."[9] Carter's troubles began in earnest with the revelations of questionable financial transactions by Bert Lance, his close friend and director of the White House's Office of Management and Budget. Carter's public support for Lance throughout the congressional inquiries and Lance's ultimate resignation plainly hurt him in the polls.[10] He was particularly vulnerable because he had campaigned heavily on

[9] *Congressional Quarterly Weekly Report* 36 (September 29, 1978): 2548.
[10] *1977 Congressional Quarterly Almanac*, p. 66A.

his personal moral integrity. The proportion of people approving of his performance remained well below 50 percent for most of 1978. A majority (in the Gallup Poll) approved his performance only after Carter had engineered the Camp David agreements between President Sadat of Egypt and Prime Minister Begin of Israel.

Many of Carter's most notable legislative successes — including the sustaining of the public works veto — took place in the wake of this rise in public esteem. Political scientists and political practitioners agree that presidential popularity is an important source of presidential influence in Congress. One official in the administration involved in congressional liaison put it this way: "When you go up to the Hill and the latest polls show Carter isn't doing well, there isn't much reason for a member to go along with him. There's little we can do if the member is not persuaded on the issue."[11] And research suggests that this conventional political wisdom is correct. Popular presidents have more success with Congress than unpopular ones.[12]

The reasoning here is clear. If constituents like and support the president, then at least some voters will reward or punish their representatives according to how consistently they support the president. Local activists, campaign contributors, and potential primary and general election challengers will consider it a factor in their decisions. Close association with a popular president will help to discourage opposition before it becomes serious. Conversely, separating oneself from an unpopular president of one's own party may also be a very wise move, as many Republicans learned in 1974. President Nixon's staunchest supporters suffered the consequences at the polls.[13] Early in the summer of 1978, few Democrats were interested in having Carter campaign for them in the upcoming election. But after the Camp David meetings, he was a welcome visitor and ended up campaigning for many Democrats. There is no evidence that presidents really help their party's candidates in the off-year elections by stumping for them, but as long as members of Congress think they might, it remains a useful way for popular presidents to accumulate political credit.

[11] *Congressional Quarterly Weekly Report* 36 (March 4, 1978): 586.

[12] George C. Edwards III, "Presidential Influence in the House: Presidential Prestige as a Source of Presidential Power," *American Political Science Review* 70 (1976): 101–13.

[13] See Gerald C. Wright, Jr., "Constituency Response to Congressional Behavior: The Impact of the House Judiciary Committee Impeachment Votes," *Western Political Quarterly* 30 (1977): 401–10.

CONGRESSIONAL SUPPORT
FOR PRESIDENT CARTER

The widespread opinion in Washington that President Carter had an unusually difficult time with Congress is borne out by empirical data from the Ninety-fifth Congress. The *Congressional Quarterly* measures overall presidential support by the percentage of times Congress votes with the president when his preference on the vote is unambiguously known. Carter's rate of success, measured against those of his predecessors going back to Eisenhower, is shown in Table 11.1. His victory frequencies — 75.4 percent and 78.3 percent for his first two years in office — are the lowest of any Democratic president in any year but one. That was 1968, Lyndon Johnson's last year in office, when he was taking the full brunt of criticism for Vietnam and was no longer a candidate for reelection. Even John F. Kennedy, who had well-publicized difficulties with Congress, enjoyed a distinctly higher rate of success. Carter has done little better than had Richard Nixon

TABLE 11.1
Proportion of Presidential Victories in Congress, 1953–78

Eisenhower		Nixon	
1953	89.0%	1969	74.0%
1954	82.8	1970	77.0
1955	75.0	1971	75.0
1956	70.0	1972	66.0
1957	68.0	1973	50.6
1958	76.0	1974	59.6
1959	52.0	Ford	
1960	65.0	1974	58.2%
Kennedy		1975	61.0
1961	81.0%	1976	53.8
1962	85.4	Carter	
1963	87.1	1977	75.4%
Johnson		1978	78.3
1964	88.0%		
1965	93.0		
1966	79.0		
1967	79.0		
1968	75.0		

Source: From Congressional Quarterly Weekly Report, December 9, 1978, p. 3407. Reprinted by permission of Congressional Quarterly, Inc.

during his first three years in office. Nixon of course faced a Congress dominated by the opposing party. And these figures may even underestimate Carter's weakness, since many of his proposals never reached the floor for a vote.

The *Congressional Quarterly* also computes how frequently individuals and groups in Congress vote in support of the president's positions. The data on Carter are quite interesting. They show, not surprisingly, that he drew more support from Democrats than Republicans; comparison with previous years indicates that this is a common pattern. Support scores since 1961 for House and Senate Democrats and Republicans are listed in Table 11.2. Notice the differences in presidential support by party depending on the party of the president. Notice also that Carter's support among House Democrats was unusually low; his first-year figures are much lower than were Kennedy's or Johnson's.

Unexpectedly, however, Carter's support among Senate Democrats was unusually high by historical standards — higher than anything Kennedy or Johnson could muster. So was his support from Senate

TABLE 11.2
Congressional Support for the President's Programs, 1961–78

Year	Party of President	House Democrats	House Republicans	Senate Democrats	Senate Republicans
1961	Democrat	73%	37%	65%	36%
1962	Democrat	72	42	63	39
1963	Democrat	72	32	63	32
1964	Democrat	74	38	61	45
1965	Democrat	74	41	64	48
1966	Democrat	63	37	57	43
1967	Democrat	69	46	61	35
1968	Democrat	64	51	48	47
1969	Republican	46	58	40	64
1970	Republican	53	66	45	60
1971	Republican	47	72	40	64
1972	Republican	47	64	44	66
1973	Republican	35	62	37	61
1974	Republican	41	51	39	55
1975	Republican	38	63	47	68
1976	Republican	32	63	39	62
1977	Democrat	63	42	70	52
1978	Democrat	60	36	66	41

Source: Congressional Quarterly Almanacs for each year.

Republicans in his first year in office. Indeed, the *Congressional Quarterly* points out that Carter's "biggest legislative victories were, in large part, the result of Republican support and were achieved despite prominent Democratic defections. Controversial proposals that did not have much Republican backing — the bill designed to control hospital costs, for example — were defeated."[14]

The House-Senate differences in Democratic support for Carter are intriguing. What accounts for them? One answer is found in the regional breakdowns in the presidential support figures. Table 11.3 lists the levels of support for Kennedy, Johnson, and Carter in their first year in office, by region, in the House and Senate. Carter's support in the House is lower everywhere; the smallest drop-off is in the south. Southern senators support him much more frequently than they did Kennedy or Johnson; his support elsewhere is similar to theirs. Thus the higher level of Democratic support Carter enjoyed in the Senate can be attributed in large part to his fellow southerners.

Even with very large Democratic majorities in both houses, Carter could not rely on his own partisans to enact his major programs. Despite consistent support from party leaders, the many forces working against individual loyalty to the party and the president were simply too strong. And so any hopes that, after eight years of divided rule, Democratic control of Congress and the presidency would bring a new era of cooperation and the enactment of an ambitious new legislative agenda were disappointed. The data in Table 11.2 suggest that they were vain in the first place. No postwar president has been able to count on the overwhelming support of his party; all have had to pick up votes from both sides of the aisle. President Carter's problems were only more acute, not fundamentally different. That they were no worse than they turned out to be is a tribute to the skills of the party leaders in Congress.

THE ISSUES

"It used to be that a central piece of information on a vote was the president's position. Now the central information is the issue," said a State Department congressional liaison official. "With the breakdown

[14] *Congressional Quarterly Weekly Report* 36 (October 21, 1978): 3000.

TABLE 11.3
Democratic Congressional Support for Democratic Presidents During First Year in Office, by Region

		House			
President	Year	East	West	South	Midwest
Kennedy	1961	82%	84%	59%	83%
Johnson	1965[a]	83	80	57	82
Carter	1977	69	66	53	69

		Senate			
		East	West	South	Midwest
Kennedy	1961	78	73	49	74
Johnson	1965[a]	73	68	49	71
Carter	1977	77	69	64	71

Source: *Congressional Quarterly Almanacs* for each year.
[a] Data are from Johnson's first term as an *elected* president.

of party discipline, it is clear that voters expect members to exercise independent judgment. That means voting on the issue, not just to agree with the president."[15]

If true, this means that the president — and congressional party leaders — must make a greater effort than ever before to convince members of Congress of the intrinsic rightness of their proposals. And given the kind of issues the federal government now faces and the surly mood of the American public, it is no wonder that success has so far been modest. The president and Congress confront a host of particularly tough issues, many of which directly affect how millions of people live and many of which do not conform to traditional party divisions.

Consider energy policy. It splits Congress — and the parties — by region and state. Oil- and gas-producing states have interests contrary to energy-consuming states. On this and other economic issues, states of the so-called "snow belt," the northeast and midwest, oppose states of the so-called "sun belt" of the south, southwest, and west. Snow-belt congressmen have even formed a northeast-midwest Congressional

[15] *Congressional Quarterly Weekly Report* 36 (March 4, 1978): 596.

Coalition, a bipartisan group with 213 members from eighteen states, to protect their regional interests.[16]

Or consider environmental questions. They divide the educated, middle-class Democratic environmentalists from traditional labor-oriented Democrats who would give priority to economic growth. The distinctive voting patterns of junior, "new politics" Democrats is a visible result. Older Democratic divisions have been crosscut by a newer one according to political scientists William Schneider and Gregory Schell. Northern Democrats are divided between traditional prolabor Democrats and "new politics" social liberals. The latter group is thoroughly liberal on race, environmental, and foreign policy issues, but that liberalism is not associated with support for the claims of organized labor. And the prolabor Democrats are hardly social liberals.[17]

Economic issues no longer conform to the familiar New Deal categories. A tax system that President Carter called "a disgrace to the human race" because, he argued, it unfairly burdened middle- and lower-income taxpayers was "reformed" by the heavily Democratic Ninety-fifth Congress — acting on a Republican proposal — to give tax relief to upper-income groups. By the 1978 elections, many Democrats were campaigning for Congress on the traditional Republican promises of lower spending, lower taxes, less regulation, and balanced budgets. This is not an anomaly but rather a logical consequence of all the trends discussed in this chapter. If members are as sensitive and responsive to district opinion as they seem now to be, it is scarcely surprising that they adjust their campaign appeals to the popular mood. Discarding old party chestnuts when they become stale hardly requires a second thought. The party and its symbols are no longer the primary political guideposts.

[16] *Congressional Quarterly Weekly Report* 36 (November 18, 1978): 3330.
[17] Schneider and Schell, "New Democrats."

12
Congressional Parties: The Future

The sources of conflict that fragment the congressional parties and hamper presidential and party leadership lie outside Congress. In a sense, Congress is too representative. American citizens are plainly divided themselves on many important political questions. But their divisions do not compose coherent patterns. Clear political battle lines have yet to form across a range of issues. There is little consensus on what issues are important, let alone on what alternative solutions are preferable. Parties, politicians, and governmental institutions are viewed with suspicion if not hostility. Insofar as people are represented by organized groups, the pressures on political decision makers will be as diverse as they are intense. Members of Congress who seek to "represent" their constituencies do not find it easy; no wonder they find it hard to cooperate on partisan or any other consistent basis.

THE 1978 ELECTIONS AND BEYOND

Like the members of Congress whom they elect, Americans like to have it both ways. They enjoy the programs and benefits the federal government provides, but they dislike paying the price in the form of higher taxes, more inflation, and greater government regulation. Public opinion polls find solid majorities for national health insurance, wage and price controls, government guarantees of jobs, and current or greater levels of spending on the environment, education, the cities, and health care. They find equally solid majorities believing that the federal government is too large, spends too much money, and is too intrusive into people's lives.[1] Senator Lowell Weicker put it succinctly: "Everybody wants to go to heaven, but nobody wants to die."

Even the publicized "tax-revolt" in 1978 generated few demands that government services be curtailed. Many Republicans campaigned as supporters of a 30 percent across-the-board cut in federal income taxes that was *not* wedded to any cuts in federal spending. (An economist's theory supported the happy notion that the economic stimulus the cut produced would keep total revenue from actually falling.) The *Congressional Quarterly* noted during the campaign that most candidates of both parties were "finding it prudent to promise that next year they will reduce taxes and still manage to prevent any of the consequences from touching anybody back home."[2]

Conflicting signals from the districts provide a ticklish problem for members of Congress and an opportunity for President Carter. The problem for congressmen is obvious. Members are expected to bring home the usual projects and benefits while holding down spending and taxes — which means rejecting the special projects of *other* members. The old solution of everyone backing everyone else's district pork will not work. This is what gives Carter his chance to lead. If there is a clear popular mandate to cut spending *somewhere*, reduce inflation, and lower (or at least not raise) taxes, the president has a clearly specified set of popular objectives to pursue. This would help him in several ways. An administration policy that members think their constituents favor finds readier support; witness the public works veto. He can also take full blame for killing individual programs and projects — in return for general credit for holding down spending, taxes, and inflation. Members can still claim credit for pursuing district benefits while blaming Carter for their failure to provide them (their use of the budget resolution is instructive here). Congressional Democrats may also legitimately suspect that the administration's success on these

---

[1] From a study by Everett C. Ladd, Jr., cited by George F. Will, "Slash 'Waste,' Cure Everything," *Hartford Courant*, December 14, 1978, p. 30.

[2] *Congressional Quarterly Weekly Report* 36 (November 4, 1978): 3238.

issues will affect how hard they have to campaign to retain their seats in 1980.

Ironically, Carter may be able to lead Congress most effectively by pushing policies that run counter to the ambitious plans envisioned at the outset of his administration. But if such an approach would strengthen Carter's hand, it would also weaken the partisan ties between the president and congressional Democrats. He could only succeed by relying consistently on Republican backing. The staunchest opponents of a tight budget that cuts back on social services and welfare programs would come from liberals in his own party. Stronger presidential leadership would engender lower, not higher party unity.

Without such a clear-cut path to follow, the 1978 elections portend more trouble for the president (and for the congressional party leaders). The high number of House retirements and the defeat of ten incumbent senators means reinforcements for the obstreperous junior contingent in Congress. Republicans picked up eleven House and three Senate seats. The new senators appear to be much more conservative, as a group, than the ones they replaced. Party loyalty took another beating in 1978. A growing number of congressional candidates scarcely mention their party affiliation in campaign literature and advertisements. It used to be that the candidate of the minority party in an area played down his party affiliation, asking voters to vote the man, not the party. Now *both* candidates have come to favor this strategy, a reaction to the public's apparent scorn of parties in general. Its implications for party loyalty in Congress are obvious.

ORGANIZING THE NINETY-SIXTH CONGRESS

Members of Congress are not entirely pleased with the results of all the changes they have brought about in congressional procedures during the 1970s. "I've voted for every reform — to open committee meetings, to reduce the power of seniority, to do a number of things which reduce the power of a few in Congress — and somehow the end product is worse than it used to be," lamented Representative Charles W. Whalen.[3] Members complain of too much work, too many subcom-

[3] *Hartford Courant*, November 28, 1978, p. 32.

mittees producing too many bills, and too much time wasted taking too many recorded votes. Some of these problems were addressed by new reforms passed by the House Democratic caucus in December 1978. Others are likely to prove more intractable, since they are a consequence of the redistribution of power to younger members, a trend not likely to be reversed by its beneficiaries.

Roll call votes were made more difficult. Provision was made for clustering some votes and eliminating other procedural votes entirely. Republicans were not pleased with these changes, since they had been using demands for roll call votes to delay legislation they opposed. But the Democratic majority makes the rules.

The Democrats also voted to limit the number of subcommittee assignments any member may hold to five. The immediate effect is to open eighty-four subcommittee slots to new members, and in this sense it continues the devolution of power in the House. The long-term intent, however, is to cut down the number of subcommittees. The issue is a sensitive one. It took years to wrest power from twenty committee chairmen; imagine the potential for resistance of more than 150 independent subcommittee chairmen.

Some of the "young Turks" from the classes of 1974 and 1976 are not yet satisfied with their work in limiting the power of the committee chairmen. One proposal would have prohibited full committee chairmen from chairing any subcommittee, a crucial blow at a time when subcommittees hold the power. It was defeated easily, but chairmen of standing committees were prevented from chairing ad hoc, joint, special, or select committees. And other minor changes opening subcommittee assignments to new members by limiting committee seniority rights were adopted.

Even the Republicans moved toward redistributing the small amount of institutional power they hold in the House. The conference voted to allow each member to be the ranking Republican (who would become chairman if Republicans won a majority in the House) of only one committee. Back in 1971 the House Republicans, like their Democratic colleagues, had opened the way to modification of the seniority system. Ranking minority members must now be officially ratified by secret ballot in the conference. So far, no senior member has been denied the post on any committee. But these are clear signs that the Republicans have not remained untouched by the forces that have affected their rivals.

Assaults on the seniority principle show no signs of abating. When committees met to organize for the Ninety-sixth Congress in January 1979, three junior House Democrats were elected to subcommittee chairmanships (on the Commerce and Government Operations Committees) over more senior colleagues. A novel circumstance was that committee members were not reacting to autocratic behavior or incompetence on the part of the senior members, but, as one of the losers said, "were voting on whether one candidate's views are closer to theirs than others."[4] The basis for voting was, in other words, ideological.

One of the winners, Representative Henry Waxman, first elected in 1974, summed up the attitude of younger members toward seniority: "We don't feel bound by it."[5] His open and aggressive campaign for a Commerce subcommittee chairmanship included campaign contributions to ten Commerce Committee members from a special fund he had established. Senior party leaders had made similar contributions in the past — it is quite legal — but it is extraordinary, to put it mildly, for a junior member to seek internal influence in the House by such means. What this innovation portends for the future is unclear; but if a trend, it does not bode well for party leadership.

It could hardly be said that the spirit of reform pervaded the organization of the Ninety-sixth Congress, however. Convicted, indicted, or reprimanded Democrats were not deprived of their committee chairmanships. Perhaps members were deferring to the judgment of the people these members represent; all had been reelected despite widely-known legal and ethical troubles. And Democratic leaders were hard pressed to find anyone at all willing to sit on the Committee on Standards of Official Conduct.

And so the process of adjustment continues. Members of Congress maintain ambivalent attitudes toward their party because electoral and policymaking incentives remain in conflict. Reluctance to follow party — or presidential — leadership grows out of the desire to stay in office. But its deeper roots must therefore lie in American society, in the moods and expectations of the diverse constituencies they represent. The parties remain, however, essential to effect collective action by Congress. They provide the machinery through which members cooperate to make national policy. Strong congressional leadership —

[4] *Congressional Quarterly Weekly Report* 37 (February 3, 1979): 183.
[5] *Ibid*.

strong party leadership — enhances the collective power of Congress. Changes in rules that simultaneously give members more independent authority and leaders more tools to manage congressional business are not really so strange. They simply reflect the conflicting needs and motives of members of Congress.

Epilogue:
A Concluding Note on Political Parties and the Future

We end this book on a speculative note. The picture of political parties presented in the preceding chapters is not a pleasant one. The American political parties do appear to be in decline, and the consequences for our democratic system are enormous. The argument made to this point can be summarized.

THE DECLINE

Concerning the Electorate

The number of voters participating in elections continues to decline to levels low enough for us to begin to question the relevance, and should the trend continue, the stability and representativeness of American political institutions. The picture is bleak. The electorate has become polarized between the higher socioeconomic-status adults who remain in the 30 to 50 percent of the eligible population that continues to participate in elections and the lower socioeconomic-status groups

247

who have dropped out. How representative is a governing system that does not include in its decision making in any meaningful way those most in need of effective political representation? You will have to answer this question for yourself.

Within the evolving electorate, political parties are becoming less relevant. The number of people identifying with the major parties is decreasing, to the point where the proportion of independents equal those identifying with the larger of the two parties, the Democrats. As the number of independents increases — as it will with the entry of new voters into the electorate, a group for whom the parties have the least appeal — independents will become the dominant group in the electorate. Within the American political system an independent identification has been associated with a lack of political interest and involvement. There is evidence that this depiction is no longer totally accurate — independents are a disparate group — but the development of such a large pool of unattached voters is not a hopeful sign for a party system that has depended on a continual stream of new adherents to replenish its ranks.

The weakening of party ties has led to a volatile electorate, one capable of swinging from overwhelming majorities in favor of one party to, in the space of one election to the next, competitive outcomes or equally decisive margins in favor of the other party. The stability, predictability, and, if you will, mooring mechanisms of the American electorate have been seriously undermined. The future suggests the evolution of a basically partyless electorate, with little of the placidity of, say, the 1950s. The normal ties of identification with the parties continue to be eroded.

To make matters worse, the voters' perceptions of the political parties and of the government continues to be negative. The turnaround in indicators of public trust, efficacy, and faith in government in less than two decades has been remarkable. However one defines it, Americans are alienated from their own government and its leaders. Jimmy Carter's 1976 prenomination and general election campaigns made good use of this negative strain to win office. It is unlikely that anything that has happened in the interim has renewed the voters' faith in the government. If anything, the ineffective leadership provided by a man inexperienced in national politics has likely deepened the distrust.

As the electoral impact of the parties has declined, issues have increased in significance as an influence on voter decision making.

Without party identification to provide a powerful (and simplifying) cue to the voter, issues decisions demand more of a voter's time and mental energy than most are willing to give. An issue-oriented electorate is one likely to increase the dominance of the better-educated and upper-income groups over electoral decisions. Lower socioeconomic groups face enormous difficulties in reincorporating themselves into the electorate without the political parties to encourage, organize, and guide their efforts. One of the strengths of the two-party system has been its ability to include large elements of the less well-off in their coalitions. The weaknesses of the parties in the electorate has already indicated that there will be future difficulties in mobilizing and attracting this vote. Specific candidates may be able to appeal to nonidentified, nonvoting adults enough on occasion to stimulate them to turn out and vote. Whether this will move, as the parties have done in the past, to incorporate these lower socioeconomic groups into the electorate in any meaningful, long-term manner and to allow them a vehicle through which to exercise a consequential influence on political decision making is doubtful. There is no evidence that the trends depicted in this book in regard to these concerns will change to any significant degree in the forseeable future.

Concerning Campaigns, the Rise of PACs, the New Technologies, and the Increasing Costs of Politics

The campaign functions of the parties have been seriously undercut. Parties are no longer the principal funders of campaigns. PACs are. Television has replaced the party as the dominant communicator of political information and, as a consequence, the preeminent influence on voter attitudes. Parties are no longer the major organizers of campaigns. Media consultants, public relations and professional experts can create "instant" parties for candidates with the funds to pay for them. As the campaign function of parties has decreased, the role of money — and hence of those who can supply it — has increased geometrically. The new politics is an expensive one.

The response of the parties to these developments has been uneven. The movement for party reform was an effort to produce a more participant-oriented party structure responsive to, and in line with, contemporary political concerns. The movement has experienced a varied success. The presidential nominating system has been remodeled. More voters are involved and the decision over the nomination is now in the hands of those who take the trouble to participate in the process. This is a pronounced change from the closed, elitist nominating politics of the old (pre-1972) party system.

The reform movement may have many commendable qualities, but it has created problems. It could be argued with justification that reform resulted from the inability of the parties, and especially the larger of the two, the Democrats, to adequately represent the major concerns of the parties' constituencies. Nevertheless, in many respects, reform has also contributed to the continued erosion of the party system by weakening the parties' control over their most vital function, the nominating process.

Reformers and party regulars both recognize the problem. Many states, to meet the reform guidelines and (not incidentally) to benefit from the exposure television can provide, adopted primaries. In a dozen years the number of primaries has better than doubled (from sixteen to thirty-five), and the number of delegates selected through primary elections has increased from an average of less than 40 percent for the two parties to over 70 percent. Since primaries neutralize the role and influence of the party, they have contributed to its demise. The void has been filled by the media (particularly television) and the groups with the financial resources needed to mount serious candidacies in a media-oriented age.

Reform has had little impact, good or bad, in other areas. The national party structures have shown little evidence of change. The parties also have failed to take command of the new technologies of politics and to use these to their own advantage. In this regard, Republican efforts have been more substantial and impressive than those of the Democrats.

The leaders of both parties pay lip-service to the problems the parties face. Given the chance to rebuild party coalitions and strengthen party services, they do little. From Richard Nixon to Jimmy Carter, the chief concern of those most in a position to help revitalize the party system has been their own political survival. If the leadership of the two parties fails to recognize the fundamental seriousness of the problems confronting the parties, it is unlikely that anyone else can be of much assistance. Party regeneration will have to begin from within. At present there is no sign that party leaders truly appreciate the extent of the parties' malaise and are willing to extend themselves to do something about it. The future in these regards is bleak.

Concerning the Party in Congress and in Policy Making

The party in Congress has been subjected to an increasing dissolution of discipline and a decline in party line voting. The congressional leadership in recent years has on several occasions lined up against the president of its own party on policy issues. There has been a continuing split between the electorate of the presidential party and that of the congressional party. At the same time, the advantages of incumbency in seeking reelection have been magnified; the congressman's relation to his constituency has become more service-oriented; and PAC funds have increasingly supplied the capital needed for campaigning.

There have been reforms within the party and within the institutions of Congress. Some have helped to strengthen the party; most, however, have weakened it. Generational differences within the congressional membership have become more pronounced, with the newer members less amenable to party and presidential direction. Congressional electoral politics, the demands of legislative performance, party needs, and the will and priorities of a president, for the most part, all appear to pull in opposing directions. As a consequence, the factionalization evident in other aspects of American politics has adversely affected the national-level policy formulation and implementation and the parties' role in, and control over, them.

These changes have been in progress for at least the last several decades. To compound the difficulties and accentuate the trends, over the last four years the nation has been led by a president with weak ties to the national and congressional party and a poor understanding of party needs (at any level) or legislative demands. It may be that the worst manifestations of the debilitating forces assessed in this book have yet to be seen. If this is the case, future years will witness the continuing decline in party performance and relevance. The question remains then as to the consequence of these developments. What does it all mean? What will American politics be like with a progressively more ineffectual party system, one characterized by weak leadership, an increasing lack of coherence, an inability to control its own activities or members, undue responsiveness to special interest funds and influences?

THE FUTURE

Again, we can only speculate at this point, but it would seem that a partyless politics contains both risks and opportunities. The biggest difficulty will be in the absence of the bonds that held party coalitions together and that allowed for some coherence among different levels of party concerns (the president, Congress, and the voter). These bonds — which were largely internal, personal, and attitudinal — allowed for a sense of order to prevail in American politics. Democrats, usually, stood for something; the voter did not need to know the details on every issue to reasonably assume that his party was different from the Republicans' and that it served different group needs. These are no longer safe assumptions.

A president, regardless of how liberal or conservative his program might be in contrast to that espoused by the congressional party, could count on his legislative party leaders to support his major recommendations, and therefore those of the party nationally, and to exercise their influence to have these enacted. Again, this is no longer the case. Likewise, party leaders within Congress had the tools — in consultation with the baronial committee chairpersons — to force a degree of loyalty to party-endorsed programs and therefore to deliver in some manner on policy commitments. The results were often a cautious, conservative muddle of programs; Congress was run by its most conservative interests (southerners; committee chairpersons from noncompetitive areas; interest groups with a personal stake in supporting or opposing legislation). Bold programs were hard to come by and it took, normally, a national crisis in order to force Congress to move (Birmingham on civil rights; the Watts rioting on urban decay; Vietnam on the war powers of the president; and so on). It was not a happy situation, and it is often forgotten. A major reason for the rise of the imperial presidency, beginning with Franklin Roosevelt and the New Deal and extending through John Kennedy, Lyndon Johnson, and Richard Nixon, was the inability of Congress and the political parties to give adequate attention to the nation's needs. More and more, voters looked to the presidency for leadership with results that in the long run (Watergate) may have been predictable.

A Congress factionalized and divided to the point that it cannot act on policy questions is an unpleasant prospect. One less under the control of the president and its own more repressive elements has some positive elements. The congressional party may be in decline but a congressional membership more in tune with and responsive (in a service-oriented way) to its constituents may allow for a more flexible approach to policy issues and one more immediately responsive to the ongoing concerns of the nation. This may be a best case example, but it is a possibility.

Toward securing the end of a Congress more in tune with its electorate, one must check the advantages of incumbency. A limitation on PAC contributions to negate their presently overwhelming influence on elections would be welcome. Also, and more generally, the public funding of congressional (and other level) elections, with spending quotas set sufficiently high to allow challengers to compete effectively with incumbents, would be a step in the right direction.

The dissolution of the party in the electorate raises other questions. To date, political parties have been the most effective vehicle found for mobilizing an electorate and, in its highly imperfect way, representing the views and serving the needs of the outgroups. Without political parties, the less well-off have no effective, consistent representational outlet. Coupled with the decline in all forms of political participation by lower socioeconomic groups, these are disturbing developments. A discontented group — and any coalition of groups not serviced by the government and its policy rewards would increase its distance from the political system — is not a happy prospect for a democracy. It has been argued that neglected lower socioeconomic groups of this type provide fertile recruiting grounds for demagogues, from the Huey Longs and Father Coughlins to the George Wallaces of the future. The threat is real enough. Political parties incorporated these groups into the government, gave them a stake in its decision making, and educated them to the nature of their own role in the political process as well as to the limits that could reasonably be expected from government activity.

The parties also acted as a restraint on the prospective candidate. To win he had to satisfy the needs of a broad coalition. To accomplish his goal, he had to be (normally) an experienced politician (thus ensuring some skill in governing) sensitive to the wishes of a diverse, but interconnected, constituency. The party provided the coherence to this coalition, and it placed limitations on what a leader could or could not do. The checks generally worked well. The system was not fool-proof — the Nixon administration's Watergate crisis is hard to explain in this context — but it did serve the ends of responsible, reasonable government managed by experienced professionals and representative of the interests of most of the groups in the nation's electorate. These functions are unlikely to be performed by any other agency. The loss to the system in these regards is incalculable.

This is not to suggest that responsible and moderate government is less likely to occur in the future. What it does argue is that the restraining influence of the political parties on candidates, campaigns, and governmental excesses will not operate as it has in the past. Similarly, the representative qualities of parties competing in a broader and more inclusive electorate is also likely to decrease.

There is no immediate or obvious solution to these dilemmas. It may be that a higher order of electorate is evolving, one with a direct concern for policy outcomes, blinded less by habitual party loyalties and more demanding of a responsive government on the contemporary issues it considers important. In such a scenario, the decline in participation — at least as worrisome as the decline in performance of its traditional functions by the party — may be a short-term phenomenon, indicative of an electorate in flux. If so, and under the right conditions, involvement in American politics could increase over the coming decades, as the governing system becomes more directly responsive to its citizenry and their concerns.

In this last regard the role of the media, especially television, could be extremely important. The failure of television to fulfill its potential as an information-distribution and educational outlet has concerned everyone from social commentators to television critics. The problems with television as they relate to the political parties are discussed in this book. There is enormous power inherent in television to reach, educate, and involve the American citizenry more knowledgeably in its political affairs. If the concept of television constituting a public service enterprise and the belief that the airways actually do belong to the people ever gains currency, and both are heard often from representatives of the television industry and from government officials, changes of consequence could occur. The debate over the role of television and its contribution to American society is not new. The very fact that it has continued so long with little to be shown for the effort expended indicates that, realistically, little change can be anticipated.

CONCLUSION

The structure of American politics has changed in fundamental ways. These changes are likely to continue over the next several decades. A new political order is emerging with consequences yet unclear. One thing is certain. The role of the political parties within this new political arrangement will be different. More than likely, their impact will be reduced and their contributions to the governing system and the society nowhere near as substantial as they have been in the past.

It is possible to anticipate many of the changes that will come, to debate their consequences, and to move to alleviate some of the worst of the potential problems that are likely to arise. The United States has been an experiment in democratic governance, and quite clearly this experimentation will continue. Part of the debate over the emerging political order should concern the proper role and functioning a revitalized party system could play.

We end on a somber note. E. E. Schattschneider, one of the more eminent students of political parties, has claimed, "the political parties created democracy and . . . modern democracy is unthinkable save in terms of the parties."[1] Maybe so. Schattschneider was writing well over a generation ago. The contemporary era may be forced to adjust to a democratic system in which political parties no longer play a dominant role. The transformation is in progress. Future decades may see the trends developed in this book accentuated. If so, a partyless era, with implications still uncertain, may be settling on us.

[1] E. E. Schattschneider, *Party Government* (New York: Holt, Rinehart and Winston, 1942), p. 1.

Index